The
CARAVAN
Handbook

BUYING • OWNING • ENJOYING

© John Wickersham 2002

First published in February 2002
Reprinted 2002, 2003, 2004 and 2006 (with minor amendments)

Haynes Publishing, Sparkford,
Yeovil, Somerset BA22 7JJ, UK
Telephone: **01963 442030**
Fax: **01963 440001**
E-mail: **sales@haynes.co.uk**
Website: **www.haynes.co.uk**

ISBN 1 85960 801 9

A catalogue record for this book is available from the British Library.

Printed and bound in Britain by J.H. Haynes & Co. Ltd, Sparkford

The
CARAVAN
Handbook

BUYING • OWNING • ENJOYING

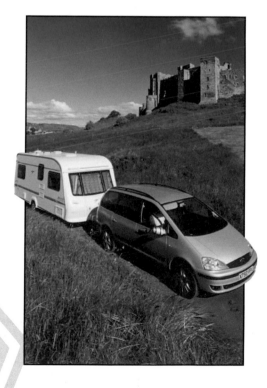

JOHN WICKERSHAM

CONTENTS

CHAPTER ONE
THE
FIRST STEPS

The adventure starts here! But you're not in this alone. It's claimed that in Britain, over 500,000 caravans are in regular, active service. Some make an annual appearance in summer whereas others are used throughout the year. Certainly the modern caravan is a sophisticated product offering all sorts of comforts irrespective of weather. Interested? If you are, you'll want to live the caravanning life to the full – and that's where this book will help. It's mainly addressed to complete beginners, although experienced caravanners will find it helpful, too.

My father was terrified by the prospect of towing. After all, there was only so much a 1939 'Flying Standard' could be expected to do.

So we hired an uncle's caravan at Whitsun weekends instead. And I took photographs with the Standard 10 reversed up to the tow hitch to pretend we were coupled together.

Whether it was the smell of the leaking gas that I remember most or collecting fresh water in a white enamel jug, I've never forgotten those holidays in the early 1950s.

Ten years later, I built a sailing boat and found its trailer was easy to tow, even behind a Mini. Then I bought a frame tent, built a camping trailer, and found that this was simple to tow as well.

However, the prospect of towing a caravan was much more daunting, even though the Mini had been replaced by an elderly Rover 2000. And anyway, there wasn't enough money in the family savings to even think of buying a brand new caravan.

Happy caravanning!

The modern caravan is a sophisticated product offering all sorts of comforts.

It was in the late 1960s, when the family frame tent developed some ominous leaks, that the caravan idea resurfaced. There was one very odd feature which added to the attraction of owning a caravan. Tax – or rather the lack of it! For some peculiar reason, 'purchase tax' as it was called in pre-VAT days, didn't apply to caravans, so new and second-hand models were quite reasonably priced.

In consequence, when a work colleague advertised a small but carefully maintained Cygnet caravan, I decided to take the plunge. A cheque was written, a towing bracket installed on the car, and a morning was spent raising and lowering corner steadies, and getting the hang of the hitch.

Simple though the amenities were, a couple of seasons in the Cygnet had revealed the pleasures of caravanning. Then the Government made an announcement: new caravans sold after 1972 would be subject to purchase tax, like everything else. Convinced that caravanning was ideal for our young family, we therefore joined hundreds of others who decided to buy a new model before tax on caravans came into force. We bought a 1972 Lynton Javelin, and the sales figures for caravans in that year hit an all-time high. In fact the figure has never been equalled.

Now I don't agree with Rousseau, the educational philosopher who said, 'learn by doing whenever you can, and only resort to books when "doing" is out of the question.' In those early moments of need, I would have paid a king's ransom for a book to explain how to do 'this or that.' The Instruction Manual unfolding the mysteries of my Cygnet had been lost by its earlier owner, and the Lynton leaflet didn't even quote tyre pressures.

So I blundered on and was impressed by the helpfulness of other caravanners when problems arose. Bit by bit I learnt the ropes and my adventure experiences were gaining momentum.

THE FIRST STEPS

But that's enough of the personal snapshots. Thousands of towing miles later, the world has changed. Caravans nowadays – like the cars which tow them – are sophisticated examples of modern technology. Safety standards have rightly arrived as well. Put all this together and there's an awful lot more for beginners to learn.

In fact, anyone new to caravanning clearly needs an illustrated book to guide them. So here it is and its 17 chapters cover a lot of ground. However, a few things are missing and that's with good reason. Guidance on Continental travel is a case in point.

That's because this Caravan Handbook is one in a family of caravan-related titles. For instance, a comprehensive book was launched recently called *Driving Abroad: skills, advice, safety and laws*. Equally, if it's caravan repair work that interests you, *The Caravan Manual* (3rd Edition) should be on your shopping list. Its sister volume, *The Motorcaravan Manual*, is another key source book, especially if a towed caravan isn't your preferred choice of leisure vehicle.

When it comes to choosing top quality caravan sites, *The Alan Rogers' Good Camps Guides* are unique. Whether you're planning to take a caravan to the Western Highlands, Portugal or Poland, these guides list good quality venues which have passed the stringent biennial inspections of experienced site assessors. Moreover, their concise reports give clear information about every site selected.

So to summarise. Don't be worried by the prospect of towing, especially when there are organised practical courses to help. Use the advice recorded here when choosing a caravan, too. Consider joining one of the national clubs because the benefits of membership are legion. And don't forget to read the caravan magazines that report all the latest developments.

So couple-up your caravan in confidence. Your travelling adventures are about to begin.

CHAPTER TWO

CHECK
POINTS FOR
PURCHASING

If you decide to buy a second-hand caravan, what precautionary measures should be taken? For example, how can you establish that a caravan being offered for sale privately is owned by the vendor and not subject to a hire-purchase agreement? Alternatively, if you're in the fortunate position of being able to buy a brand-new model, what points should be borne in mind? These are just a few of the topics raised in this chapter.

Whether you buy new or second-hand, there are many points to consider when buying a caravan.

Buying new

- Choosing a dealer
- Buying at an exhibition
- Delivery calendar
- Dealer 'specials'
- Warranty terms and conditions

Buying second-hand

- Purchasing privately
- Dealer sales
- Caravan auctions
- Obsolete models
- Owners' clubs
- Imported models
- Pre and post 1980 models
- Caravan Registration Identification Scheme

BUYING A CARAVAN

You might imagine that buying a caravan is much the same as buying a car. Both are costly commodities and a good dealer should be able to give advice. Alternatively there are dozens of classified advertisements in monthly caravan magazines if you're looking for a pre-owned private purchase.

There's no doubt there are similarities in buying procedures, but there are also differences. For instance, a caravan doesn't have a mandatory registration document. This means that if you're looking at a second-hand model, its true age is often hard to establish. And can you be absolutely sure that the pre-owned 'van available for purchase is being sold by its rightful owner? Add to this the fact that there's no form of MOT test for caravans, and the differences become even more apparent.

As regards brand-new caravans, you'll also find that factory warranties differ from one manufacturer to another. Moreover, choosing a dealer isn't quite as simple as you might imagine, either. For example, an impressive discount from a caravan specialist whose base is a long way from your home carries a problem that isn't evident when buying a car. If a warranty repair is needed at a later date, you will usually have to take the caravan all the way back to its original supplier. It's not the same with a car where warranty work can be done at any franchise dealership.

It's matters like this which are raised here, with the new or second-hand alternative providing a natural division. Points discussed are outlined in the adjacent panels.

NEW OR SECOND-HAND?

In the opening chapter, the merits of buying new or second-hand were discussed briefly. Further considerations are also described in Chapter Three where changes in manufacturing methods are explained. For instance, improvements in thermal insulation need to be borne in mind. Similarly, when looking at a relatively old caravan with a view to purchase you should be aware that obtaining spare parts isn't always straightforward.

This might sound as if the best way forward is to buy a brand-new caravan and if you're in the fortunate position to be able to take this step, the advantages are obvious. However, if you decide to do this, there are several points you need to bear in mind before placing your order, as explained overleaf.

Most dealers tend to specialise in a particular marque – although some retail new caravans from two or three manufacturers.

Getting model details and the addresses of manufacturers

Most monthly magazines include 'Buyers' Guides' in which key information is laid out in tabular form. This allows you to single out models which meet your particular needs using criteria such as weight, size, bed accommodation and so on. These magazines also include the addresses of manufacturers thereby enabling you to send away for brochures. In addition, a growing number of manufacturers run web sites which can be informative, too.

Where are caravans built? Most monthly caravan magazines include an address list of manufacturers.

BUYING NEW
Choosing a dealer

Most dealers specialise in a particular brand of caravan although this usually extends to include products from two or three manufacturers or importers. In other words, if you merely call at your nearest supplier, you are only going to see a small selection of caravans currently available on the market.

In fact if you look at the tables in one of the monthly caravan magazines you'll see there are around 18 different marques made in Britain and nearly ten imported brands. To be strictly accurate it's true that the Swift Group accounts for Abbey, Ace, Bessacarr, Sterling and Swift caravans at the time of writing, just as the Explorer Group manufactures models under the brand names of Buccaneer, Compass, Crown and Elddis. However, there's plenty of choice even if there are less manufacturers today than there were twenty years ago.

Moreover, these two major manufacturing groups retain individuality in the different models, just as British Leyland did when major take-overs brought cars like Austin, Morris, MG, Rover and Triumph into a major conglomerate. Notice, too, that if a caravan dealer is franchised to sell Swift Caravans, this doesn't mean the dealership will retail all the 'badged models' coming from this East Yorkshire manufacturer.

So to see what's on offer, a good way to gain a broad picture of models available is to purchase several of the major monthly magazines. For instance, *Caravan Life*, *Caravan Magazine*, and *Practical Caravan* all publish monthly test reports and in some instances there are back-issue departments where you can catch-up on feature articles that you've missed.

CHECK POINTS FOR PURCHASING

A large selection of caravans are on show at indoor exhibitions such as the National Boat, Caravan and Leisure Show held at the NEC, Birmingham.

In other words, if you're prepared to get hold of brochures and to read test reports in magazines, a 'phone call to the manufacturers or importers will reveal where different dealers are located.

This is a good way to find out what is on the market. However, there's another approach worth consideration – and that is to go to one of the major indoor exhibitions or outdoor shows.

Buying at an exhibition

The two largest caravan exhibitions are as follows:

1. The Caravan and Outdoor Leisure Show is held at Earl's Court, London late in the year – e.g. November or early December.
2. The National Boat, Caravan and Outdoor Leisure Show is held at the National Exhibition Centre, Birmingham in February.

In addition, there are regional shows held in Cardiff, Glasgow and Manchester, albeit on a smaller scale.

There are also a number of outdoor shows where caravans are on sale and details of venues and dates are given in caravan magazines. Typically these are held at agricultural show grounds or race courses so there's plenty of room for exhibits and visitors alike.

By visiting a large event you are able to look closely at products and to make your own assessments. Moreover, on a caravan manufacturer's stand there are sales people from several of the manufacturer's dealers as well as staff from the factory. Hence you can place an order at a caravan show and this facility is very different from the arrangement at a motor show where dealer representatives are seldom in attendance.

Models held in stock
Occasionally a dealer might have an example of the model you want back at his or her base. In reality that isn't always the case because to stock every model with all the different permutations of internal layout and equipment would take up a large amount of space on a dealer's forecourt.

Sometimes there are special prices or 'add-on' accessories when orders are taken for caravans at an exhibition.

Not surprisingly, if you show interest in a caravan on a show stand, a dealer is likely to approach and strike up a conversation. He or she will often enquire if you are already a caravan owner, and for anyone visiting a show as a potential purchaser, here is a good opportunity to conduct business. There may also be some show discounts either in the form of a price reduction or additional items 'thrown-in' as an inducement. Overall it's a good way to compare prices and products, but there are important words of warning.

First you should establish where a sales person's base is located since that is usually where you'll have to visit in order to collect the 'van. Equally, you will usually have to return to the dealer who conducted the sale if warranty work needs carrying out at a later date. So if you get the best selling price from a dealer situated two hundred miles from your home, the cost of travel to and from the base can quickly eliminate the apparent benefit of an attractive price.

Secondly you should appreciate that when purchases are 'signed and sealed', it is often many months before the caravan is built, supplied to the dealer, given its pre-delivery inspection (PDI) and made ready for collection. Orders taken at shows held early in the New Year are not always ready for use in time for Easter. Delivery is certainly a point to discuss with the dealer.

CHECK POINTS FOR PURCHASING

Lastly, you should check all the technical points raised in the accompanying chapters before placing an order. Some sales specialists are well-versed in details about their products and a few may even own a caravan themselves. On the other hand, there are others whose understanding about technical detail is woefully limited. At a show, this need not be a serious handicap because there is usually a technical member of staff present who comes from the factory. So don't be reticent to pose important questions; a less-knowledgeable salesperson should be able to find answers by consulting one of the manufacturer's representatives.

Delivery calendar

The fact that most new caravans are ordered rather than purchased directly from a dealer's forecourt inevitably means there is usually a waiting period.

Furthermore, the curious calendar in the caravanning industry sees new models launched annually. As it often turns out, the changes might be cosmetic rather than radical but there are yearly changes nonetheless.

Many manufacturers finish making the prototypes of models to appear the following year as early as June or July. These are then unveiled to members of the caravan Press in July and August. After this, one of the first trade shows falls in September and public exhibitions follow in late autumn.

Without doubt, the annual exhibition at Earl's Court, which falls around November time, is one of the best times to order a new caravan if you want to ensure delivery in the early spring. Orders placed here set the pattern of manufacture over the winter period although at Christmas/New Year time, many caravan factories have a traditional extended shut-down. Then there are spring shows and spells of frenetic energy on the production

Annual post-season sales
With the advent of new models not far away, there are typically late autumn sales where dealers make strenuous efforts to clear stock in readiness for new models. Some of the mark-down prices are notable, although for most people the summer has passed and the idea of caravanning with winter approaching acts as a purchasing disincentive. But there are bargains at the close of every season.

This is the same as the smart interior of a 2001 Lunar LX2000 – but it's actually Campbells' Caravans 'Dealer Special' re-badged as a Lunar Gemini 524.

lines. Some deliveries can get delayed quite considerably – partly because many manufacturers produce caravans in batches according to model. Hence all the twin-axle models might take the production line for a week, thereby putting on 'hold' the manufacture of other models.

Spring is especially busy both at the factory and the dealers. Even caravan workshops at dealerships are stretched to the limits as customers arrange their annual pre-season service.

So be mindful of this annual roundabout when planning a new purchase and arrange the dates so that your intended purchase will arrive in time for your first planned trip.

Dealer 'Specials'

As a way of boosting sales, several large retailers make arrangements with a manufacturer to produce a model specific to their dealership. Typically this is a model already in the line-up, albeit with the addition of a new name, different decals on the outside and a package of extras like a gas barbecue point on the side, an additional chest of drawers inside, and so on.

Similar techniques are employed, of course, by car dealers – particularly with high volume models such as the Ford Fiesta. The offer of something 'special' which includes extra items at no extra cost usually acts as a buying incentive.

How this strategy affects a resale at a later date is a little less clear. In truth, the benefits bestowed by a few 'add-ons' is most unlikely to be reflected in a trade-in price. Moreover, a model associated with a particular dealer might not be so favourably viewed when offered as a trade-in to a rival dealer. Apart from that, there's little against buying a dealer special, especially if you like some of the extra items that have been thrown-in as part of the package.

Warranty terms and conditions

When comparing new models in a shortlist, don't forget to compare the warranties as well. These differ in a number of ways, especially with regard to the period over which the external fabric of a caravan is insured against leaks arising from faults in construction. This particular affliction is often referred to as 'water ingress'.

Over the years, some caravans have been disappointing in respect of workmanship and water ingress problems have often been reported. Without doubt, a survey undertaken by The Caravan Club in 1999 found some disturbing facts. Manufacturers duly responded and the confidence of some constructors led to longer-than-usual warranties being offered. So it's worth checking the details.

Warranty conditions

You should take note what has to be done in order for a warranty to remain valid. As a rule there's a stipulation that the 'van has to have a full service at regular calendar intervals at an approved workshop. Overlook this at your peril! Equally, you should establish what is deemed to be an 'approved workshop'.

When purchasing a pre-owned caravan, ask to see the results of its last damp check conducted at a service centre.

BUYING SECOND-HAND

Private purchases

Specialist magazines and local newspapers usually contain a classified advertisement section devoted to caravans. There are certainly some very good caravans on sale privately – as well as plenty of poorer products. The term caveat emptor, or buyer beware, is particularly relevant here.

In truth, every transaction has to be evaluated individually and it is quite impossible to give any more than a few guidelines here. Suggestions include these points:

- if you are not very familiar with caravans, read Chapter Three with care. This identifies some of the features to check.
- establish when the caravan was last serviced and ask to see the signed service schedule to establish the extent of the work undertaken.
- ask to see approval certificates that the gas and electrical systems have been checked and deemed safe.
- ask when the last professional damp check was carried out using an electrically operated damp meter and ask to see the certificate.
- follow up the CRiS registration as described later, where appropriate.

CHECK POINTS FOR PURCHASING

In practice these recommendations are all very easy to list but the hard fact of the matter is that many caravans are never serviced professionally. Others have been given a cursory service but the 'van is returned without any documentation showing the extent of the work carried out. Equally, there are thousands of caravans which have never been damp checked with a meter. Nor for that matter are many pre-owned models sold with certificates from appropriately qualified gas and electrical engineers to verify that their supply systems are in safe working order.

In acknowledgement of this, a cautionary purchaser might wisely decide to avoid anything not supported by this kind of documentation. On the other hand, if the price is attractive and you are prepared to get this work done as soon as taking ownership, you might decide to proceed. There are certainly some cared-for caravans on sale which have been lovingly cherished and kept clean by fastidious owners. Many pre-owned examples like this have also brought much pleasure to their next owners. Conversely there are also appalling potential purchases that have proved to be disastrous. So all I can add is look closely, compare critically – and caveat emptor.

Checking a caravan's credentials

A particular worry is establishing whether a caravan being offered for sale is wholly owned by its vendor. On one hand it might still be the subject of a hire purchase or loan agreement; on the other, it might be a 'van that has been stolen. This is where the CRiS scheme is so helpful and this is explained on page 28.

Inclusion of accessories

Most dealers sell their pre-owned stock empty of accessories. Not surprisingly, a dealer will willingly direct you towards the accessory shop when you realise you need cutlery, crockery, a leisure battery, water containers and costly items like an awning. In contrast, private sellers often include these accessories as part of the sale. Admittedly some items might be transferred where the private seller is purchasing another caravan in its place but things like awnings might not fit the new model. So they tend to be included as part of the deal.

Dealer prices might be higher than private sales, but you can insist that the caravan is sold fully serviced before collection.

Dealer pre-owned models

Whereas there are inherent risks when purchasing privately, buying a pre-owned caravan from a dealer generally provides a measure of post-purchase support in the event of a subsequent problem. Admittedly, the degree of cover offered by a warranty on a second-hand caravan varies from dealer to dealer but there's far more likelihood of after-sale support. Needless-to-say, this is one reason why the asking price is usually higher than a private transaction.

A further benefit of purchasing from a dealer is the fact that a caravan offered for sale is likely to have been serviced and fully checked over. In addition a post 1992 CRiS registration transfer of ownership would normally be carried out on your behalf – a topic dealt with under the CRiS section later in this chapter.

All-in-all, many purchasers prefer the support that accompanies a dealer-sale; it's just that you normally have to pay slightly more to secure the additional peace of mind.

There's usually some form of after-sales warranty accompanying pre-owned caravans sold by a dealer.

CHECK POINTS FOR PURCHASING

Local auctions are sometimes conducted by local auctioneers and estate agents at venues such as storage centres.

23

Caravan auctions

Broadly speaking, caravan auctions appear on two levels. On one hand there are local affairs conducted by a local auctioneer and estate agent. These are comparatively unusual and can be staged at a caravan storage centre, near a factory or a dealer which has gone into liquidation.

More easy to track down are sales conducted by a specialist like British Car Auctions (BCA). This specialist's occasional 'Leisure and Caravan' auctions have taken place at several of the 23 or so BCA centres around the country but nowadays most are held at the Measham branch in the Midlands. Caravan sales are timetabled on a fairly regular basis.

While the popular image of auctions depicts a situation where there's little purchaser protection, this is not necessarily accurate. Legislation affords rather more support than is often appreciated and there is plenty of opportunity at Measham for a purchaser to scrutinise caravans thoroughly prior to the sale itself. Occasionally there are even brand-new caravans included in the sale as a result of company liquidations. Not surprisingly, the purchase prices are often very attractive.

British Car Auctions

At present, you would expect to find around 60 to 70 caravans and motorhomes at a Measham Centre auction and there are guidance leaflets produced by BCA on bidding procedures.

For more information and dates of sales contact: The General Manager, British Car Auctions, (Measham Branch) Tel: 01530 270322.

Thorough inspection is most important before placing a bid at a local auction.

If you buy a really old caravan – as kept at the back of a dealer's forecourt – you might have difficulty buying spare parts.

Obsolete models

In the last twenty to thirty years many caravan manufacturers have ceased trading. Some have been taken over by larger conglomerates while other factories have closed down.

When it comes to spare parts, this can present a problem, but spares for post 1980 chassis parts are usually easy to obtain and many appliances e.g. refrigerators, hobs, water systems and so on can usually be repaired as well.

However, it is items like matching furniture, unusual catches, window glazing, and upholstery products which are often impossible to replace with identical units. This is where owners' clubs (next section) can be helpful points of contact. So, too, are caravan breakers and a list of yards is available to members of The Caravan Club from its head office in East Grinstead.

The Caravan Club can supply members with a list of breakers like this specialist dealer in Stopsley, Luton.

Models no longer in manufacture

There are many familiar names of caravans which are no longer in production. These include the following, although there are many more lesser-known brands:

A-Line, Astral, Buzzard, Castleton, Cavalier, Cheltenham, Coronet, Cygnet, Deanline, Europa, Fisher, Fleetwind, Forest, Knowsley, Lynton, Mardon, Mustang, Panther, Robin, Royale, Safari, Silverline, Sprite, Sunseeker, Thomson, Trophy, Viking Fibreline and Windrush.

Further historical information can be found in Caravans From 1960 *by Andrew Jenkinson* (1999, Veloce Publishing).

25

Known for its range of ultra narrow caravans, Silverline finished production in 1992.

The Forest was produced for several years in Nottingham before its demise in 1977.

High quality woodwork, a glass-fibre body and rainwater downpipes with a hopper head were features of this 1950s Cheltenham – a marque that finished production in 1974.

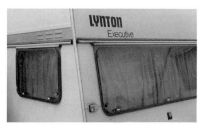

The Lynton ranges from Manchester were often lively in style; production ceased, however, in 1986.

Very early caravans are now collectors' items; towed by cars of the period; they often appear at outdoor shows.

Old and even older

Some owners' clubs are concerned with caravans which went out of production in the last few years whereas others support models of much greater heritage. There are even two clubs catering for the owners of very early caravans and these charming products – usually towed by a car of the correct vintage – are often seen on display at outdoor caravan rallies.

Owners' clubs

There are currently around 45 clubs devoted to particular brands of caravan and the addresses of their secretaries are published regularly in magazines like *Caravan Magazine* and *Practical Caravan*.

Those clubs concerned with models still in manufacture often attend major exhibitions, like The Boat, Caravan and Leisure Show held at the National Exhibition Centre. Furthermore, a section is usually provided for them on the stand of the host manufacturer.

Many clubs concerned with obsolete models are also surprisingly active and interest in old caravans is not dissimilar from the enthusiasm shown by owners of classic cars. Here are important contacts if you need advice on an older model that you have purchased.

Pre- and post-1980 models

When buying an older caravan, it is important to recognise that many radical changes in construction took effect around 1980. Externally, these features are not very obvious to the lay-person, but 'below the skin', the revised building techniques are most significant.

To find out more about these developments and their implications for ownership, refer to the following chapter.

CHECK POINTS FOR PURCHASING

Imported models

With caravans being built in several European countries, several potential owners enquire whether they can import a model independently. While this is certainly possible there are a number of potential disadvantages to bear in mind.

First the caravan door is normally situated on the opposite side to suit right-hand driving. When parked by the roadside in Britain, this presents a possible danger when you step outside the 'van.

In addition, an imported caravan might not comply with British Standards. For instance all UK-manufactured caravans now have to comply with the Furniture and Furnishings Fire (Safety) Regulations 1988 – which means that any foam in mattresses has to be fire-retardant. This requirement is not obligatory in many European countries.

As regards the gas supply system, some foreign caravans have been built in the past with different gas jets because their tourers operate on a supply system whose regulator creates a different operating pressure.

Then there are different fixtures and fittings as described in the accompanying panel.

In practice, caravans imported by specialist importers in the UK are often fitted with the items that British caravanners usually want. So whereas the door position would not be changed, if you prefer an imported model, it is better to buy through a specialist who carries out small modifications like changing a cooker and altering the mains electricity provision.

Imported caravans

Whereas some imported caravans have much to commend them, they are seldom fitted with a grill. Our friends from overseas seem not to have discovered the pleasure of toast. Equally, many imported models lack carpet and while a vinyl floor covering is distinctly practical, many British caravanners prefer a carpeted floor. And not surprisingly, a mains installation will have different switches, sockets and control units.

Not that all is negative. Some caravans, especially Scandinavian models, are fitted with a greater level of thermal insulation to suit the lower winter temperatures.

Since its inception, the CRiS registration scheme has involved etching an identification number on a caravan's windows.

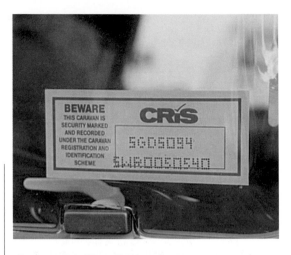

Caravan Registration Identification Scheme (CRiS)

Unlike cars and other motor-driven vehicles, caravans had no registration document until the CRiS initiative was launched in 1992. This wasn't a mandatory registration but all new caravans launched with National Caravan Council badge accreditation were included from 1992 onwards.

The visible evidence of CRiS registration is given on each window where the caravan's identification number is etched. Other features that developed later were:

1997 – from July of that year, all new caravans from NCC member manufacturers were fitted with a hidden electronic tag which also carries the VIN (Vehicle Identification Number).

1999 – from October of that year, owners of pre-1992 caravans could also register them on the scheme. Points about this are as follows:

- The registration fee is £19.95.
- A VIN is allocated.
- A DIY etching kit is supplied for marking the 17-digit number on the windows.
- At the time of initial registration, a DIY electronic tag can be supplied for an additional £12.50.

The benefits of CRiS are especially evident to anyone purchasing a pre-owned caravan and these are explained in the panel opposite. Information about a caravan you might purchase is obtained as follows:

Calling CRiS
You can make contact by 'phone:
01722 411430
Lines are open:
8am–8pm Monday to Saturday and 10am–5pm on Sunday
There's also a web site on
www.crischeck.com

CRiS benefits for buyers and owners

Through the CRiS scheme, caravan keepers have: '...access to a vital register that can help protect the security of their caravans and help the police in returning stolen caravans to their rightful owners.'

Alternatively, if you want to purchase a second-hand model, you can verify that it hasn't been stolen, or can find out if any hire purchase payments are still outstanding. As a potential purchaser you can pay £5.95 for a history check. All you have to do is to submit the caravan's 17-digit VIN number, a description of the 'van, and the name and address of the seller. This will then be checked with the database to see that everything matches.

But note: CRiS won't give away confidential information about the owner – merely whether your information and theirs is matching.

You will also be able to establish if the caravan is:
- Currently recorded as stolen.
- Officially written-off by an insurance company.
- Still the subject of a loan from a finance house.

Finally, when purchasing a CRiS-registered caravan, change of ownership procedures are as follows:

a) A private seller has to complete the Notification of Sale section on the registration document and send it to CRiS.
b) The private seller should pass the rest of the document to the purchaser.
c) You, as purchaser, have to fill out the Notification of Change section on the document and send it to CRiS with a £10.00 change of ownership fee.

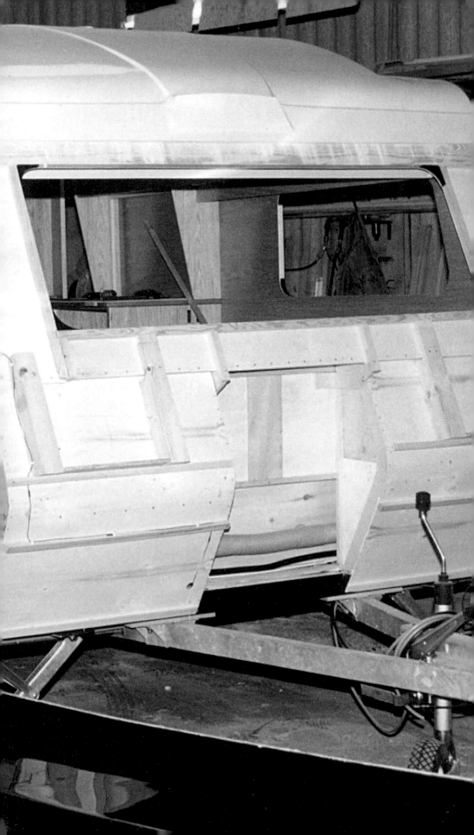

CHAPTER THREE

DESIGN AND CONSTRUCTION

Not surprisingly, most people buy a caravan on the basis of its appearance, layout and suitability for towing. It is not until much later that the qualities relating to its overall design and construction become apparent. This chapter takes you beneath the surfaces and explains building details and their implications. With this knowledge, you'll be able to make a more informed judgement when buying a new or second-hand caravan.

A discerning and knowledgeable purchaser pays particular attention to details like these when comparing caravans.

- The materials used for the roof, side walls, front and rear panels.
- The chassis and running gear.
- Type of windows fitted.
- Body trims – checking that they won't be a weak spot when rain streams down the sides.
- External lockers, gas storage, battery location, and space for stowing leisure equipment.
- The installation of appliances such as the space heater and the refrigerator.

To conduct an appraisal along these lines, you need to know what you're looking for – and that's the reason behind this chapter. Unfortunately many prospective purchasers only make their decision on the basis of the soft furnishings, overall layout, and sleeping capacity. The wider implications of a caravan's design, construction and possible weaknesses only become apparent when something starts to go wrong.

Some caravans are still constructed using a skeleton framework which is later clad with aluminium sheet, as this Carlight model shows.

Technical Tip

The traditional build technique in which a skeleton structure of timber struts is assembled first and later 'skinned' was largely superseded in the early 1980s. The use of prefabricated bonded sides and floors became the preferred form of construction.

Some manufacturers continue using the traditional coachbuilding approach, especially companies specialising in high quality, low volume products. Carlight Caravans are an example of a craftsman-built product using a traditional construction. Buccaneer caravans were also built traditionally until the brand was taken over by the Explorer Group. Buccaneers were then constructed using pre-fabricated sandwich panels.

CARAVAN BODY CONSTRUCTION

At first sight, caravans look much the same regardless of model. But the differences are more than skin deep. The construction of a caravan's body, for example, can differ significantly and this has implications if a repair has to be carried out.

Whilst there are some excellent caravans around, there's no doubt that a few models are poorly designed, badly built and hard to repair. So here are some points you'd be wise to check.

a) Structure of the shell

If you are buying an old caravan at a low price, it is important to realise that around 1980, the way that most caravans were built underwent a radical change. The change speeded up construction – which helped to bring the price down – and it also led to considerable weight saving.

Prior to 1980, caravans were built using a skeleton of timber struts which was subsequently clad on the outside with aluminium sheet whereas thin ply was the usual choice for the interior. As a rule, the void in between was filled with glass-fibre; this provides insulation but it has the tendency to slump down over time leaving cold spots. Floors were heavy structures comprising thick plywood fixed to timber joists which spanned the steel chassis members.

The major structural change which took place involved the introduction of prefabricated panels. Wall panels, for example, comprise block insulation (usually polystyrene) which has been bonded to an outside skin (usually aluminium sheet) and an interior layer of 3mm decorative plywood. However, a caravan's front panels – and sometimes the rear sections – are generally built using a moulded plastic panel supported by a timber framework. Only budget models are

DESIGN AND CONSTRUCTION

constructed with the same flat panels used for the side walls.

To bring things up-to-date, a few caravans now have side walls covered with a flat sheet of glass reinforced plastic (GRP) instead of aluminium sheet. This alternative idea first appeared in 1996 on the Abbey Domino and the benefit of this alternative outer material is that a skilled 'fibre-glass' repairer can sometimes repair a damaged GRP skin. In contrast, if an aluminium-clad panel gets dented, the whole side section usually has to be covered with a new layer fixed on top of the old one.

When the techniques for producing bonded wall panels was first developed at the close of the 1970s this coincided with new thinking about the design of caravan chassis as well. In fact the radical changes that took place went hand-in-hand because both the shell and the chassis interact to produce strong, but light living accommodation.

Note: With these constructional points in mind, if you're planning to purchase a second-hand 'starter' caravan, bear in mind this important period when many constructional features were undergoing radical changes.

Most modern body panels are now prefabricated separately.

The bonded sandwich panel used for side walls has a core of polystyrene insulation.

Today, caravan floors are built using a prefabricated sandwich panel; this one has blue Styrofoam in the core for insulation.

Buyer's Tip

Delamination

When caravan floors and walls are prefabricated using three relatively weak materials in a 'sandwich', strength is achieved because they are bonded together. Indeed the whole success of the system depends on the effectiveness of the bonding adhesive. If the adhesive fails, rigidity is lost and it's common knowledge that a polystyrene or styrofoam block – as used in the core – is as brittle as a biscuit. So delamination – which the problem of bond failure is called – can be a serious matter.

Fortunately you don't often find the aluminium skin on side walls bubbling and losing its bond with the insulating core; nonetheless, it can happen so it's something you should check carefully when buying a pre-owned caravan. Floors, however, do sometimes give trouble and this happens when the ply in the living area loses its bond with the insulating material below.

Not only does the floor then start to flex; the overall strength achieved by the combined bracing effect of the floor, the axle and the chassis is going to be reduced. As explained in the section on lightweight chassis, a rigid floor panel is one of the important elements that contributes to the overall effectiveness of the chassis members.

If the floor ply does break away from the foam core, a delamination repair involves drilling holes and injecting a special adhesive.

So you need to look out for delamination. Check the following points:

• Make sure the corner steadies are lowered and go into the 'van.
• Walk around inside and listen for pronounced, tell-tale creaking sounds.
• Look for slight rises in parts of the floor which in essence are blisters where the plywood has flexed upwards away from the foam.
• Check for a feeling of movement and floor flexion when you walk around.
• Particularly check areas which the occupants use often. Classic weak spots are just inside the door where everyone steps on entry. Look around the kitchen units because a lot of time is often spent here.

Note: Delaminated sections can usually be repaired and a service specialist rebonds a faulty area by injecting a liquid adhesive into the damaged zone to recreate adhesion. This aside, it's obviously wise to avoid buying a caravan with the problem in the first place.

Older chassis are comparatively heavy in structure and the steel sections have to be painted periodically.

b) Chassis

Caravans built before 1980 also featured a heavy chassis which was usually painted. Products from Peak Chassis and B&B (Bird & Billington) were especially well-known. Then it was discovered that by using a sandwich-bonded floor panel, its inherent strength could be used to contribute a bracing effect to the steel chassis members. The result? A new breed of notably lighter, computer-designed chassis where the overall strength was derived from an interplay between the floor, the axle tube and purpose-designed lightweight steel chassis sections.

Lightweight chassis made by AL-KO or BPW are now fitted by nearly every manufacturer. However, the swing to these products was a gradual process. For instance until the mid 1990s, Lunar caravans were built on an aluminium chassis made in Lancashire. In addition, the well-known manufacturer of Sprite caravans continued to use a more traditional and heavier chassis until the early 1990s. And Carlight Caravans are still built on a robustly constructed British chassis to this day.

If you buy a 'van with an older chassis, it will be heavy, though robust. It will also need painting occasionally when it gets chipped because very few were ever galvanised. Even some of the lightweight chassis from AL-KO were painted in the early 1980s. Nowadays, however, all AL-KO and BPW chassis are galvanised and this means that unless there is abrasion damage, they are maintenance-free constructions.

c) Running gear

This term includes items like the suspension and the braking system. Again you should note two differences between the older type of chassis and the lightweight versions which replaced them in the post-1980 period.

On older chassis, the suspension usually comprises two coil springs together with telescopic shock absorbers. If you purchase one of these models, crawl underneath and check that no oil is seeping out of the shock absorber casing. Whereas a shock absorber can be replaced, it's not an easy job so the labour charge can be surprisingly high.

On the more modern lightweight types of chassis, the ride is cushioned by rubber installed in the axle tube instead of a coil spring. This is maintenance-free and on most 'rubber-in-compression' systems there's no need for shock absorbers. This is because rubber doesn't create the bouncing effect that you get with a coil spring.

The other difference on old and new chassis designs relates to the brakes. Apart from minor differences in the operating rod arrangement, there is a rather inconvenient feature in the older models. Before you can use your towcar to reverse a 1960s and '70s caravan, a brake-disabling lever near the coupling has to be engaged. It's so much simpler on an AL-KO or BPW lightweight chassis because an automatic release mechanism is built into the brake drums. This senses when a caravan is being reversed and it automatically prevents the brakes from engaging during the manoeuvre.

Overall, there's no doubt that the undergear systems on models made in the last two decades embody many improvements.

Prior to 1980, a caravan window was glass which was mounted in an aluminium frame.

d) **Windows**

In November 1977, it became mandatory for caravans to be fitted with safety glass. At this point, manufacturers decided to move away from glass units set within an aluminium frame and frameless moulded acrylic plastic units were installed instead. To begin with, most plastic windows were single glazed, although double-glazed versions were fitted on several top-of-the-range models. During the 1980s, these subsequently became standard because the higher level of thermal insulation was clearly beneficial. So windows should also be checked if you're buying a second-hand caravan from around this period.

DESIGN AND CONSTRUCTION

If a stone cracks a window on the front of your caravan, a small unit is not too expensive to replace.

Buyer's Tip

Windows

a) Windows fitted to pre-November 1977 caravans which comprise glass held in an aluminium frame are virtually impossible to replace.

b) Replacement double-glazed plastic windows are surprisingly expensive and can take a long time to obtain from a dealer. Useful contacts are breakers' yards and members of The Caravan Club can obtain an address list of breakers from the Club's Head Office.

c) A specialist who buys surplus stocks of new products from caravan manufacturers – including windows – is:
Magnum Caravan Surplus (Grimsby).
Tel: 01472 353520

d) Stones can get thrown up when you're towing and windows on the front occasionally get cracked. When it comes to buying a replacement, the cost will be considerably less if it's one of the three small windows fitted at the front as opposed to one large single unit.

e) If you really cannot find a replacement plastic window – for instance if your caravan's manufacturer has ceased trading – EECO (near Halifax) makes 'one-off' windows with a reasonably fast turn-around time.
Tel: 01274 679524.

Caravans built with a single window on the front are going to cost the owner a considerable amount of money if a flying stone causes damage.

The wooden framework and ceiling board of a caravan roof is often built as an independent section.

e) Roof design and construction

Irrespective of the age of 'van that you're planning to purchase, have a look at its roof design. Nowadays many manufacturers assemble pre-insulated sectional panels which are subsequently offered-up to the supporting walls and then skinned with aluminium sheet.

Flat roofs are less good at discharging rainwater and this is not always a good feature. On the other hand, if you plan to fit a roof-mounted TV aerial, a solar panel or an air conditioner, there's no doubt that these fit more successfully on a flat surface.

On a flat-roofed caravan, the roof skin is usually pulled into place from a large roll of aluminium sheet.

DESIGN AND CONSTRUCTION

Boat-style roofs have a slightly raised ridge that runs from end to end. Separate aluminium sheets are mounted on either side of this ridge and a trim cover bedded on sealant covers the join. In this design, rainwater is more quickly discharged outwards.

You may also come across the old-style 'lantern roof' where a central raised section is fitted with narrow windows on either side. Caravans like the Safari adopted this pattern and this style is now a patent design of Carlight Caravans. It's a distinctive feature on these craftsman-built models.

Lastly you'll find that some roofs are built using a one-piece glass-reinforced-plastic (GRP) moulding. Avondale has been one of the companies using this type of construction on certain models. The moulded roof fitted to the latest Avondale Landranger is especially impressive and its thoughtful designers have ensured that rainwater is appropriately discharged with efficiency.

Sealant under the central cover strip of a 'boat-style' roof may need to be renewed periodically.

Avondale has been noted for single-piece GRP roofs which are fitted on models such as this Landranger.

Is the front panel on this Fleetwood made from GRP or acrylic-capped ABS plastic? An inspection soon shows that it's made from the latter.

This 1990 Compass Rallye is built with GRP panels on both the front and rear walls.

Running a hand over the rear of the front skirt on this Compass Rallye immediately reveals that it's made from GRP.

f) Moulded front and rear panels

All but the least expensive caravans now have moulded panels at the front and rear. However, when purchasing a caravan, whether new or old, it's helpful to know if these moulded sections are made from GRP or acrylic-capped ABS. There's a good reason for this and the box below explains how you can tell the difference.

Technical Tip

Checking for GRP and acrylic-capped ABS moulded panels.

The key feature of GRP is that it has a shiny side and a reverse side that is usually quite rough to the touch. The roughness is not a problem when the reverse face of a panel is not going to be seen. However, on expensive caravans, items like GRP locker lids often have a secondary inner skin of GRP to hide the rough texture.

In contrast, acrylic-capped ABS (acrylonitrile-butadiene-styrene) has a natural shine on both faces. Admittedly, a textured surface is sometimes created on one of the sides – as it is on many car bumpers made from ABS. But when you rub your hand over the reverse face, you'll see how ABS differs from GRP. In fact, many A-frame fairings at the front and items like flared wheel arches are made using ABS mouldings.

DESIGN AND CONSTRUCTION

Replacing the front panel of a caravan is an expensive operation and repairs to a damaged section can often be done by a skilled specialist.

The reason why it's helpful to establish which material has been used is related to repair work. Whereas a GRP panel is often both heavier and more expensive, it is often quite easy to repair. Boat builders, car body specialists and many others familiar with GRP repair techniques can effect neat repairs if you have the misfortune of damaging a panel.

In the last couple of years, special repair kits have now been formulated to repair ABS panels as well. Regrettably, however, not many staff at caravan service centres know about ABS repair procedures at present. With just a few exceptions, repair specialists would normally replace an entire caravan front or rear panel if it gets damaged. If you have the misfortune of merely cracking the spoiler section of an ABS front or rear wall section on a high kerb, it is most upsetting to hear that the entire panel will need replacing. The cost for this normally runs into four figures.

So until the skills of repairing ABS panels are more widely learnt, there's a degree of wisdom in looking for a caravan where these panels are made in GRP. Unfortunately, however, this material is becoming less used on more recent models.

The centrally located gas locker on this Avondale means that the weight of the cylinders is close to the axle.

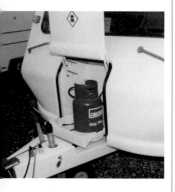

On a Carlight caravan, the gas cylinder is easily accessed by sliding its support tray forward out of the locker.

The imported Knauss 'Sport & Fun' is one of the few caravans which has large locker accommodation for outdoor activity gear.

g) External lockers

Lockers often didn't exist on caravans made thirty years ago and gas cylinders were merely mounted on an exposed rack fitted to the A-frame near the coupling. Today, however, it's standard practice to have a purpose-made gas locker and you should check that its lid fits well and isn't damaged. Most lockers are situated at the front although on a few models, the locker is situated over the wheel which has advantages in terms of weight distribution.

Check that access to the cylinder section of the locker is easy and don't expect to find the sliding base that makes cylinder replacement so easy if you own a Carlight caravan.

As regards a location for the caravan's battery, this should have its own separate locker. A few caravans built in the 1980s had a cage to house a battery installed alongside the gas cylinders. This is bad practice because gas can seep from a faulty cylinder valve and sparks are not unusual when coupling up a battery terminal. Hence to avoid any likelihood of an explosion, gas and battery lockers are now kept completely separate.

Beyond this, check to see if there are any external lockers built to house outdoor leisure gear. Regrettably, only a few caravans include this provision.

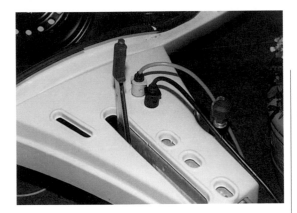

Fairings which cover a caravan's A-frame are often made of ABS plastic.

h) Fairings and other body parts

Caravans are built with a number of external components like a moulded fairing over the projecting axle at the front – called the A-frame. Then there are wheel arch extensions and it's not unusual to find the rear road lights mounted in a moulded housing.

These components are usually made either of GRP or ABS. If you intend to purchase an older model which was built by a manufacturer who is no longer trading, replacement items will be virtually impossible to obtain. However, it has already been explained that a skilled service specialist is usually able to repair GRP and ABS components.

The wheel arch extension here is made from ABS plastic and it might be hard to obtain a replacement for this 1990 model.

There are rather a lot of aluminium trim strips on this caravan; the screws which hold them in place can become points where rainwater enters.

Trim strips on a caravan often need rebedding on a strip of fresh sealant to ensure that leaks don't develop.

Another point to check is the aluminium trim strips. I make no secret of the fact that where embellishment is concerned, I'd rather see a painted stripe or an adhesive transfer. This is because an aluminium strip is usually held in place using screws and a bedding of mastic. When the mastic goes brittle, each screw hole becomes a potential drain hole for the entry of rainwater. Damp in caravans is something to look out for with great care when planning a purchase as mentioned in Chapter Two.

DESIGN AND CONSTRUCTION

This Carver appliance is a heater with sealed burners and separate intake and outlet air ducts.

i) Main appliances

In a modern caravan, the gas-operated space heater will be a sealed unit. This means its gas burners are fitted inside an enclosure and combustion air is drawn from outside via a ducting and not from the living space. Similarly there will be a flue which takes exhaust fumes directly outside. This arrangement is for safety.

If you purchase an older caravan which has an open-burner gas fire, you should have this removed and scrapped. Not only does liquefied petroleum gas give off moisture when it burns – which leads to condensation problems; open burners are no longer considered safe. Under no circumstances should the fumes be able to reach the living area.

Turning to refrigerators it is a matter of concern that a number of caravan manufacturers do not fit these units in accordance with the Electrolux installation instructions. When correctly fitted, the whole of the rear section of the unit should be completely enclosed and shielded from the living quarters. If the caravan manufacturer has failed to construct a proper enclosure around the cooling unit, two problems arise:

1. Draughts blowing towards the outside wall vents are able to enter the living area.
2. In hot spells, the refrigerator will not run efficiently and you won't be able to obtain the level of cooling of which the appliance is capable.

After removing a cutlery drawer it was easy to see through the upper vent in the side wall; so this fridge wasn't properly sealed off at the rear.

So when comparing new or second-hand caravans, peer through the outside wall vents and make sure you cannot see into the living space. Alternatively remove a kitchen drawer near the fridge to check if you can see light through one of the outside ventilators. If the vents are visible from inside, the appliance is not fitted with the rear shielding that the refrigerator manufacturer specifies. There is no danger involved here, but comfort and the appliance's efficiency will be compromised.

Summary

Using the advice in this chapter, now have a critical look at some caravans. While it's true that caravans look broadly similar to an uninitiated observer, you'll soon recognise many of the important features discussed in this Chapter.

ESTABLISHING THE AGE OF A CARAVAN

Whereas cars have a Vehicle Registration Document, there is no obligatory form of registration to accompany a caravan. It can therefore be quite difficult to establish a caravan's age. Chassis plates, for example, are not always helpful and there's no doubt that some second-hand models on sale are older than the seller suggests. The notes which follow record changes that have occurred and these act as helpful clues for anyone trying to establish when a caravan was manufactured.

1970s caravans:
- Caravans of this period are heavy and are built very differently from post-1980 models.
- Bargain buys for around £500–£800 certainly exist and sometimes provide a pleasant introduction to caravanning. But be careful if you're not prepared to carry out repairs or improvements yourself.
- Spares can be difficult to obtain for earlier models – particularly spare parts for appliances, fittings for furniture, chassis items and coupling components.
- Locker boxes to house gas cylinders – previously clamped to the draw-bar and open to the weather – became common after 1971.
- Refrigerators like the Morphy Richards models of the early 1970s had to be lit using a match and often failed to provide cooling because of an air lock.
- Chassis made by firms like B&B, Peak, and CI need periodic painting.

- The running gear of the period employed spring suspension and shock absorbers; damaged items may be difficult to replace.
- To reverse a 1970s caravan, you usually need to operate an override catch on the coupling head before starting the manoeuvre. This is an annoying chore.
- In the early 1970s, fluorescent lights became popular but gas lamps were often fitted, too, in order to provide back-up lighting.
- In the early 1970s, water pumps were usually foot or hand-operated devices.
- Bodywork construction comprised a framework made of wood. This skeleton structure was clad with aluminium sheet on the outside and a coated hardboard or plywood wall on the inside.
- Insulation was poor on most 1970s 'vans. Usually fibre glass wool was placed in the void between the wall panels – but this slumps down in time leaving cold spots.
- Floors were made from plywood with supporting joints underneath and seldom had any form of insulation.
- Windows were single glazed and glass was used. However, in November 1977 it became obligatory for new caravans to be fitted with safety glass.
- In response to legislation, the industry introduced acrylic single-glazed windows comprising a frameless moulded pane. Aluminium frames were discontinued overnight.
- Not long afterwards, double-glazed versions of these 'plastic' windows became the standard fitting.
- After October 1979, it became mandatory for all new caravans to include a rear fog lamp. Absence of a fog lamp suggests a 'van is a pre-1979 model.
- From 1978, a double socket system was used – the 12N socket for caravan road lights; the 12S socket was reserved for internal supplies.

DESIGN AND CONSTRUCTION

1980s caravans:

- A new approach to building was introduced using pre-manufactured bonded sandwich floors and wall panels; most manufacturers soon adopted the system.
- New computer-designed lightweight chassis were introduced around 1980–1981.
- On lightweight chassis, the coil springing system together with its shock absorbers was replaced by a rubber-in-compression suspension system.
- A few chassis as late as 1984 were still painted, but galvanising was more usual now as a standard finish.
- In April 1989, all caravans manufactured had to have auto-reverse brakes; manually operated levers fitted to the coupling head became obsolete. Automatic brake disengagement mechanisms were now built into the drums.
- More and more low-voltage appliances appear in caravans including electric pumps, reading lights, fans and stereo systems. Now a separate 'leisure battery' becomes an essential item.
- Fused distribution panels were introduced so that low voltage circuits could be separated and fused independently.
- In the mid-1980s, caravans lost their symmetry and became wedge shaped using sloping fronts to achieve better fuel economy.
- From 1986, virtually all gas storage lockers were built into the body itself. A separate locker box mounted on the drawbar was no longer fitted.
- From the mid-1980s many caravans were equipped with water heaters and the Carver Cascade storage heater was the most popular of these appliances.
- Around 1987, the cassette toilet arrived, revolutionising bathroom design and vastly improving emptying arrangements.
- From 1 May 1989, smoke alarms had to be fitted to all new caravans and all second-hand 'vans sold by a dealer.

1990s caravans:

- Road lights set high on the sides – called marker lights – became obligatory on caravans manufactured after 1 October 1990.
- Combustion Modified High Resilience Foam (CMHR) became mandatory in UK caravans built after 1 March 1990.
- From April 1991, all fabrics have had to be of a fire-resistant type.
- Hardly any caravans have been sold in the 1990s that haven't been wired for mains electricity by the manufacturer.
- In the latter part of the 1990s, reeded and stucco surfaces were used less and less on external walls. Smooth aluminium finishes became popular again.
- In 1992, ALKO-Kober announced that their latest lightweight chassis must not be drilled – even for mounting a stabiliser bracket on the drawbar.
- The CRiS (Caravan Registration and Identification Scheme) was introduced in 1992 and UK-manufactured caravans were issued with a Vehicle Identification Number (VIN). This is documented with owner-information recorded at CRiS headquarters and a number etched on windows.
- Since 1994, flame failure devices have been fitted on stoves.
- Around 1992, BPW chassis and running gear featured maintenance-free sealed bearings.
- The Al-Ko Euro-axle with sealed bearings appeared in 1994 ranges. The sealed bearings are well enginered, but to inspect the brake shoes an expensive torque wrench is needed to

DESIGN AND CONSTRUCTION

remove/replace the 'one-shot' nut which holds the drums in place.

* In Spring 1995, the Abbey Domino was launched with GRP impact-resistant sheet on its side walls instead of aluminium sheeting. Other models have followed using this easy-repair material.
* From 1 January 1996, gas appliances have had to bear a CE mark to indicate that they meet European standards.
* In caravans manufactured from 1997 onwards, a small 'tamper-proof' tag containing the Vehicle Identification Number is hidden within the bodywork and this can only be identified using a CRiS reader device.
* AL-KO Kober introduced a universal chassis with bolt together main members in Spring 1999. This meant that models of different lengths in a manufacturer's range could be accommodated using the same chassis components.
* In Spring 1999, AL-KO Kober introduced the Euro Over-Run Automatic Self-adjusting Brake. This detects movement when a 'van is parked on a backward facing slope and will re-apply a slipping brake automatically.
* A CRiS Scheme was launched in 1999 in which caravans manufactured before 1992 can be retrospectively CRiS registered and tagged.

Note: If planning to purchase a CRiS-registered caravan, you can have the age of the 'van confirmed together with verification that it has not been reported as stolen by 'phoning CRiS on 01722 411430.

CHAPTER FOUR

STORING YOUR CARAVAN

A point that often worries potential purchasers is where to keep their caravan. In practice this isn't the problem that many people imagine and seven suggestions are proposed in this chapter. There's certainly more scope than you might have thought.

A caravan usually takes up more space than the car which tows it. So storing it between holiday trips is a matter that needs some thought. Here are a few ideas you might like to consider:

- On hard standing alongside your house.
- In a commercial compound specifically designed for caravan storage.
- At an indoor facility intended for storing caravans.
- In a storage compound at a privately owned caravan site or a club site.
- On a short-term seasonal pitch on a club or privately owned site.
- On a farm, either inside a barn or outdoors.
- At a storage facility abroad near a venue you return to on a regular basis.

On farm sites, arrangements can sometimes be made to leave your caravan in a barn.

To draw a caravan up a drive when parking alongside their home, some owners install a manual or electric winch.

Don't let storage put you off buying a caravan. There are caravanners who live in high rise flats, in split-level houses on the side of a steep hill, or in properties where there's a dreadfully tight chicane in the driveway. Some own a house which offers sufficient parking space but cannot contemplate reversing a caravan on to the allotted position. A number of caravanners solve this by installing a manual or electric winch so that their 'van can be pulled over a kerb and along difficult terrain to the parking place. Others purchase a battery-driven pulling device or have an electrically driven Motor Mover fitted. Where there's a will there's a way.

So let's look at the plus and minus points about different storage solutions.

If you feel uneasy reversing a caravan on to a parking place at your house, a Motor Mover usually eases manoeuvring problems.

ALONGSIDE YOUR HOUSE

Of the seven alternative storage possibilities, parking a caravan alongside your house is the only one that doesn't involve a fee. On the other hand, this isn't always permissible. For instance there's sometimes a covenant which a property developer imposed when your house was originally built. Covenants occasionally forbid the storage of a caravan and these restrictions are often established on open-plan estates where front gardens are unfenced to give an overall impression of space.

Notwithstanding the existence of covenants, there are instances where stored caravans are screened from sight alongside a house and when this is done discreetly, neighbours seldom raise an objection. Common sense usually prevails although there's no doubt that a conspicuously parked caravan can occasionally spoil the views of other residents.

In addition to covenant restrictions, it is equally likely that a Local Authority's Permission is required to park a caravan on council-owned property. And be aware that in both these examples of possible restrictions, the references relate to an empty caravan; it stands to reason that using a caravan for additional permanent accommodation would not meet with approval.

With these points in mind, it should also be pointed out that several Acts of Parliament do permit a home owner to store a caravan on his or her driveway in certain circumstances. The legal departments of both the Camping and Caravanning Club and The Caravan Club are able to provide members with more information about rights and restrictions.

When restrictions are absent, there are both advantages and disadvantages of storage at your place of residence. These are:

Advantages
- You can keep an eye on your caravan.
- It's easy to keep it clean on a regular basis and you can also heat the interior periodically when winter temperatures plummet or damp weather arrives.
- Within reason a caravan can provide useful storage space for summer chairs, a picnic table and your patio sunshade.

Disadvantages
- When shielding is difficult or if there's not access to the side or rear of your house, a caravan stuck in the front garden is not an asset to your home's appearance.
- If you take a holiday in your caravan, everyone in the area knows you're not at home. Indeed a caravan can become a conspicuous landmark and you don't have to be a house-breaker to spot a 'van is missing from its normal resting place.

So there might be better storage strategies.

COMMERCIAL STORAGE COMPOUNDS

If you look at the entry entitled 'Caravan Storage' in the *Yellow Pages* covering your area, you're likely to see addresses of commercial storage compounds. Furthermore, if you're a member of The Caravan Club, a list of storage specialists is available free from their head office.

Outdoor storage centres vary a great deal in respect of security, service and price. It's no secret that caravan theft has been a growing problem and some commercial storage centres have a resident warden living on site, and with security fences, alarms and closed-circuit cameras. That's one extreme. At the other end of the spectrum you'll find a few compounds merely protected by a five-bar gate and a tractor.

Security at many high-quality commercial storage venues includes CCTV camera systems.

Storing caravans in a compound merely protected by a padlock and gates is not going to present a thief with much of a challenge.

Not surprisingly, insurance companies ask for detailed information about the place where clients park their caravan and some storage specialists fall far short of the minimum level of security that the insurers specify. So check this point most carefully before towing your 'van to a compound and parting with money.

And one more point. Not all owners using a storage facility choose a site which is close to their home. Owners who particularly like to return to the same area year after year sometimes prefer to select a storage site near their holiday venue in order to reduce the towing distances.

TIP
Caravan Storage Site Owners' Association

Recognising the security problem, a professional trade body was instituted in 1999 to represent caravan storage owners. Known as CaSSOA (Caravan Storage Site Owners' Association), this demands a high level of security at member storage facilities and the growing national chain of approved centres is in excess of 400.

A team of inspectors checks storage sites applying for membership and issues a gold, silver or bronze badge depending on the level of security. This takes note of the location of the site, protection from the elements, security, safety and control of access. An item like a sound, secure perimeter fence, for example, is deemed essential.

A list of centres region-by-region can be accessed through the web site,
www.cassoa.co.uk
or by telephoning 0115 941 1022.

STORING YOUR CARAVAN

Addresses of commercial storage compounds are often listed in Yellow Pages.

Once again, there are advantages and disadvantages of this storage option:

Advantages
- Your caravan is not taking up precious garden space at home.
- The level of security on a high-quality storage facility is likely to be much higher than it is at your home.
- Some storage specialists offer additional services like caravan cleaning. A few can carry out servicing work as well.

Disadvantages
- Out of sight, out of mind. Once the 'van is sited, some owners completely forget to remove their battery for winter charging. Equally, end-of-season jobs like the water drain-down are overlooked.
- If you want to collect something left in your caravan, or perhaps you've got repairs to carry out, it isn't always easy to gain access to a storage compound at short notice.

Indoor storage ensures that a caravan is kept out of inclement weather.

COMMERCIAL INDOOR STORAGE

Specialists offering indoor storage for caravans and motorhomes are relatively uncommon. However, there are a few in Britain and one of the largest is Calvers Caravan Storage in Bedfordshire. Not only are there caravans here owned by UK residents from all over the country; there are also clients from as far away as South Africa and the United States of America. These are people who enjoy touring the United Kingdom and other European countries but who prefer the versatility and flexibility of a caravan rather than stopping at hotels.

Taking this particular storage centre as an example, caravans are closely packed inside darkened and thermally insulated storage buildings. Items like the upholstery or curtains are thus unlikely to fade and the caravan is not exposed to the extremes of weather.

STORING YOUR CARAVAN

At this indoor storage centre, caravans are skilfully parked and retrieved whenever the client requires.

The intricate task of manoeuvring a caravan into or out of its bay is undertaken by personnel at the storage centre and clients simply drive up to a parking area near the entrance to collect or return their caravan. During a six- or twelve-month storage period there are no restrictions on the number of times you request the use of the 'van.

Whereas a layer of dust will inevitably accumulate on a caravan stored under cover, there is no likelihood of leaks, algae deposits or bird droppings leaving their unwelcome marks.

Advantages
- There's greater security when a caravan is locked away and packed tightly amongst many others in a storage building.
- A caravan remains cleaner when kept indoors and any model afflicted by occasional leaks in very bad weather will benefit from indoor storage pending repair work.

Disadvantages
- The fees charged for under-cover storage are usually quite high.
- There are not many covered storage centres in Britain.

Storage is often available at caravan sites although the compound is usually discreetly located.

STORAGE AT CARAVAN SITES

Both The Camping and Caravanning Club and The Caravan Club offer storage facilities at some of the sites they own. Appropriately the compounds are not always conspicuous and it's a useful service for members which often passes unnoticed.

In practice, storage is only available on selected club sites although you don't have to choose a venue close to home. Equally, many other caravan sites and holiday parks also get involved in storage as a sideline. Take Highfield Farm Park near Cambridge, for example. This is a privately owned site that is in membership of the Best of British Holiday Park group. Manicured lawns and screened sections are part of the charm and it is not unusual for visitors to be wholly unaware that there's a small storage compound at the site. This is because it is appropriately shielded by trees and strong steel posts provide security at the entrance.

STORING YOUR CARAVAN

Another discreetly located compound can be found on a site with landscaped, reseeded and rolling hills that was once a coal mine at Oakdale, not far from Newport in South Wales. Again, you may not see the fenced compound and it certainly doesn't detract from the site in any way.

These are just two of the hundreds of caravan sites around the country which also offer a discreet storage service. So if you stop at a caravan park in an area you find particularly pleasing, you might like to enquire about storage. But be aware of the advantages and disadvantages of this arrangement.

Advantages

- You can easily return to an area you enjoy with the knowledge that your caravan can quickly be transferred from the compound to a pitch.
- Towing – which for some owners is a chore – is reduced and for a quick weekend getaway that's especially beneficial when fighting Friday's traffic.

Disadvantages

- Don't be surprised to find a dusty and streaky caravan on your arrival. And remember to make arrangements for its transferral from the locked compound.
- Levels of security vary and some sites don't have the sophisticated provision of surveillance equipment found on many purpose-built commercial storage centres.
- There's a discouragement to have a caravan regularly serviced when it's stored some way from home. And most site owners do not allow you to wash or repair a caravan once it's transferred to a pitch.

Entry to Caravan Club sites sometimes requires either a swipe card or a security code.

Seasonal pitches are organised both at Club and privately owned sites.

SHORT-TERM SEASONAL PITCHES

On both club and privately owned sites it is often permitted to leave your caravan on one of the pitches for an extended period. This is not strictly storage in the normal sense of the word, but it enables you to have a base away from home. The term, 'seasonal pitch' is used for this facility.

From a site owner's point of view it is always a gamble knowing how many pitches to allocate for long-term use. On occasions, caravans with drawn, faded curtains and a fair share of long grass around their perimeter can detract from a site's appearance. Equally they effectively curb the chance of more lucrative pitch lettings if the season is blessed with long spells of summer sunshine. But, of course it's a guaranteed income for a pre-agreed period of time.

As far as the co-ordinating staff of the club sites are concerned, they constantly review the position, knowing that touring members will not be pleased if they find pitch availability much reduced on account of 'sitting tenants'. So the position is reviewed regularly and venues offering seasonal pitches are intentionally changed from year to year.

As far as a caravan owner is concerned, this is a splendid way to establish a 'second home' and a place of escape. You can even keep an eye on the weather and defer an away-weekend until the last minute. However, the booking conditions relating to seasonal pitches are strict. For instance, the sub-letting of a touring caravan is normally not permitted and you would need to read the 'small print' carefully.

Also, be aware that a caravan kept on a pitch

At some Caravan Club sites, the level of security is especially good.

STORING YOUR CARAVAN

in the main part of a site is unlikely to be as secure as it would be in a locked and fenced compound. On the other hand at some Caravan Club sites, entry for all visitors is via a security barrier for which you need a card or key number. This is certainly a praiseworthy provision.

As a postscript, it is also crucial that you keep in close touch with the site proprietor, particularly at times of severe weather. The photograph alongside shows a situation during extreme wet weather in 2001 when the owner of a suitably wheel-clamped caravan on a seasonal pitch couldn't be contacted by the warden. Anxious 'phone calls went unanswered and the flood waters kept rising. Unclamped 'vans, meanwhile, were pulled to safe ground by tractor.

Advantages
- During the caravanning season, you can have a leisure base properly established and ready for occupation.
- Home storage inconvenience is eliminated for extended periods during the year.

Disadvantages
- Being 'locked-in' to one site discourages you from travelling more widely.
- Security on a pitch in the main part of a site doesn't match the level of anti-theft provision achievable when a caravan is locked in a fenced compound.
- Seasonal pitches can be costly and if circumstances prevent you from using the caravan on a regular basis, this strategy is hardly cost-effective.
- Wardens cannot crop the grass close to a caravan parked for a long period, so you may need to take some shears to keep your caravan's perimeter tidy.

If you leave a clamped caravan on a seasonal pitch, make certain you can be easily contacted by the warden, especially if it's near a watercourse.

STORING ON A FARM

If you visit some of the small location sites that both The Camping and Caravanning Club and The Caravan Club list in their Members' Site Book, you'll find that many are farms. Bearing in mind that farmers have been experiencing tough times in the last few years, it's hardly surprising that a number are willing to store your caravan in a barn or within the farmyard itself for an appropriate fee.

You might like to take up this opportunity but don't overlook the realities of rural life. Farm animals sometimes break through a fence and it's always amazing what they decide to eat. You might also find that manure which is so beneficial on the land is less welcome on a caravan's drawbar.

So whereas you might decide to leave an inexpensive elderly caravan on a farm, I'd seriously doubt the wisdom of making this arrangement for a more expensive and newer model.

Advantages
- Points made earlier in respect of seasonal pitch arrangements and storage away from home all apply once again.
- Farms which take no more than five caravans under special exemption arrangements described in the adjacent panel can be enchanting places to visit.
- The fee to leave your 'van on a farm is often extremely reasonable and sometimes there's space in a barn which provides weather protection.

Disadvantages
- Security is often open to question.
- Movement around a farmyard – both of livestock and agricultural implements – can easily lead to a brush with your paintwork.
- Be prepared to find a dirty caravan on every visit.

Tip

Both major clubs list 'five-van only' sites in their directories. These are known as Certificated Locations (CLs) with The Caravan Club (around 3,000) or 'Certificated Sites' (CSs) with The Camping & Caravanning Club' (around 1,500). These venues obtain a special exemption under the 1960 Caravan Sites and Control of Development Act and a large proportion are based on farms. A number are able to offer small-scale storage as well – sometimes under cover in outbuildings.

STORING ABROAD

Caravanners who embark on long trips to Southern France, Spain and other more distant European venues will often see advertisements for caravan storage. Signs announcing Gardiennage Caravanes are often seen in France and a number of farmers advertise storage opportunities on roadside notice boards. In addition, you'll often find a leaflet left on the door of your caravan when stopping at a large holiday site. Recognising that journeys to these warm venues are costly on fuel, costly on ferry tickets and often rather tiring, it is no surprise that local entrepreneurs offer to store your caravan.

But the position is not straightforward. Current EU Law appears to allow these storage arrangements, provided your caravan is strictly used for pleasure purposes. However, the legal responsibilities, insurance and security situation are complex. For instance your roof light might get blown off in a gale-force wind, striking a neighbouring caravan in the process. This raises Third Party considerations, not to forget the damage to your caravan which will now allow wet inside whenever it rains.

Similarly it is normal for storage specialists to want to move caravans around to achieve access and so your request to fit a robust wheel clamp as a security measure will probably be refused.

On a practical note, it is also likely that the higher temperatures in more southerly countries will hasten the drying out of the sealant along your caravan's seams. Similarly, direct sunlight won't be kind to the side walls of your tyres. And, if you leave a caravan at a distant venue for several seasons, when will it be serviced and by whom? This is likely to be a problem when you finally decide to tow it back to the United Kingdom.

In rural France, you often find Gardiennage Caravanes signs announcing the storage of caravans.

Add to this the fact that you'll need to take an awful lot of caravanning clobber in your car whenever heading for the distant venue, and you begin to see why this is a very questionable strategy.

In reality, the savings on a ferry and fuel are counterbalanced by a number of disadvantages. In fact when a friend of the author was rather slow to renew storage payment on his elderly caravan which he left at a site in Spain, he subsequently found that the impatient proprietor had destroyed it.

Advantages
- You will save on ferry costs, fuel costs and avoid the aggravation of towing over large distances.

Disadvantages
- Insurance problems, security doubts, damage to the fabric of the 'van from heat are just a few of many imponderables that place a big question mark over this idea.
- When and by whom will the caravan be serviced?
- A touring caravan left hundreds of miles away cannot provide the pleasure of travelling around closer to home.
- A lot of caravan equipment needs stowing in your car when travelling to and from the venue.

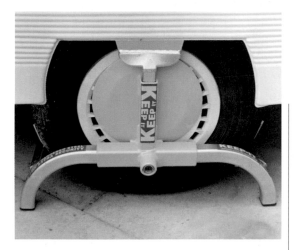

Provided a storage site owner doesn't insist that your caravan should be easy to move, fitting it with a security device is much to be commended.

INSURANCE

These seven alternative approaches to storage provide a number of possibilities. However, it is most important to emphasis that all caravan insurance companies will want to know where your caravan is kept. This is clearly stated in their literature and if you contravene the agreed arrangement, it is likely that a claim will not be met.

Furthermore, if you check the insurance position with storage proprietors, they normally point out that insurance is your responsibility. Some storage centres are as secure as the Tower of London and have a blemish-free record. Other's are less impressive.

With this in mind, it's a matter of considerable concern that caravan theft has grown considerably in recent years and determined thieves go to great lengths to secure certain models. Whereas some storage specialists happily take your caravan off your hands, they sometimes make it all-too-easy for thieves to take the 'van off your hands in a way you didn't anticipate. Just because there's a high fence and an alarm system, you are urged to fit security devices as well.

So be especially careful, even if you park a caravan outside your home. Wheel clamps and other security products need to be considered too, and these are discussed in Chapter Six.

CHAPTER FIVE

TOW CARS AND TOWING

Most people buying a caravan are constrained in their choice by the ability of their car to do the towing. A few go about things the other way round. They become so eager to own a particular 'van that they are fully prepared to buy a more powerful car. Either way, the focus here is about creating a matching partnership. How can you work out what sort of caravan your car will be able to tow efficiently and safely? And is it easy to tow a caravan on today's busy roads?

If the letters sent by readers to caravan magazines are anything to go by, there are a lot of caravanners who find it difficult to work out what size and weight of caravan their car could tow. To find this out, there are several simple guidelines to follow and one of the aims here is to take you through the process.

73

If you want to tow a large caravan like this Abbey Spectrum, you'll need a powerful and heavy towing vehicle.

MANUFACTURERS' LIMITS

Car manufacturers usually publish the maximum overall weight of a fully-packed trailer that can be towed – and the term 'trailer' includes caravans as well. Sometimes this is called the 'towing limit' and the term is described further in the adjacent box.

As regards the weight of a tow car, this is often referred to as the 'kerb weight'. Check the box on

Unsuitable tow cars

A few cars cannot be used to tow at all. These models are examples:

Ford Ka
Audi A2 (model launched in 2001)
Vauxhall Tigra
MGF
Aston Martin DB7
some Mazda MX5 models

In reality these are hardly the kind of vehicles you'd choose for caravan towing duties. In addition, there are others where the manufacturer's towing limit is so low that it excludes caravans. Some Ford Fiestas have a very modest towing limit, the Zetec 1,250cc for example, has a maximum of 250kg – which hardly covers a camping trailer.

Weight (Mass) Terminology – the towing vehicle

KERB WEIGHT: Defined by the vehicle manufacturer and which normally –
Excludes:
the weight of passengers
any load apart from essential tools e.g. a wheel brace and jack
the weight of towing add-ons like a bracket, 12V sockets, mirrors, etc
Includes:
a full tank of fuel
other liquids forming part of the engine system

MAXIMUM TRAIN WEIGHT: Defined by the vehicle manufacturer as the maximum permissible combined weight of both the laden tow car and the laden caravan. 'MTW', sometimes called gross train weight or gross combination weight, is the total sum of the tow vehicle weight, the weight of its occupants, the weight of its other load items and the weight of the caravan and all its contents. The stated limit must not be exceeded.

TOWING LIMIT: Sometimes specified by a car manufacturer and usually referring to the maximum weight a car can tow based on its re-start ability on a 1:8 (12.5 per cent) uphill gradient.

the opposite page for an explanation of this.

Another limit stated by a manufacturer is the 'maximum train weight'. This is similarly explained in the box opposite.

The data section in your vehicle's owner's manual, should provide these all-important limits. Alternatively a Type-Approved vehicle will have its maximum towing weight stamped on the VIN plate which is usually mounted in the engine compartment. Still working on matters of weight (or 'mass' as a physicist would prefer) let's look further at contributing factors to towing stability.

CAR AND CARAVAN WEIGHT RELATIONSHIP

Whereas maximum train weight is one limiting factor to the size of caravan your car can tow, the stability of the outfit is also influenced by the car's weight in relationship to the weight of the fully laden caravan. The box opposite explains terms relating to the caravan.

Using this information, you should always ensure that your fully laden caravan doesn't exceed its designed limit. Reacting to the fact that some owners overload their caravan with no regard for safety, the Police are carrying out an increasing number of roadside weight checks. Overloading may lead to prosecution and it is also likely to render your insurance policy null and void.

The only way to get a clear picture of the fully laden weight of your caravan is to take it to a public weighbridge. These are usually listed in the *Yellow Pages* but you can also contact your local Trading Standards Department (Weights & Measures Section) for information.

Once you have these figures, you can now carry

What can be used for towing?

Without doubt, most cars can be used to tow a caravan but some models are much more suitable than others. As a rule, the best cars are:

1. Equipped with a powerful engine
2. Fairly heavy

This is a simplification, of course, but it stands to reason that an engine needs to be powerful. In addition, the towing vehicle should be heavier than its fully laden caravan and this factor contributes to the stability of the combined unit as explained later.

out a comparison between the kerb weight of your tow car and the actual weight of the packed caravan. A recommendation adopted by the caravan and trailer towing associations is that to ensure you have good stability – **the weight of the loaded caravan should not be more than 85 per cent of the kerb weight of the tow car.**
This gives the recommended maximum weight of a caravan to achieve a stable pairing.

Weight (Mass) Terminology – the caravan

(These are terms introduced in conjunction with the European standards for caravans EN 1645 Pt 2. Terms used before these definitions were adopted are also given below.)

MAXIMUM TECHNICALLY PERMISSIBLE LADEN MASS (MTPLM), formerly Maximum Allowable Mass or Maximum Technical Permissible Weight: Stated by the manufacturer, taking account of elements like tyre ratings, suspension weight limits, material rigidity etc.

MASS IN RUNNING ORDER (MRO), formerly Ex-works Weight: Weight of the caravan with factory-supplied equipment as defined by the manufacturer.

USER PAYLOAD, formerly Caravan Allowable Payload: The weight limit is established by subtracting the **MRO** from the **MTPLM**. The user payload comprises the following three elements:
i) **Personal effects payload:** items you take including clothing, food, drink, cutlery, crockery, cooking utensils, bedding, hobby equipment. The formula for the expected minimum provision is:
(10 x number of berths) + (10 x length of body in metres excluding draw bar) + 30 = Minimum allowance for personal effect payload.
ii) **Essential habitation equipment:** any items, including fluids, deemed by the manufacturer as essential for the safe and proper function of equipment for habitation.
iii) **Optional equipment:** the weight of optional items like a cycle rack, spare wheel, an air-conditioning unit, and an extra bunk must now be itemised by the caravan manufacturer. The weight of items subsequently installed by the owner, e.g. a solar panel will also fall into this category.

TOW CARS AND TOWING

But note:
1. If the answer is greater than the stated maximum towing limit of a particular vehicle, you must obviously work to the lower figure.
2. The weight distribution of your possessions in the caravan and its noseweight are important, too. These topics are discussed in Chapter Eight.
3. Remember that the 85 per cent recommendation is not a legal requirement and caravan specialists add the following comment.

A driver with extensive towing experience who drives with great vigilance, and whose towing vehicle is suitably powerful, may choose to extend the tow car/caravan weight relationship to 100 per cent.

However, a trailer should never weigh more than its towing vehicle. Should this occur there's a great risk that the 'tail' (i.e. the caravan) might start to wag the 'dog' (i.e. the tow car). It is at this point when the stability of the entire outfit is under severe threat.

Some examples of questions

Q. In 2001 I purchased a Rover 45 2.0-litre diesel saloon car; what is the maximum weight of caravan I could tow without breaking the 85 per cent recommendation?

A. The kerb weight of your Rover is listed at 1,230kg and the 85 per cent rule would suggest you can tow a loaded caravan up to 1,045kg. However, in this case, Rover have put a towing limit on your car of 1,000kg so you must not exceed the lower figure.

Q. I want to keep my elderly (1989) Swift Corvette but need to buy a new tow car. I like the specification on a Citroën Xantia 1.8-litre Dimension – but is it suitable for towing my Corvette?

A. No problem! The car is listed as having a weight of 1,264kg, together with a maximum towing weight of 1,500kg. A Swift Corvette weighs around 762kg unladen – presuming that you haven't added any accessories like an air conditioner. Its maximum payload is listed at 150kg which all adds up to a caravan with a total permitted laden weight of 912kg. That's well within the capacity of the Citroën, although it's still prudent to check these figures by taking your packed caravan to a public weighbridge.

OTHER TOW CAR CONSIDERATIONS

Let's return now to the subject of engine power which is rather a vague term. Also think of the time-honoured phrase about 'horses for courses'.

Engine characteristics and torque

A fast, powerful horse likely to win a flat race at Newmarket might seem an impressive equine performer, but if required to pull a cart laden with beer crates it would be pretty ineffective. Conversely a large shire horse which displays stunning strength when required to pull a heavy farm cart would hardly feel at home running in the Cheltenham Gold Cup.

Cars are much the same. In fact many of the 'GT' type of 'sports' cars are swift performers but achieve their peak power characteristics (or 'torque' as it's usually called) when the engine is running at high revs. One of these cars being driven in top gear and at high revs would easily achieve an illegal speed of 120mph or more. That's fine on a private track but of no interest whatsoever to a caravanner who in the UK is not permitted to exceed 50mph on single carriage roads (where there is not a lower enforced restriction in place), or 60mph on dual carriageways and motorways.

What the caravanner wants is a car which achieves its best pulling power when it's in top gear and the engine is still running at low revs. Hence you'll hear technically-minded caravan specialists saying that it's best to own a car which achieves its maximum torque at a low engine speed.

It's worth commenting that diesel engines are especially noted for achieving their best pulling power when the engine is turning over quite

Weight and a powerful engine are important – but you don't need the latest model to achieve safe and certain towing performance.

TOW CARS AND TOWING

slowly, but there are plenty of petrol-driven cars which achieve good torque at low revs as well. Although diesel vehicles often make good tow cars, but you certainly don't have to buy a diesel car to tow a caravan.

Automatic
In recent years, it has been agreed that vehicles with automatic transmission instead of a conventional gearbox often make good towcars. That used not to be the view of automotive experts, but today, however, it's recognised that an automatic is good on hill starts and certainly affords relaxing driving when you're moving at irregular intervals in a serious traffic jam. However, many owners prefer manual gearboxes and that's fine where towing's concerned.

There's also a serious problem with an automatic if its transmission fluid starts to overheat when outside temperatures are high and the towing task is a tough one. To combat this some owners have an additional oil cooler fitted in the system and if you have any need for advice, either consult a main dealer or contact:
The Federation of Automatic Transmission Engineers,
PO Box 25,
Clacton-on-Sea,
Essex, CO15 2GG
Tel: 07885 228 595.

Vehicles with an automatic gearbox usually make good tow cars, as long as the transmission fluid doesn't overheat in extreme temperatures.

Many suspension aids are available, but check if the type you plan to purchase is deemed suitable by the vehicle manufacturer.

Suspension

The suspension of a towing vehicle faces extra load when a caravan coupling head (or 'hitch') is bearing down on the towball. Caravan noseweight, as it's called, is an important contributor to stability as explained in Chapter Eight.

Where a vehicle has a long overhang to the rear of the back axle, the noseweight load is magnified and the rear of the tow car might start to sag excessively. This will cause the headlight beam to lift to an unacceptable level and it also has the effect of lightening the load on the front tyres. On front-wheel-drive cars, this can also cause a loss of traction between the tyre tread and the road.

Many vehicles have a stiff enough suspension to cope with noseweight but others need reinforcing products to assist the standard springs. Seek advice on this subject – especially from the customer service department of the car manufacturer. The technical departments of the caravan clubs also have useful free literature on this subject available to members.

The trouble with some devices is that by stiffening-up the suspension for towing means there's a hardened ride when the car is being driven solo. However, there are a few devices on the market which offer progressive resistance, and only harden the suspension when a caravan or trailer is coupled-up.

TOW CARS AND TOWING

Tyres

Good stability is also dependent on having car and caravan tyres of the appropriate type, in good condition and correctly inflated. Some car handbooks suggest that tyre pressures are increased when the vehicle is heavily laden and this usually relates to towing as well. It's not unusual, for example, to increase the rear tyre pressure by 4psi to 7psi (0.3–0.5 bar) prior to towing – but to avoid false readings, only alter pressures when the tyres are cold.

Off-road 4x4 vehicles

Some owners presume that the 'ultimate' tow car for caravans is a 4x4 'all-terrain' vehicle. That's not entirely true.

Certainly on a campsite in muddy conditions, this type of vehicle is ideal for hauling a large caravan from a slippery pitch. On the road, the weight of this type of vehicle also helps in the tow vehicle/caravan weight relationship. But there are other elements which are less advantageous including the tendency of 4x4s to have a poor turning circle.

All-terrain vehicles offer several benefits as towing vehicles, but there may be some less suitable features if you want to pull a caravan.

A recent Land Rover fitted with an approved tow bracket and drop plate did not allow this caravan to tow at a suitable level, or slightly nose-down angle.

Moreover, the chassis rigidity of a true all-terrain vehicle can place a relatively light chassis on a modern caravan under surprising stress. In contrast, a conventional monocoque car has more resilience in its body construction.

To ease the unyielding nature of true chassis-based 4x4 vehicles, some owners fit proprietary 'cushioning' devices between a bolt-on towball and the mounting flange of the bracket. This strategy was fine until new legislation required that all tow brackets fitted to non-commercial vehicles registered post 1st September 1998 had to be TUV approved. The requirement also meant that large bolt-on devices like this were deemed illegal, unless they had been included in the original TUV test of the bracket to which they are fitted.

A further problem with some 4x4 off-road vehicles concerns towball height. Even though a towball height is now required to fall within certain limits, there are some instances where the towball on manufacturer-supplied brackets for all-terrain vehicles is too high, even when a drop plate is fitted. Whilst the ball height might prove fine for towing an agricultural trailer, it can cause a caravan to tow nose up and tail down as the accompanying illustration shows.

Towing brackets

Whether you decide to have your vehicle fitted with a bracket that accepts a bolt-on towball, a swan neck version, or a removable type, is a matter of personal choice. It's the same with the sockets. Most British owners prefer twin seven-pin sockets for coupling with the caravan's electrical system. However, there are single 13-pin sockets being used on the Continent now, especially in Germany.

While there's an adaptor to fit a 13-pin socket, some owners dislike this addition. However, cars of German manufacture and their dealer-supplied towing brackets give you no choice – unless the

In Britain, the traditional towball is held to the faceplate of the bracket with two large bolts.

TOW CARS AND TOWING

There are more swan neck towballs appearing in Britain now, but they don't allow certain accessory items to be fitted so easily.

towbar fitter is asked to cut off the supplied socket and rewire the lead to two separate 12N and 12S versions.

With these variations in mind and the increasing complexity of car wiring, it's important to have the work done by an accredited fitter. Recent changes in towbar legislation are described in the panel on page 84, and changes in the pin allocations on the 12S (supplementary) socket simply haven't been noted by a few ill-informed fitters. Even main dealer garages have wired up sockets incorrectly in a few reported cases.

If a car is fitted with a 13-pin socket to ISO 11446 standards, an adaptor lead is available to suit the twin plugs supplied on British caravans.

Because an adaptor cable adds more bulk around a coupling head, some caravanners have the 13-pin socket replaced with 12N and 12S types.

The authorisation plate fitted to the right of these sockets confirms the bracket has achieved type approval and can be fitted to post 1 August 1998 vehicles.

Which bracket?

Cars registered before 1 August 1998
- A non-EC Type-approved towing bracket can be legally fitted. But purchase a good quality product from a well-respected manufacturer.
- The bracket should comply with BS AU113 and BS AU114. Ball centre height must be between 350 and 420mm above the ground when the vehicle is fully ladenand more details are given in the 'Technical Tip' box on page 133. The ball centre should lie a minimum of 65mm rearwards from the vehicle body.

Changes in the law
The recent implementation of European Directive 94/20 insists that certain requirements have to be met. This directive now has legal standing in Britain following an amendment in the Road Vehicle (Construction & Use) Regulations 1986. However, older cars fall outside the regulations as described above.

Cars registered after 1 August 1998 (S registration or later)
- Almost all cars registered on or after this date will have a VIN plate bearing an 'E' mark and number to denote EC approval.
- All cars bearing the 'E' mark must only be fitted with a towing bracket that complies with European Standard 94/20/EC and which similarly displays a plate or label to confirm compliance.
- Vehicles exempt from these requirements include specialist cars built in small numbers whose accreditation is achieved by passing the Single Vehicle Approval (SVA) scheme.
- Also exempt are vehicles imported directly from a non-European country, often referred to as 'grey imports'. These are different because they do not bear a European VIN plate, but they may have different bracket mounting points – causing difficulties when trying to fit a Type-approved bracket. The Mitsubishi Pajero (grey import Shogun) is an example although Witter Towbars produces a Pajero conversion kit and Watling Engineers builds bespoke brackets.
- Light commercial vehicles (LCVs) fall outside this legislation so motorcaravans built on a commercial base are permitted to have non-TUV-approved brackets designed, built and fitted.

TOW CARS AND TOWING

The National Trailer and Towing Association now runs courses so that tow bar fitters can learn all the latest requirements and legislation.

Recognising that a number of changes have taken place recently, it's fortunate that the National Trailer and Towing Association has created a national programme of training courses for fitters, together with a growing chain of accredited tow bar fitting specialists. Without doubt, this NTTA Quality Secured Scheme is one way to ensure that the installation of a towing bracket and its electrical connections is carried out correctly as the panel below explains.

The NTTA Quality Secured Scheme means that accredited centres:

- Have qualified fitters with the right knowledge, skill and training.
- Have adequate resources and the right equipment.
- Are subject to regular assessment and approval by independent assessors.
- Adhere to the National Trailing and Towing Association code of practice.
- Use the best quality components and work to established standards.
- Charge a fair rate for each job.
- Offer good customer care.
- Give a guarantee of good workmanship and component quality.

The list of Quality Secured fitters can be checked on the NTTA website: www.ntta.co.uk. Information is also obtainable from Quality Secured Tel: 0161 273 6664; Fax: 0161 273 5641

Have a bracket and its accompanying wiring carried out by a qualified towbar fitter.

To find out more about towing, this book is specifically devoted to the subject.

Further information

Overall, the subject of towing is detailed and complex. Since this book is written for newcomers to caravanning, I have purposely omitted some of the more complex matters.

On the other hand, if you want to find out more, one of the best sources of advice is *The Essential Towing Handbook* by Philip Coyne, initiated by the Police Foundation at the suggestion of the National Trailer and Towing Association and Brink UK. The first edition was published in 2000 by the Stationery Office and has nearly 200 pages devoted to towing matters.

In addition, the chapter entitled Towcar Preparation in *The Caravan Manual* by John Wickersham and published by Haynes also goes into much greater detail than here and explains several tasks that DIY caravanners might want to carry out themselves.

Similarly, literature available to members of the Camping and Caravanning Club and members of the Caravan Club is also extremely helpful.

TOWING SKILLS

There are many caravanners who started towing without receiving any instruction. It is generally known that when there's a large trailer coupled behind, you have to take a wider sweep around tight corners. Ignore this in a town and the caravan may ride up on the kerb and scatter pedestrians.

Parking against a kerb is difficult too, because of the width of most caravans. And then there's that elusive skill of reversing.

There's no doubt that to acquire the relatively simple skills of towing, it is wise to join one of the caravan manoeuvring courses organised by the two major caravan clubs.

TOW CARS AND TOWING

Club manoeuvring courses include advice on choosing and using extension mirrors.

Manoeuvring courses

Both The Camping and Caravanning Club and The Caravan Club run manoeuvring courses at venues around the country. These take place on venues such as old airfields and agricultural show grounds – so there's no worry about other traffic.

Illustrated technical talks, supporting literature and instructional videos usefully support the practical sessions. There's only one warning – these courses are popular and you usually need to book a place a long time in advance.

The topics usually cover items like selecting and adjusting extension mirrors, coupling-up a caravan with and without a helper, checking noseweight, and general safety tips about key items such as tyres.

Practical tasks include straight line reversing, reversing into an offside location and the harder

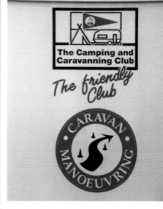

The Camping and Caravanning Club provides you with a caravan with which to practise manoeuvres on the instructional courses.

Using guide poles, participants on towing courses are able to practise coupling up a caravan on their own.

Working on a traffic-free agricultural show ground, a course member is advised how to carry out a tricky reversing manoeuvre.

task reversing into a nearside opening. Plastic cones usually define the target zones and are flattened on a regular basis by wayward caravans. But practising manoeuvres with an experienced instructor is the way to learn these skills even though many drivers regard reversing as a black art beyond their compass.

Restricted vision means reversing into a nearside opening is harder than reversing into an opening on the offside.

Other issues

a) Driving test

Remember that you if passed a driving test or obtained a full driving licence before 1 January 1997, this automatically permits you to tow a caravan. If you passed the test after this date, however, you will be required to pass a further test if the intention is to tow a very heavy outfit. Frankly, the obligatory test does not apply to the majority of UK caravans and the specification is as follows:

The need to take a special towing test applies where the combined weight of the tow car and caravan exceeds 3,500kg and the maximum weight of the caravan exceeds the unladen weight of the towing vehicle. If you're thinking of towing a colossal caravan with a very large vehicle and need to take a test, contact the Driving Standards Customer Services Unit, Tel: 0115 901 2515.

b) Motorway lane use

When towing a caravan you are not permitted to use the right-hand lane of a motorway with three or more lanes – unless special notices indicate

You seldom see heavy caravans in Britain like America's long-established Airstream models.

TOW CARS AND TOWING

An imported Airstream needs a heavy towcar and owners who passed their driving test after 1 January 1997 would need to take a supplementary test to tow a heavy outfit like this.

otherwise. Permission may equally be given when roadworks have caused lanes to be closed.

c) Parking
When parking a car and caravan, you are not permitted to use parking meter zones.

d) Passengers
It is illegal – and highly dangerous – to carry passengers in a caravan when you are towing on public roads.

e) Deflection and snaking
When towing on fast roads, large overtaking vehicles will cause your caravan to deflect from side to side. This buffeting is quite normal but if you're not paying attention to your rear-view mirrors these unexpected movements can be rather frightening. Once the vehicle passes, a well-balanced outfit will re-align itself quickly and if you take your foot from the accelerator, the dissipation of movement is usually hastened. But don't try to cure deflections by braking heavily! Stabilisers which help to reduce lateral deflection are discussed in Chapter Eight.

Note: These deflections are NOT what is meant by a 'snake'. A snake occurs when an ill-matched or damaged outfit gets out of control with the help of strong side winds and thoughtless driving. In a snake the caravan swings so far to one side and then the other that the articulation of car and caravan approaches an angle of 90°. In the unlikely event that you experience a snake, the advice is to immediately lift your foot from the accelerator, resist the temptation to apply the brakes, and hold the steering wheel steady rather than trying to steer with the movement.

Happily, anyone heeding the advice in this book will enjoy the pleasure of caravanning without ever experiencing a frightening reptilian attack.

Whether you are overtaking the lorry or the lorry is overtaking you on a motorway, there's usually a brief moment of buffeting which affects the caravan's stability.

CHAPTER SIX

ACCESSORIES

To describe all the accessories available for caravanners would take a whole book – and a very thick book at that. Many products have arrived with a flourish and then disappeared without ceremony. Others, however, are 'must have' items which are not supplied when you buy a caravan from a dealer. Accessories like water containers, gas cylinders and a spare wheel are virtually essential. In addition, a good quality security device is a crucial purchase whatever the age of your caravan.

It is only recently that caravan manufacturers have been required to include a mains hook-up lead with a new caravan. On the other hand, a wheel brace has been provided as a standard item for rather longer – although some have been pretty fragile. However, the situation is improving and more and more key components, like a spare wheel, are likely to become standard items. In fact, current regulations even require that a step of stipulated size is now supplied with every new tourer.

This is pleasing news if you're intending to take delivery of a brand new model. But in reality, most purchasers start their caravanning experiences with a pre-owned 'van – a strategy which makes good sense. So this chapter intentionally refers to a wide range of accessories to suit new or second-hand models alike.

Incidentally, towing items like extension mirrors are discussed in Chapter Eight so they're not mentioned here. Nor for that matter is there reference to awnings, which are the focus in Chapter Seven.

A locking post is worth considering if your caravan is stored outside your house.

It is most important to have a spare wheel and it's sometimes possible to stow this on an under-floor carrier.

Note: Virtually all caravans are fitted with radial tyres. Never fit a cross-ply tyre with a radial tyre on the same axle. Note that some caravans are fitted with a car-type tyre where the pressure tends to be in the 35–45psi region (but see handbook); others are fitted with commercial tyres which need a much higher pressure. This is typically around 50–65psi (but see handbook). More information on this is given in *The Caravan Manual,* published by Haynes, Chapter Four.

ROAD ITEMS

Spare wheel

You can caravan for years without getting a puncture, but if it happens, the mishap can prove costly if you're not carrying a spare wheel with a sound tyre. Prior to the launch of 2002 models, most new single-axle caravans were built on 13-inch wheels, and when touring abroad, buying a tyre to fit a 13-inch rim is usually very difficult.

So in 2001, a few manufacturers introduced 14-inch wheels on their single axle caravans. The idea gathered momentum and in the 2002 model year, most (although not all) new caravans have 14-inch wheels. Again, this is no help to owners of older caravans and it's one of many reasons why you should always carry a spare.

When you buy one, be absolutely sure it fits. It's surprising how often dealers supply a spare wheel where the fixings do not match those on the caravan, or where the tyre is incorrect. This often passes unnoticed until a puncture necessitates a road-side wheel change . . . which is neither the time nor the place to find the error. As regards the tyre, this should be:

• The correct size (both in diameter and width).
• The correct type.
• Of the appropriate speed rating.
• Of the appropriate load rating.

ACCESSORIES

Tyron Safety Bands

When a car or caravan tyre punctures badly, the collapsing tyre often falls into the well of the wheel whereupon its steel rim starts skidding along the road surface. A sudden loss of adhesion with the road can cause all sorts of problems.

To cure this, Tyron Safety Bands comprise steel sections which are bolted into the well of the wheels thereby preventing a deflated tyre from dropping into this recess. In consequence, the rubber of the tyre continues to intervene between the rim and the road so that the caravan doesn't slip all over the place. Even though the tyre is likely to be ruined, both car and caravan can be driven with reasonable control and steered to a safe point by the roadside.

Towing demonstrations held on redundant airfields in which a tyre is punctured by a detonation device are extraordinary to witness. The Tyron Safety Band certainly achieves what its promoters claim and some caravan manufacturers fit them as standard. The product can also be fitted at a later date by tyre-fitting specialists.

The Tyron Safety Band is bolted into the well of a wheel.

With a Tyron band fitted, this punctured caravan tyre still maintained contact with the road surface rather than the wheel rim.

Jack

When lightweight chassis were introduced in the early 1980s, the positioning point for a jack became critical in order to avoid damage to the main members. Most caravans are lifted using a portable jack although some caravans now incorporate a side jacking system. It's a good arrangement and if you own a recently-built caravan, this jacking assembly can sometimes be fitted retrospectively.

Where this isn't possible, you need a jack which can be positioned under the axle, even when your caravan has slumped close to the ground due to a puncture. A compact scissors jack usually meets the requirement, but these devices take considerable arm strength to lift a heavy caravan. It's certainly worth doing a 'practice run' at home or in a storage compound rather than carrying out your first wheel change by the roadside.

A scissors jack is compact enough to be positioned under a caravan's axle even after a bad puncture.

ACCESSORIES

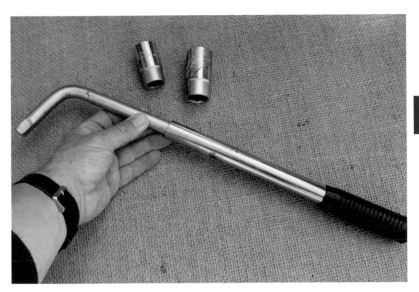

Telescopic wheel brace

This is probably the best way to loosen wheel fixings on both cars and caravans. The additional leverage offered by an extending telescopic bar means you don't need great strength to loosen an over-tightened wheel bolt. Telescopic wheel braces are obtainable from most car accessory shops and are sold with sockets to fit four different sizes of fixing.

Chocks

These are obligatory in Germany and if you have to change a wheel after a puncture, chocks are most important accessories. Being able to chock the wheels is also appropriate if you park on a steeply sloping pitch. Frightening stories of caravans rolling down slopes are well documented.

Regrettably, however, some of the plastic chocks on sale have a habit of slipping when used on a smooth road surface. This can cause a serious problem if you've just removed a wheel. Sticking a layer of rubber matting on the underside of the chocks often helps, but you might prefer to get some larger wooden wedges constructed by a carpenter in which the curvature matches the shape of your caravan's wheels.

A telescopic wrench makes it notably easier to loosen over-tightened wheel fixings.

*The Flexator from
Airmuscle makes lateral
levelling much easier.*

*A portable inflator is
useful if you use a
Flexator lateral leveller.*

SITE ITEMS

Spirit level

There are several levelling aids on the market but
a small spirit level takes some beating. Positioning
this on the floor directly above the axle is a logical
place for both lateral and longitudinal checks.
However, a few owners position this on the A-
frame at the front; others use the horizontal line of
a front or rear window to check lateral levelling.

Ingenuity is often used as well. Some
caravanners carry a rectangular plastic jerry-can
which they part fill with water and then lay this on
its side over the axle

Levelling boards

Getting a caravan level from side to side is harder
than levelling from front to back – which a jockey
wheel soon achieves. The classic and inexpensive
answer is to pull your caravan forwards on to
some wooden boards prior to unhitching.
Alternatively there are several types of wedge
available such as the products in Fiamma's range.
There are also wind-up devices which lift a wheel;
but these are usually heavy and rather
cumbersome to carry. A few owners use inflatable
pads which pair-up well with a portable air
compressor that runs from either a cigar lighter or
its own rechargeable battery.

ACCESSORIES

Corner steady pads

To prevent lowered corner steadies from sinking into soft ground, four small pads help distribute the load. Small blocks of wood are perfectly adequate although a number of owners like to use purpose-made moulded plastic pads. These are often attached to corner steadies with a steel pin although a few examples have a nasty habit of shaking around when you're towing. One type of pad has a channel which you fill with water. This acts as a very effective moat, preventing colonies of ants from climbing up a corner steady intent on sharing the caravanning experience.

Step

There are plenty of step designs on the market, some of which offer uncertain stability. A number of caravanners take DIY steps which double-up as tool boxes. Heavy tools help hold them in position, but there's the risk that their contents can easily be stolen. Milk crates with a ply top are also popular – and provide extra bottle storage when you're towing.

Pads to fit corner steadies are available from most accessory shops; this type incorporates a 'moat' to keep out inquisitive ants.

SERVICE SUPPLY ITEMS

Hook-up mains lead, socket adaptors and socket tester are described in Chapter 12 and the quality of cable needed to connect with the hook-up pillar is clearly explained. There have been instances where sub-standard cable has been sold at an attractive price – but whose specification does not comply with European Standards.

Leisure battery

Choosing, using and understanding the purpose of a leisure battery is discussed in detail in Chapter Thirteen.

Fresh and waste water tanks

Trolley types, rolling barrels and simple jerry cans will all be seen on caravan sites. Some of these are described and illustrated in Chapter Ten.

Gas cylinders and regulator

Important tips on choosing the right type of gas and regulator are given in Chapter Fourteen.

A battery designed for use in a caravan is usually refered to as a 'leisure battery'.

ACCESSORIES

Many hitchlocks include a metal insert which takes the place of a towball.

SECURITY DEVICES

There are two main concerns in respect of security. On one hand there's the risk of a break-in while your caravan is unattended. On the other, there's the risk it might be towed away.

The latter has become increasingly worrying in the last few years and these are some of the points to bear in mind:

- It's claimed that 'buying time' is important. Most security devices can be beaten by an experienced thief, but more robust types take much too long to defeat. So anxious not to be caught in the act, most thieves move on to 'easier pickings'.
- It often pays to fit more than one device. Whereas hitch locks are useful, a well-designed wheel clamp is usually harder to overcome. Fitting both is an extra deterrent.

This Bulldog hitchlock is robust and will even enclose the coupling head when your car is attached – that's useful when using a roadside restaurant.

Some wheel clamps are heavy duty models for storage use; this portable version, however, is more compact to take on holiday.

- The locking mechanism is usually the easiest element to overcome. Devices reliant on an unsophisticated padlock within their design are often surprisingly easy to force open.
- Note the difference between heavy duty wheel clamps designed to protect caravans when stored for long spells and lighter 'portable' wheel clamps intended to be taken on holiday for caravan site use.
- Locking poles and barriers are often worth considering if your caravan sits outside your house on a drive. Some types are made to couple-up with a hitch lock as well.
- Electronic devices are reliant on a battery and some have a nasty habit of leaping into life due to a false alarm. Whereas some are mainly to register a break-in, others include a switch which incorporates a blob of mercury that starts rolling whenever a caravan is moved. This immediately triggers the alarm.
- Check the advice in the accompanying panel regarding the Sold Secure testing scheme.

The Centinel locking post is one of several security barriers and posts used when a caravan or trailer is being stored by a house.

ACCESSORIES

The attack tests conducted at the Sold Secure test house use an armoury of portable tools as well as sophisticated machines and lock picks.

Tips

Sold Secure Test House

It is extremely hard for caravanners to evaluate which security devices are most likely to deter someone who wants to break into a caravan or defeat a thief who wants to drive off with the whole lot in tow.

So the Sold Secure initiative is particularly noteworthy. Not only is this a way manufacturers of security aids can gain recognition from an independent, non-profit-making agency. It's also a means whereby a caravanner can check which products have passed the very stringent attack tests conducted at the Sold Secure Test House.

Understandably you won't be able to find out which products fail these tests, but at least the published Approved Products list gives you guidance on successful ones. Note, too, that products passing the test are re-checked on a regular basis just to ensure that no short-cuts or quality faults subsequently creep into the manufacturing process.

A lock is usually the most vulnerable part of a security device – but some types are very resistant to sustained drilling.

With a new blade fitted for every test, hacksaws are used in an attempt to defeat a security device.

The testing involves a five-minute sustained onslaught by locksmiths with all manner of picks, together with heavyweight attacks with all kinds of wrenches, bolt cutters, drills, hammers and so on. There's also a salt water bath to check rust degradation and a parallel test facility for checking the integrity of electronic systems.

Caravan accessories are the key interest here and products tested by Sold Secure include parking posts as well as wheel clamps, hitch locks and other devices. However, some caravanners take bicycles on holiday and there are also Approved Products lists for cycle locks. Other Approved Product lists cover house alarms, car alarms, motorcycle alarms and so on.

Information and Approved Products lists are available free by telephoning: 01327 264687

Alternatively this is available on the web site: www. soldsecure.com

A long bar is used in an attempt to lever a clamp away from a caravan tyre.

ACCESSORIES

A fibrous non-slip underlay from The Natural Mat Company helps overcome the problem of damp patches forming under mattresses.

INTERIOR ITEMS

Bedding

This is really a personal matter. Some caravanners use the sleeping bags they previously used for camping. These are often easy to stow whereas duvets can take up rather a lot of space in a bed box. Other caravanners hate being 'bagged-up' and prefer a traditional bed in spite of the extra effort involved in its making.

Underlay

If a bed mattress rests on a sheet of plywood (as opposed to a slatted support), air cannot freely move around underneath. This leads to large damp patches appearing on the underside of mattresses and damp areas soon encourage mildew if the mattresses are not turned and aired periodically. The phenomenon seems to be worse in winter.

Putting large towels under mattresses makes a very small improvement, but it's not a cure. However, there are several products now available which help air to circulate. These include:
- The Natural Mat Company's 15mm fibrous rubberised, non-slip underlay,
- MMG VentAir underlay.

Cutlery and crockery

This is another personal matter. However, to save weight, most owners buy melamine or similar crockery from a caravan accessory shop. Only when you purchase a top tourer like a Carlight can you expect to find a bone china dinner service provided as standard.

Caravan and motorhome accessory shops are able to supply lightweight cutlery and crockery.

It's always wise to check the distribution of Fire Points when you visit a site.

Fire precautions

Smoke alarms are now required in all NCC Approved caravans, but they're unlikely to be found in older caravans. Their inclusion is well-reasoned although in the close confines of a caravan they have a habit of reacting extremely easily.

When visiting a caravan site, it's also wise to check the provision of fire extinguishers and alarms. In addition you should strongly consider the merit of fitting a fire blanket (made to EN 1869) in your caravan. The problem of fat fires in caravans and the terrible mistake of trying to extinguish one with water is often demonstrated with devastating effect at outdoor caravan shows. So a fire blanket is important and once in place it should be left covering the pan for up to 30 minutes; that's because hot fat has an ability to re-ignite.

For some fires, a fire blanket is extremely useful to have readily to hand.

In this demonstration, the moment half a cup of water on a long rod was emptied into a burning chip pan, a large explosion of flame erupted.

ACCESSORIES

A dry powder fire extinguisher is strongly recommended for caravan use.

It's also wise to install a general purpose fire extinguisher. A dry powder type of extinguisher is recommended as the best 'all-rounder' for typical caravan problems.

When fitting these items, remember to have them within easy reach but not at a place which is near the source of heat or enveloping flames.

Carbon monoxide alarm

These battery-operated devices are now readily available and can be purchased at DIY Superstores.

First Aid

It's obviously wise to take a First Aid outfit on holiday just as you'd have this provision at home. Some modern cars include one of these as a standard item but if that's not the case, it's a matter to address in respect of the caravan.

Toilets

Caravans have been fitted with cassette toilets for a number of years. If you've bought an old caravan, a cassette toilet can sometimes be installed if the washroom is large enough. Don't worry if that's not the case. Portable toilets from Elsan and Thetford are almost as convenient. Turn to Chapter Ten to find out about treatment chemicals and so on.

Omnidirectional aerials are neat in design and convenient for caravanners; but a directional aerial will receive a stronger signal.

In hilly areas where TV reception is usually poor, a directional aerial is much more likely to capture a signal than an omnidirectional model.

Small amplifiers which run from a 12V supply are provided with most TV aerial kits fitted in caravans.

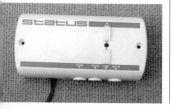

TV aerials

Nowadays, most caravans are supplied with a roof-mounted TV aerial as a standard item. The circular types are known as omnidirectional aerials because they don't need to be pointed towards the nearest transmitter. This ability to receive a signal irrespective of which way the caravan is parked is undoubtedly convenient. However, many caravanners do not realise that omnidirectional aerials are not able to pick up signals as efficiently as 'directional' types.

Either way, many caravan aerials are also fitted with a 12V booster amplifier which includes a signal-reducing facility, too. On one hand, this helps improve a signal in a weak reception area or it can also reduce its strength when your site is too close to a transmitter.

One of the best ways to obtain good TV reception is to use a pole-mounted directional aerial like the Status 530. This is pushed upwards into position from inside your caravan and rotated while you're watching the TV screen. It means you can fine-tune everything from indoors – and even tilt the mast-head unit through 180° to suit those transmitting stations which need the reception elements of an aerial in a vertical plane. The Status 530 can usually be fitted easily to older caravans as long as the retracting pole can be suitably hidden inside. Usually it pulls down into the side of a wardrobe.

The Status 530 directional aerial is easy to fit; its elevating pole and orientation is controlled from inside the caravan.

ACCESSORIES

Caravan movers like this model from Carver use powerful 12V motors and a knurled wheel to engage against the tyres.

OTHER ITEMS

Many other accessories could be discussed in this chapter but it is appropriate to conclude with:

Caravan movers

When a caravan has to be manoeuvred into a difficult storage place, it can be a tough assignment. Elderly and disabled owners can find things pretty difficult, especially if the ground is sloping.

There are several answers to the problem and electrically driven tugging trolleys are one popular answer. Run by a 12V battery, these usually have a tow ball on top of the casing. A few couple-up with the jockey wheel clamp although some specialists feel that this pulling point might cause minor chassis damage. Overall, these are tough products – but they're costly.

Another answer is to fit electric motors which drive the caravan's wheels and the Carver Caravan Mover is probably the best-known example. Other versions have followed, some of which have remote controllers. This allows you to move your 'van backwards, forwards or around corners – just like a large version of a radio-controlled car.

Unfortunately, units like the Caravan Mover take up payload weight because they're permanently fitted to a caravan. On the other hand, they enable many incapacitated owners to continue enjoying their caravanning experiences. And that is certainly pleasing to note.

The Carver Caravan Mover has been manufactured with a remote handset so that a tourer can be driven into the most difficult spots.

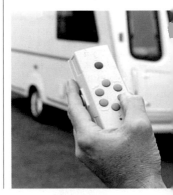

CHAPTER **SEVEN**

CHOOSING
AND USING
AWNINGS

If you park your caravan on a pitch for an extended period, an awning is always an asset. Not only does it add to your personal space, but it also provides useful undercover storage for wet clothing and bikes, or simply somewhere to sit while you prise off your muddy wellies. Some caravanners use their awning as a summer cooking area, an extra place for sleeping, or a venue for camp-site banquets. The choice is yours ...

A full-size awning can more than double your living space.

A good way to gain extra living space without buying a bigger caravan is to purchase an awning. However, these valuable accessories come in all sorts of sizes, styles and materials. Types currently on sale include:
- The simple sun shade consisting of just a roof and supporting poles.
- A sun roof, but with the extra facility of a zip-in front panel and side walls to increase protection against mild winds and moderate rain showers.
- A porch awning which is ideal in winter to keep draughts from your caravan door.
- A 'combi', 'universal' or 'half awning' which describes a series of models falling midway between a porch and a full awning. Most of these have the special advantage that they fit a wide range of caravans – which is important if you're changing your caravan but don't want to buy another awning.
- A full awning of basic rectangular shape. Side panels may be permanently stitched-in or removable using zips so you can simply opt for a roof-only sunshade for a brief stop or the full construction with sides for a longer stay.

A compact porch awning will keep draughts from the door and can be erected in minutes.

- The full awning whose design is specifically intended for folding caravans.
- A facility to add an extra bedroom to one of the sides.
- A massive multi-sided unit whose overall internal dimensions are far greater than those of the caravan to which its attached.

Points to note:

a) Large awnings are especially heavy to handle and transport. Can you carry a large awning in your tow car? Is there sufficient scope within the personal effects payload of you caravan to add a heavy awning to the weight of all the other items you normally carry on board?

b) Universal and porch awnings are usually easy to transfer from one caravan to another. However, you need to check that there are no obstructions where the sides of the awning are going to locate against the wall of the caravan. For instance if they cross the face of an acrylic window, this is likely to get scratched by fabric blowing in the wind. Similarly the canvas shouldn't cross a refrigerator vent and it is even more important it doesn't touch or obscure the fridge flue outlet.

c) A resourceful owner is usually able to erect an awning unaided, although it's not always easy. When it's dark and especially if it's breezy, it is wise to wait until later. Either way it is much easier if you have helpers when you go caravanning. Bear this in mind before buying one of the grand mansion-like structures that look so good in catalogue illustrations.

d) Some motorcaravan owners install large roll-out blinds on the sides of their vehicles as an alternative to using free-standing units. On account of the sheer simplicity of setting up one of these extended covered areas, it's likely that we'll see similar units being fitted to touring caravans in the future.

Free-standing kitchens are especially popular on the Continent for summer use.

The zip-on bedroom extension shown here simply takes the place of a side-wall panel.

MATERIALS

As regards constructional materials, there are several choices to consider. For example, the fabric itself can be either a synthetic product or a natural cotton canvas. Similarly, the poles are available in various materials as described in the box alongside. There are also pole systems incorporating special clip-together couplings which considerably speed up the erection process. Awnings from Khyam are an example of products using this kind of system.

The unusual Khyam Futura is suspended from its quick-erect poles – so the whole lot can be put up at remarkable speed.

ATTACHMENT TO THE CARAVAN

Manufacturers use different ways to fit their awnings to the side of a caravan. Some models use large rubber suction pads on the ends of the roof poles, but these fail to achieve a sound location on aluminium which has a textured finish.

Fittings featuring an eyelet which has to be screwed to the wall are more successful, but most of these necessitate drilling the sides of the caravan. Typically you won't find any wood behind the aluminium skin to give a really firm fixing so you usually have to rely on a tight-fitting self-tapping screw. However, as long as these small items are mounted using stainless steel screws on flexible sealant, they normally fulfil their purpose. Moreover, the puncture holes made by the fixings are unlikely to act as leak points because far less rainwater runs down the side walls of a caravan than down the sloping ends. It's the end panels which have to cope with most water discharging from the roof.

In spite of this, there's a growing preference to use flexible pads to hold the inboard end of the roof support poles. Sometimes these are stitched to the main seam that runs just below the awning rail. Occasionally you'll find versions which slide into the awning rail groove as well. Either way, rubberised pads usually achieve the objective of anchoring a pole without problems.

MEASURING-UP

It is important that an awning fits well. If the fabric starts to flap in a wind, it not only keeps residents awake at night; it can also damage a caravan's painted side panels and the surface of acrylic windows.

CHOOSING AND USING AWNINGS

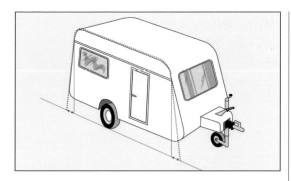

Measuring up a caravan for an awning. See 'Measure-up tips' below.

113

With a conventional full awning, as opposed to a porch or combi design, it's most important that the measurement from the ground and all along the trackway is going to match the dimension of the awning you plan to purchase. In a good handbook, the caravan manufacturer will prescribe exactly what size awning is needed for your particular model of caravan. If this information has been overlooked you sometimes find that awning manufacturers and retailers hold records of measurements on more popular recent caravans. Failing that, check the panel below.

Measure-up tips

To establish the size of awning required you will need to carry out the following procedure:

1. Park your caravan on level ground and lower the corner steadies.
2. Working from the diagram above, hold a tape measure around the awning channel which normally runs round the perimeter of the side walls and the roof. Include in your measurement the bottom projection from each end of the trackway down to the ground.
3. Even better is to run a length of non-stretch cord around the trackway itself – just as the attachment cord of an awning would do. Carry both ends down to the ground and then remove it to be measured carefully.
4. Since the angle on the sides of an awning usually splays outwards, you need to take this into account when establishing the point where the bottom of the awning will touch the ground.

Pole Materials

- **Coated steel** – Strength is a point in their favour: weight is their disadvantage. A good quality anodised finish is featured on more expensive awnings; but cheaper products often start to rust when the coating material gets damaged. Budget models may only have painted tubing.
- **Aluminium** – Some manufacturers offer alternative alloy poles which are light and more resistant to corrosion. However, they seldom lack the strength of steel and good quality aluminium tubing is also quite costly.
- **Glass-fibre** – This hollow tubing will neither corrode nor discolour. It is also very light in weight although it tends to be costly. The trouble is that it's rather flexible and if large areas of canvas are unsupported the pole structure can distort and might even break. In winter conditions, for example, an overnight fall of snow will place considerable weight on a roof. Experience has taught me that glass-fibre poles can fare badly on Alpine campsites in wintry weather.

Fabrics

- **Cotton** – Although usually less expensive, cotton has the advantage of its light weight and 'breathability'. This means that it doesn't suffer from condensation problems often associated with man-made fabrics. At the same time it's less tolerant to ill treatment. Pack it away damp for several days and the rotting process starts. What's more, the inevitable marks left by mould are almost impossible to remove. Conversely if you look after a cotton awning, it can easily last 15 years of regular use – as I know from experience.

- **Synthetic** – There are several types of synthetic material used and some are as soft as cotton but more resistant to wear. Good synthetic fabrics are expensive and the proofing process means that most types are not able to 'breathe'. So venting is essential to disperse condensation. The condensation problem is especially acute if you use your awning as an alternative kitchen or a drying room. However, it's not as bad as it is inside a small tent – there's a much greater air-flow in an awning to disperse developing damp.

Of the synthetic products:

Acrylic is light in weight, hard-wearing, virtually rot-proof, resistant to fading and it doesn't shrink.

Polyester fabrics, in contrast, sometimes offer a small measure of 'breathabilty' depending on the coating used. The product is lighter than acrylic but not as hardwearing. To improve its performance it is coated with proofing treatments like polyurethane (PU) or polyvinyl chloride (PVC).

Note: In some products, more than one material is used. For instance, there are awnings where the roof is a weather-resistant coated polyester whereas the sides are cotton. You may also find PVC-coated panels at the foot of the walls. This provision is specially advantageous because it copes with splash-up damage in downpours and spray damage from canine leg-lifters.

A good quality awning has taped edges and impeccable stitching on all the seams.

When comparing awnings, look carefully at the quality of the zips.

Fancy curtains and Georgian-style glazing bars on the windows are popular at present.

BUYING TIPS

- When comparing products, look at the list of optional extras. Some manufacturers can supply a useful pocket panel for storing holiday items. Inner tents are also available if you want to use an awning as an over-spill dormitory.

- Look for storm guy fixing points. Some models are better suited to exposed, windy locations than others. There may also be storm straps listed in the catalogue.

- Ask if there's an after-sales service in case of an accident. It's not unusual for a pole to fall over when the awning is being erected and sharp spikes on the top can easily puncture the fabric.

All sorts of 'extras' are available – including a rack of coat hooks.

CHOOSING AND USING AWNINGS

Note the white tags for the addition of storm guys and a bottom panel made in dirt- and water-resistant material.

- Enquire if you can purchase spares like rubber expansion loops for the pegging points. Find out how easy it is to purchase a replacement pole. In a strong wind, it's possible for a pole to become so badly bent that it cannot be straightened.

- Consider what ground cover you will use. Traditional ground sheets kill the grass so there are special carpeting materials with a breathable structure. Some examples can even be bought from the roll and these are priced accordingly.

- Check the colours of awnings as well. Some manufacturers have moved to light pastel shades which look very pretty. However, colours that look good on their own might not match the colour of the caravan.

Ground sheets left down for a long time can ruin a pitch; breathable floor coverings are much to be preferred.

Awning storm straps from Gardners of Wakefield help to hold down the structure when a wind blows up unexpectedly.

Porous floor covering materials which help the grass to 'breathe' are sold from a roll.

Spare poles are often on sale at major outdoor shows like The Camping and Caravan Club's Feast of Lanterns event.

SPARES AND EXTRAS

If you need spares for an awning, it's unlikely that you'll be able to purchase these at an indoor exhibition. The smaller companies who specialise in this type of product are more likely to attend the outdoor shows and rallies which are held in the warmer months of the year.

On a different note, if you have the misfortune of compressing the awning channel, then W4 accessories has the answer. A tiny dumbbell with bullet-shaped ends is designed to be tapped through the channelling with a hammer, re-establishing the shape of the aperture as it goes. In addition, W4 markets a specially shaped brush which is designed to shift any spiders which have decided to set up a permanent home in your awning track-way. However, don't try prizing open a track with a screwdriver or pliers because you'll damage it. It's better to use a scrap of wood which is tapped along the opening using a mallet.

Independent specialists sell awning spares – and you'll see them at outdoor rallies.

CLEANERS AND REPROOFING PRODUCTS

Marks and stains are a fact of life, so there are several specialist fabric cleaners available at most caravan accessory shops. For instance, Camco Awning cleaner has been particularly popular in the last few years. The Camco range from America is stocked in many caravan and motorhome accessory shops.

Stains like bird lime should be removed at the earliest opportunity whereas mud is best left until it's completely dry. Other stains include car exhaust marks. Apart from proprietary awning cleaners you can often shift marks using warm, soapy water – but never use detergent. Sometimes there's a tendency, of course, for a tide mark to appear around the area. So you then have to extend your effort and clean the entire panel – although this might not be a particularly large section between stitching boundaries.

The trouble with determined and regular cleaning, of course, is that this hastens the need for reproofing. However, specialists like Grangers and Nikwax market a number of reproofing products and their application is straightforward provided weather is on your side.

As a rule, it's best to erect an awning before tackling the reproofing work and it also needs to be clean. Ideally you want warm, dry weather – but not hot, direct sun. On the other hand, Nikwax Aqueous Technik for PU-coated materials is better when used on a damp fabric. Similarly, Nikwax Spray-on TX Direct and Nikwax TX 10 Cottonproofer can be applied to wet or dry fabrics. So before getting to work, check carefully the instruction leaflet supplied with the product that you intend to use.

Many treatments like Granger's Fabsil would normally be applied with a brush although some owners use a pressurised garden atomiser spray which is rather more convenient. Using a long lance attachment, for example, allows you to reach the roof panels much more easily.

Needless to say, a full reproofing operation will take an hour or more. However, if you merely want to reproof a small area – perhaps where you've carried out a spot cleaning operation – you can purchase reproofers in aerosol cans for localised applications.

Tips

Avoid bad locations.
If you ever make the mistake of erecting an awning under a lime tree or similar tree which exudes a sticky sap, you'll never do it a second time. The substance that soon coats the entire roof fabric needs washing off at the earliest opportunity. And even then, you might find you remove the water-resistance of the fabric and need to reproof it.

On many brand-new awnings, the needles which have been used to stitch the seams often leave large puncture holes – especially in a treated, synthetic fabric. When it rains, you sometimes find that your brand-new awning starts to leak badly. But this isn't unusual.

As long as the dampened thread and fabric swells and then closes the tiny puncture holes, the problem solves itself. If it doesn't then you may need to get an aerosol proofing compound to spray along the seams.

Some manufacturers even advise you to erect an awning before leaving for holiday and spraying it down with a hose. It's only a one-off job with a new awning – and it really is necessary with a lot of products!

PACKING AN AWNING AWAY

If circumstances force you to pack away an awning in a wet condition when leaving a caravan site, you need to open it up and dry the fabric at the very earliest opportunity. In a very short space of time, mould marks appear whatever the type of fabric. Hence on long trips back to the UK from abroad, many caravanners realise the importance of taking an over-night break to re-erect a damp awning in order to start the drying process.

At the end of a season, the need to ensure that the fabric is completely dry is again very important. With some awnings costing a four-figure sum, these are expensive products that need care and attention, and whereas it's fine storing an awning in a caravan when the weather's warm, it gets much too damp during the winter months. So if you've got the room, transfer it into your home.

REPAIR WORK

Damage can occur in a number of ways although the spike on a falling awning pole is one of the most popular ways to tear an awning. Whilst a few owners use their own domestic skills to carry out repairs, most would want to seek the help of a professional who has industrial sewing machines at their disposal. Advertisements for awning repairers are often listed in the classified advertisements of caravan magazines – and camping magazines as well. In addition, both the major clubs can advise. For example, The Caravan Club currently records 19 specialists around the country in the latest awning repair address list.

Repairers can also replace a damaged zip. However, it's worth noting that Frank's Caravan Spares at Stopsley near Luton cuts out zips from awnings that come to their caravan breaking yard. The adjacent shop displays a huge bundle of second-hand zips of all lengths, sizes, and colours which are sold for modest prices. Worth noting if you are ever in that part of the country.

ERECTING AN AWNING

A number of awnings are sold with very poor erection instructions. In fact if you are not setting your awning up on a regular basis, it's a good idea to colour-code the ends of poles with PVC tape.

If the awning is being erected for the first time, you might also find that the feed points on the caravan's trackway need widening slightly. Do this very carefully and try to use a blunt tool; the sharp corners on a slotted screwdriver often damage the surface of the aluminium extrusion. Even better is to tap a wedge of wood through the slot so there's no metal-to-metal contact.

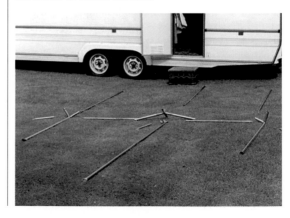

Check the poles and the way they assemble. If you need a step to reach the roof, have it in place.

Find the openings in the awning track where the cord on the roof panel can be inserted.

123

Carefully pull the roof section around the awning rail. On this Combi awning it has to leave the groove at a specially formed outlet.

Once the roof panel is centralised, the frame is assembled and coupled to the caravan – but its vertical legs are kept partly folded.

However, once this preliminary preparation is complete, the awning should go up fairly easily. The accompanying photographs show a Combi awning being erected and I'm quick to admit that my caravan's free-standing step proves especially useful when reaching up to the awning rail. Drawing the roof panel through the channelling can be quite a stretch!

Incidentally, different people put up awnings in their own favourite ways. This is my preference in which the sides are zipped out and re-instated later. It means the roof section, which goes up first, is much lighter to handle.

Lengths of foam are coupled to one part of the vertical wall using white sleeves. This is where a Combi awning touches the mid point of the 'van's wall.

The size of Combi awning was chosen so the caravan window wouldn't be obscured; foam pads attached to the awning protect the caravan's paintwork.

With the roof still untensioned, the legs are now lifted. Now the side panels can be zipped-in, the canvas tensioned and the pegs driven into the ground.

Tip

Before pegging-out the skirt around the bottom of an awning, make sure all the wall sections and doors are zipped-up. Then drive in your pegs, secure in the knowledge that the zipping sections will open and close freely later on. If you ignore this and peg-out the structure with the doors left open, you'll usually find the zip struggles to create a complete closure later on.

To prevent the walls flapping in a breeze, tie tapes allow the canvas to be secured to the poles.

For 'fine tuning', there's usually a facility to adjust the position of poles and telescopic couplings which allows the tension of the fabric to be altered.

CHAPTER EIGHT

HITCH-UP
AND GO

When getting ready for a trip away, there are several jobs to carry out before leaving. Packing the caravan correctly, checking its noseweight, fitting the extension mirrors on your car, and pre-cooling the fridge are just a few of the points discussed in this chapter. Then you have to couple the car and caravan together. Nothing's particularly difficult, but it's helpful to have some guidance.

Let's imagine the situation. Your caravan has been serviced, it bears the same number plate as your tow car, you've turned all the gas cylinders 'off', tyre pressures were checked when the tyres were cold and you're ready to load your personal gear. This may not be a huge undertaking, but understanding noseweight is closely linked to the job in hand.

A raised arm positioned directly over a caravan's coupling head provides a good sighting point when you start to reverse a tow car.

NOSEWEIGHT

The weight that bears down on the rear end of your tow car will be determined by *where* you place your possessions. This is known as the 'noseweight'.

If the entire weight of a caravan is distributed so that everything balances over the axle, there will be no weight at all bearing down on the car's towing ball. That might sound a wise strategy, but it's a recipe for disaster. You'll find that the balanced load over the caravan axle will start to see-saw up and down as you drive down the road. Your car will receive relentless lifting and lowering effects and the whole outfit will be dreadfully unstable.

For safe towing, noseweight is a crucial commodity. What's more, it's an easy thing to adjust. Repositioning items of equipment like an awning or a tool box inside the 'van, will immediately change the noseweight.

To achieve the most stable arrangement, it is generally accepted that the noseweight should be around 7 per cent of the weight of your fully laden caravan. To calculate this in a precise way necessitates having your loaded caravan checked on a weighbridge. The total weight of the 'van is then divided by 100 and multiplied by 7 to establish the ideal noseweight for achieving good stability. But wait. There's a bit more to the noseweight matter than this 7 per cent recommendation.

It's important to recognise that towing bracket and vehicle manufacturers will have both declared *maximum* noseweights for their products. So whereas 7 per cent of the caravan's actual laden weight is a useful guide, there are times when the calculated figure *exceeds* the maximum limit permitted by the car and the bracket manufacturers. So have a look at the Technical Tip opposite.

Technical Tip

Noseweight limits

As a general rule, stated maximum noseweights typically fall between 50 and 75kg (around 110–165lb). In fact it was mentioned in Chapter Five that nearly all tow-brackets fitted to post 1 August 1998 vehicles have to bear a Type Approval plate which declares maximum loading capacities – including the bracket's noseweight limit.

It's true that a few cars have remarkably high limits, like 4x4 all-terrain models and vehicles with self-levelling suspension such as some of the Citroën models. But that's not much help if the bracket itself is designed to work with a lower limit. So remember:

- Generally it's helpful to have as heavy a noseweight as the situation permits.
- You should look at the tow bracket limit and the limit stated for the towing vehicle and ensure you don't exceed the lower of the two figures.
- Only within this framework of possibility can you then work out how close you can get to the ideal of 7 per cent.

To measure noseweight, the coupling head is lowered on to a noseweight gauge.

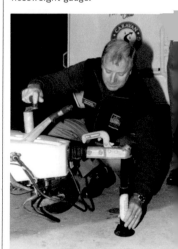

Checking noseweight

Some owners check noseweight using a purpose-made device shown in the photographs alongside. You use it as follows:

1. Park the caravan on flat ground. If there's the slightest chance of movement, chock the wheels.
2. Make sure the jockey wheel is in contact with the ground and the caravan brake has been engaged.

Noseweight is indicated on the graduated scale.

3. Raise all the corner steadies.
4. Insert the top of the noseweight gauge into the coupling head and hold the device vertically. If you can't do this because the coupling head's too low, turn the jockey wheel handle to gain extra height.
5. Once the device is in place, lower the front of the caravan until all the noseweight is being borne by the gauge.
6. Take the noseweight reading.

Altering noseweight

Increasing or reducing noseweight is achieved by moving stowed items either towards the front or the rear end of your caravan. But there's a warning. If there's excessive noseweight you could eliminate this in one easy move by putting a compensating heavy item at the extreme back of the 'van. **That, however, is bad practice**.

Loading heavy items at the opposite extremities creates a 'dumbell' effect. In other words, if the caravan starts to sway laterally from side to side during towing, the inertia in these heavy items tends to perpetuate a pendulum action. Even with a stabiliser fitted, this instability takes longer than usual to rectify.

The space might look inviting, but it's all-too-easy to exceed the noseweight limit if you pack too much into a front-end gas locker.

So when you want to reduce noseweight it's better to move items you've stored well forward in the 'van to a location much closer to the axle. In fact, as many heavy items as possible should be loaded low down and over the axle. You certainly don't want a large amount of weight at the extrimeties. This is why you mustn't be tempted to use up all that inviting space in some of the latest caravans' huge gas cylinder lockers at the front. In fact on a few caravans, a correct noseweight can only be achieved by carrying no more than two small gas cylinders in this locker – even though the available space is sufficient to accommodate larger products.

LOADING A CARAVAN

Not only does wise loading of your personal possessions help to achieve the optimum noseweight; it has other implications for stability on the road.

When negotiating a sharp bend in the road, a caravan travelling at brisk speed is likely to develop a measure of body roll. This is why heavy items should never be stowed in roof lockers. Just because caravans are fitted with rather a lot of lockers these days, doesn't mean you have to fill them all! A diagram showing you where to load your personal items is shown on the following page.

Technical Tip
'Dumbell' effect and cycle racks
A contributor to instability on the road is the installation of a spare wheel on a caravan's rear wall. This is a poor design feature because a spare wheel is heavy. Similarly it's most unwise to fit a cycle rack on the back. Instability arising from having heavy items at the extreme ends of a caravan could easily lead to a serious accident. But you'll still see caravanners who pay no attention to this whatsoever.

A rear-mounted spare wheel might seem convenient but positioning heavy items at the extreme ends of a caravan can make the reduction of lateral instability difficult.

Inclination

When you're towing at normal speeds, both the car and caravan should assume a level stance. This inclination should be checked on level ground when the outfit is stationary. However, it's worth noting that a very slightly nose-down inclination is usually regarded as acceptable when your caravan is parked. This is because there's generally a small lifting effect brought about through turbulence which helps the 'van to assume a level ride height once you're on the move.

When loading up a caravan, the weight of items should be distributed as follows:

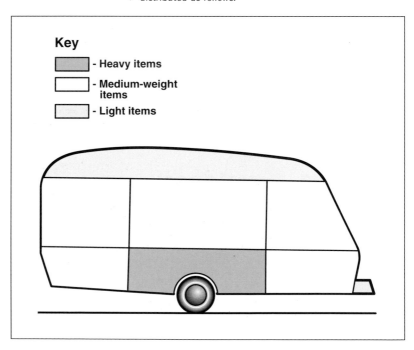

Key

☐ - Heavy items

☐ - Medium-weight items

☐ - Light items

To achieve a level car and caravan, it is sometimes helpful if a drop plate is fitted to the bracket so that the tow ball height is lowered.

- If you've achieved the correct noseweight for your caravan but find that the rear end of the towing vehicle sags when the caravan's coupled, your car might need replacement rear springs or an approved spring-reinforcing device. These were mentioned in Chapter Five.
- If it's the caravan's tail which sags, then you might resolve the problem by fitting a drop plate. See the comments on drop plates in the box below.

Note

The Type Approval regulations have an exclusion clause regarding tow ball height for off-road vehicles. In consequence the ball height for these vehicles may be too high to allow a caravan to adopt a level stance when hitched up.

Technical Tip

Tow ball height and drop plates

Nowadays, tow brackets are manufactured to produce a standard towing height. Directive 94/20/EC specifies that the centre of a tow ball should be between 350mm and 420mm (13.8–16.6in) to the ground when a vehicle is laden to maximum weight.

Problems arise, however, with some older caravans which have an unusually low coupling head. The same effect occurs, too, if a car is only partially laden and is riding high. In these instances, it would help if the tow ball was slightly lower.

Unfortunately the height of a swan neck tow ball cannot be altered. However, to suit a bolt-on tow ball, drop plates are sold which allow you to lower the ball height. In fact if your towing vehicle was registered before 1 August 1998 fitting a drop plate enables you to cure a nose-up inclination of a caravan very easily. Unfortunately, however, this practice is not permitted on the more recent Type Approved towing brackets unless a drop plate was tested with the bracket when it went through its Type Approval tests. Check this with the tow bracket manufacturer.

134

A nose-up caravan is unstable because the caravan will be susceptible to a wind lift effect which develops under the forward end of the floor panel.

Note

1. *Whereas a drop plate can be used in some instances to lower a tow ball, it should never be used to raise the height of a tow ball.*
2. *If there's a problem, take the matter up with your vehicle manufacturer. There are certainly examples of some modern vehicles fitted with approved towing brackets which do not permit a caravan to assume its required stance.*

Loading food

The old habit of loading up a caravan's cupboards with as much food as possible is fortunately losing its appeal. Even if a caravan site doesn't have a shop of its own, supermarkets are seldom far away – both at home and abroad. So why give the tow car a tough assignment by transferring half your kitchen to the caravan?

To repeat the point made above, don't carry heavy items in roof lockers. Even if a roof locker might seem a logical place to store the marmalade jar on-site, it's not the place to keep heavy items when you take to the road. (Should we ever meet on a future occasion, ask me to relate the story of the jar of red cabbage in vinegar and my first, brand-new caravan fitted with primrose yellow carpet.)

As regards refrigerator products, try to pre-cool the fridge before taking to the road. And make sure you load it correctly following the advice in Chapter Eleven.

Mirrors

The so-called 'through vision' created via a car's internal mirror is not likely to be very helpful. Even if your caravan has large windows front and back, a few drops of rain will turn a rearward image into a fuzzy blur. Even in good weather, modern plastic windows rarely provide accurate information about road conditions behind you.

So you need to use external mirrors and since most caravans are considerably wider than their towing vehicle, extension mirrors are needed. Many types have been marketed in the last 30 years and frankly, the ones which clip on to a door-mounted mirror are usually the best. Sometimes they fail to fit snugly and paintwork on the mirror housing can get scratched by road dirt trapped under the clamping straps. So the application of some protective tape may be worth considering. Similarly, some PVC electrical insulation tape is often useful for remedying a vibrating or ill-fitting unit.

Most people opt for convex rather than flat glass in an extension mirror because it provides a wide angle image. Unfortunately its greater capture of visibility is spoilt by the fact that following vehicles are really much closer to you than the reflected image suggests.

Once both external mirrors are fitted to a tow car, carry out some checks to confirm their adjustment. A bit later, after you've left home, it's often necessary to pull into a lay-by to make further 'fine adjustments'. This is also a good opportunity to double-check that the 12N and 12S cables haven't started to sag more than expected.

Coupling-up

Reversing a car up to a caravan coupling head is very much easier if you've got a helper. Whilst a

Extension mirrors which strap on to a door mirror are usually good – although you might need to add adhesive tape to assist the clamping straps.

136

Once you've taken to the road, it's not unusual to have to pull into a lay-by fairly promptly to make fine adjustments to the towing mirrors.

This diagram shows the coupling components at the front of a typical caravan.

garden cane can act as a helpful bump marker, you'll need to hop in and out of your driving seat several times if working alone. But what makes a good assistant?

Organising clear signals and some agreed words is important. For instance the word 'good' to a reversing driver might mean, 'good . . . keep coming slowly' or 'good . . . you've got there'.

I wouldn't dream of giving adult readers a prescriptive list of commands. Develop your own but make sure they're not ambiguous – especially

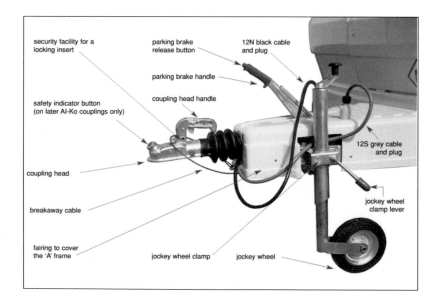

security facility for a locking insert

parking brake release button

12N black cable and plug

parking brake handle

coupling head handle

safety indicator button (on later Al-Ko couplings only)

12S grey cable and plug

coupling head

breakaway cable

jockey wheel clamp lever

fairing to cover the 'A' frame

jockey wheel clamp

jockey wheel

HITCH-UP AND GO

if you use different assistants to help you. It's not unusual to find that well-meaning neighbours on the caravan site employ a completely different sign language.

Normally, a partner will start by raising an arm vertically above the caravan's coupling head. This conveys a visual impression to the person in the driving seat regarding both distance and direction.

Then, as the car reverses, agreed hand-signals will reveal progress and deviations from the intended course. Note that the height of the caravan's coupling head should be further above the ground than the top of the tow ball. If that's not the case, wind up the jockey wheel.

Technical Tip
Running out of jockey wheel elevation
Sometimes the threaded spindle inside your jockey wheel tube reaches the end of its travel. That's annoying if you still need to raise the coupling head even further to clear an approaching tow ball. Here's the remedy:
1. Temporarily lower the front corner steadies to support the 'van.
2. Wind up the jockey wheel with the handle so the wheel pulls away from the ground.
3. Unclamp the jockey wheel and lower it further than you had before in its clamp assembly. Re-lower it until the wheel touches the ground.
4. Tighten the clamp firmly again.
5. Return to elevating the caravan using the jockey wheel handle. It will now have a lot more threads available on its spindle
6. The front corner steadies have now completed their brief supportive function, so raise them once again.

In the final stages of coupling preparation, experts recommend you give the driver progressional guidance from a side position.

To complete a coupling-up exercise, the handle on the coupling head has to be held in a lifted position while you turn the jockey wheel to lower the front of the caravan.

Some caravanners like to reverse the car until the coupling head is directly over the towball. Others are content if the coupling head is slightly to one side, as long as the caravan is light enough to nudge across to align with the tow ball. That's not so easy with a long, twin-axle model.

Once the towing vehicle is stationary, the lever of the coupling head should be lifted to its highest possible position and held in place. At the same time, the jockey wheel handle should be turned to lower the coupling head on to the towing ball, but still holding the lever upwards.

When the coupling has completely seated on the tow ball, the handle can then be released. You'll often hear a click as the coupling head finally encloses the ball.

Now it's most important to check that the coupling has clasped itself around the ball and isn't merely resting on top of it. A simple way to confirm this is to raise the locked-on coupling head a small amount using the jockey wheel. If coupling has been correctly achieved you'll see the rear of the towing vehicle starting to lift. Lastly, wind up the jockey wheel completely using the handle and then releasing the clamp to pull the whole assembly to its high level towing position. To achieve maximum ground clearance, some owners prefer to remove the jockey wheel completely and stow it in the back of the tow car. There are 'fors' and 'againsts' in both strategies.

Note: On recent caravans, many coupling heads feature a red/green warning button which confirms when there's correct engagement with the tow ball. When the red predominates, the coupling is incomplete. Green signifies the union has been achieved.

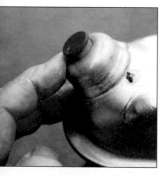

On recent AL-KO coupling heads there's a button with red and green markings which confirms when a tow ball has been correctly engaged.

Attaching the breakaway cable

British caravans have a breakaway cable attached to the caravan handbrake. The other end has to be attached to the towing vehicle.

Function: if, for some reason, a caravan becomes detached from the tow ball, its breakaway cable will tighten, apply the caravan's brakes and then promptly snap under the intense load. This provision should leave the 'van unattached and with its brakes safely engaged. It's believed that parting company like this is better than dragging a caravan behind a tow car by a back-up chain or cable. To achieve this severance, a sacrificial clip on the cable is designed to break open immediately after the caravan brakes have been applied.

Several technical specialists point out that a breakaway cable shouldn't be clipped directly to an eyelet; it's intended to pass through this and clip back on to its own cable

---

Technical Tip

Attaching a breakaway cable

It's unfortunate that many towbars are still not being fitted with an eyelet to accept a breakaway cable; then there are other towbars which DO have an eyelet but it's too small in diameter. That poses a problem because the type of clip normally fitted on a caravan should be passed THROUGH the eyelet and clipped back on to the cable itself.

This precautionary measure must be followed because the traditional clips which have been specified for more than twenty years can get wrenched apart if clipped directly to an eyelet as shown in the photo. When that happens the cable cannot apply the brakes in an emergency.

To overcome this, a new pattern of clip has recently become available (see photo). It costs around £4.00 – £7.00 (complete with cable) and is made to replace the existing components. This one CAN be fitted directly to an eyelet.

The new clip held in the hand has a spring-loaded hinging gate; the older type on the ground merely has a flat spring steel tag which can be distorted easily.

Safety warning

Some owners don't attach breakaway cables correctly and there have been recent reports of caravan brakes being engaged prematurely and burning out. Many of the incidents have occurred with handbrakes which have a gas strut. This activates the hand lever at the lightest of touches and FULLY activates the caravan's brakes and keeps them fully engaged.

Incidents also seem more likely to occur with a 4 x 4 off road vehicle – probably because their pulling power is so good that a driver doesn't always detect that the caravan's brakes have been engaged.

In response to this, an advice sheet has been compiled by a team of experts and it's available FREE from The National Caravan Council, and the two Caravanning Clubs. It can also be downloaded from their websites. It's headed "Correct Attachment of Breakaway Cables: Braked Trailers (up to 3500kg)", and is strongly recommended.

When the grey (or white) 12S plug and the black 12N plug have been attached, their cables need enough slack for the car to articulate – but they mustn't drag on the road.

Regrettably, not all manufacturers fit eyelets to their towing brackets.

Whilst recent tow brackets have an eyelet to accommodate a breakaway cable, many offer nothing at all. Some owners buy a bolt-on 'pigtail' from an accessory shop which affords an attachment facility. Others wind the cable around the neck of the towball. This isn't the preferred method of attachment because in an emergency breakaway situation, the cable might flip over the top of the towball, failing to achieve its purpose. On the other hand, in the absence of eyelets or bracket attachment points, this is often the only way to attach the cable.

Plug connection

The 12N and 12S plugs are now eased into their respective sockets, noting that a small notch in the plug in its 'six o'clock' position, engages with a lug in the socket. Thus the plug is inserted the right way up.

You also need to ensure there's enough 'cable slack' for the caravan to articulate at sharp angles without wrenching the plugs from their sockets. But make sure there's not so much slack that the cable drags along the road. That's a very costly error.

Now you need to engage in a caravan light test operation to confirm the connections are sound. Again a partner makes the whole procedure quick and efficient. I always establish the same light sequences and personally favour: right flasher, left flasher, brake lights, side and number plate lights, and fog lamp, where fitted. The checker at the rear has to call these words out as well, to signify success.

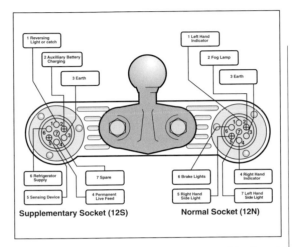

Pin allocations for 12N and 12S sockets (up to 31st August 1998).

Pin allocations for 12S socket from 1st September 1998 onwards.

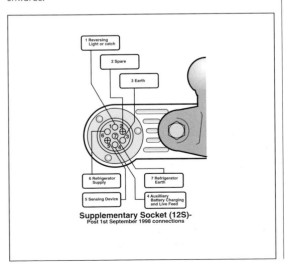

Technical Tip

Caravan road lamp failure

1. If a lamp fails to light on your caravan, give the plug a wiggle in the socket. This often creates a better connection and signifies the pins are probably dirty.

2. The connection points on road bulbs sometimes become coated and it might only be a simple cleaning job.

3. There may be a faulty bulb – and spares should always live on board the caravan.

4. If there's a detached wire somewhere in the system, you may need to call a mobile tow bracket fitter.

5. Further advice is contained in *The Caravan Manual* which is about repair work. However, wiring diagrams applicable to 12N and 12S sockets are reproduced here for reference.

The long-established AL-KO AKS 2000 stabiliser will control lateral instability but it isn't able to dampen unwanted vertical movements.

This AL-KO stabiliser introduced in 2001 is unusual for coupling head devices because it reduces instability in both lateral and vertical planes.

A friction turntable must be tightened periodically in accordance with its manufacturer's advice to ensure the right amount of resistance is provided.

Stabiliser fit

There is good sense in having a stabiliser. But note: this is not a device intended to cure instability caused by poor loading, worn tyres or a damaged chassis. A caravan must always be inherently stable, but that still doesn't stop an unexpected side wind on an exposed road or the buffeting effect from a large vehicle overtaking.

Most stabilisers use friction components to dampen down articulation around the tow ball. In other words, the caravan coupling head doesn't pivot quite so freely which means there isn't such a sensitive response to outside forces like gusts of wind. Equally if deflections occur, they are corrected much more quickly by the product.

If you use a coupling head stabiliser, these are convenient products to use, as long as you always keep the tow ball totally free of grease. Unfortunately there are only a few coupling head stabilisers that dampen down sudden vertical movements – typically caused by a bad road surface.

Blade-type stabilisers that have a steel arm mounted alongside a caravan's 'A' frame usually dampen down unwanted movements in both horizontal and vertical planes. They're fairly easy to couple-up as the accompanying illustrations show. However, make sure you have the resistance system on your stabiliser checked periodically.

1. A short bar by the friction turntable is inserted into the car plate – that's a docking point installed on the tow ball assembly.

2. The single leaf spring – which looks like a long blade – is lowered into a plastic cradle fitted to the side of a caravan's A frame.

3. If the friction turntable is equipped with a quick release system, you now clamp this down using a short length of tubing supplied with the product.

4. The clamp handle is removed and stowed away safely. The stabiliser can now be seen in its ready-for-the-road position.

Rather a lot of caravanners attach a stabiliser whose friction surfaces are worn and its retention bolt has neither been checked nor adjusted since the day the product left the factory. In other words, the stabiliser is probably having little or no effect.

Note: Stabiliser checking devices for both coupling head stabilisers and blade-type stabilisers are available from the Stabiliser Clinic.

Other checks before driving off

Checking that everything is secured inside the caravan including roof vents, windows, cupboards doors and so on is very important. However, these procedures are discussed in Chapter Nine and both Site Arrival and Site Departure check lists are given. Have a look at these because they're equally applicable when you're about to leave home.

If you have a coupling head stabiliser the resistance test kit from the Stabiliser Clinic includes a dummy tow ball insert and a torque wrench.

CHOOSING
AND USING
A SITE

Selecting a site, picking a pitch and working through a simple routine is part of the pleasure of caravanning. Here's some advice on how to select the kind of site you like best and what to do when you get there. Sometimes the pitches are sloping and often there are trees to avoid. Don't worry! The hints and tips which follow will help you handle arrivals and departures in masterful style.

There isn't necessarily a right or a wrong way to site your caravan on a pitch. Some things, of course, have to be done correctly for safety reasons, but other elements are often governed by personal preference.

Procedures also vary from place to place. In fact, many newcomers to caravanning are often surprised by the diverse range of places to stay – so it's useful to know what's on offer. You'll come across examples of the following:

There are hundreds of attractive commercial sites throughout Britain, like this water-side base at Thrapston in Northamptonshire.

Banned! A growing number of sites are exclusively for adults, and children are not accepted.

• Club sites

These are owned or managed by The Camping and Caravanning Club and The Caravan Club. Most are purpose-built, well-managed and have high quality facilities. A few, however, are racecourse sites which are used for caravanning between meetings. These tend to be slightly less well-equipped but have a fascination of a different kind. Some club sites are exclusively for members whereas others welcome non-members, albeit with a surcharge. You can often join the club on arrival as well.

• Holiday parks

Owners sometimes prefer the title of 'park' rather than 'site' and there's often a distinctly 'holiday' focus. The provision of facilities is usually aimed at families so expect to find children's amusements, mini water parks, club houses, restaurants, discos and on-site supermarkets. One holiday park even boasts an on-site theatre, a betting shop and donkey rides.

Sites like the well-equipped Sandy Balls venue in the New Forest are referred to as 'holiday parks' and they have facilities for all ages.

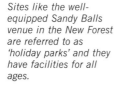

• Restricted sites

Recently there has been a growing number of 'Adults Only' sites, which doesn't mean they run sleazy night clubs. In fact, they're usually quiet, football-free places and one of these accepts no-one under 30 years' of age. Another Adults Only site accepts children at certain times, but requires them to reside in a special compound – which doesn't sound very welcoming for future generations of caravanners. Other sites with restrictions include venues where dogs are disallowed such as on farms where there are sheep. In contrast, other sites welcome dogs and have special 'dog walk' routes.

Sites run by the Forestry Commission such as this one in the New Forest, have an attraction of their own.

• Naturist sites

Whilst it's presumed that most naturist visitors will prefer to leave their 'kit' in their caravan, these sites sometimes accept clothed caravanners. Naturist sites are normally in warmer areas, particularly France, and they draw a nature-loving clientele whose environmental sensitivity often results in their venues being amongst the tidiest and cleanest you'll find anywhere. Naturism isn't everyone's cup of tea, but the sites are often most impressive.

• Standard commercial sites

The majority of commercial sites are fairly standard in provision although you'll usually find all the important facilities like showers, washrooms and toilet blocks. Most offer a limited number of pitches with mains hook-ups, and the overnight fees at these sites are normally much less than they are at all-singing, all-dancing holiday parks.

• Forestry Enterprise sites
(formerly known as Forestry Commission sites)
These wooded locations can be found all around the UK; some have fairly extensive facilities whereas others are much more limited. If you like woodland and wildlife, these are delightful places. They're usually peaceful, too, and don't suit caravanners who want an on-site restaurant, a bar or bingo.

• Small informal sites

Some caravanners seek out small sites which offer no formally marked pitches, where the grass in the field may rise above the ankles and the roads are muddy tracks. Facilities are usually abundantly simple and the fees give change for a fiver.

Cadwallader's farm site, not far from Ludlow, is typical of many farm venues which just take a few caravans – although facilities are limited.

• Certificated locations/Certificated sites

These are venues whose owners are permitted under planning regulations to accept up to five caravans or motorhomes at a time. Typically in rural areas, these spots are usually quiet and often on farms. Many provide no more than a tap and a toilet emptying point, so your caravan has to be well-equipped. Fees are remarkably modest and The Camping & Caravanning Club and The Caravan Club record several thousand examples in their Members' Site Guide Books.

• Year-round sites

This descriptive term usually implies there'll be some hard-standing areas – a provision which assumes special importance when winter weather renders grassy pitches unusable. Although not usually open for a full 365 days, a few owners organise Christmas Packages which include a seasonal events programme. These celebratory occasions are popular and have to be booked well in advance.

The Caravan Club site at Chapel Lane south of Birmingham is open for most of the year.

CHOOSING SITES

Recognising that there are many different types of site, you need to make your choice carefully when reading guide books. Using the benefits of modern technology, the publishers of some guide books work with a large computer data base of addresses. This means that an impressive list can be assembled, but experience will show that sometimes you'll find the information is dreadfully out-of-date.

CHOOSING AND USING A SITE

There are also special marketing groups whose site owner members pay for inclusion in a free site-guide booklet. In this country, the Best of Britain chain is an example and the parks of member-owners have to fulfil certain criteria before acceptance into the scheme. Typically these are high quality holiday parks. In France, the Camping and Castell Group is a similar marketing initiative for high quality sites which have a chateau or historic building within the grounds. There's also the Sites de Paysage chain which offers well-equipped sites in country settings. In most cases, a site guide booklet is distributed free of charge at major indoor caravan exhibitions.

Then there are guides which only contain sites which have been inspected by specialist assessors. The *Alan Rogers' Site Guides*, for example, are published by a committed team of caravanners, supported by site assessors who travel all around Europe. The close scrutiny of each listed site takes a considerable time to complete and the owner is visited un-announced and at least every two years. In fact if standards slip, a venue is immediately taken out of these annually published guide books.

On a different note, there are also site-searching facilities on the Internet. For instance, the developing documentation of sites throughout Europe on a web site known as Oakwood Village (www.oakwood-village.co.uk) is particularly useful.

Then there are national competitions organised to find the best site of the year in England, Scotland and Wales. There are usually various categories of site in these awards schemes and the competitions are contested eagerly by owners. Not surprisingly, the winning sites are always very impressive and well worth visiting. On a similar note, The Caravan Club also conducts a contest to find the best Certificated Locations of the year.

Lastly, there are 'tick' and 'star' schemes run by tourist boards and the motoring organisations, thereby adding further guides to quality.

The Pencelli Castle site is a national award-winning location near Brecon.

When it comes to booking a site, procedures vary from place to place. Normally the process starts with a telephone call and, in some instances, a deposit might later be required. However, like other commercial ventures today, caravan sites can sometimes be booked on the Internet and this booking procedure will undoubtedly become increasingly popular.

ARRIVAL PROTOCOL

Prior to your arrival, it's important to establish when the site reception office is open, especially if you expect to arrive late in the evening. For security, more and more sites are now protected by a barrier and you need a code number or a swipe card to lift the bar.

Tick and star schemes often give a clue about the quality of a site and its facilities.

If you can arrive on time, there may be an opportunity to make your own choice of a pitch. Whether the view over the sea is more important than a pitch close to a toilet block or the club house is a matter for you to decide. However, always try to avoid pitches under trees which shed sap; as Chapter Seven on awnings points out, this can cause you a lot of work later.

Should you decide to use a mains hook-up, ask how many Amps are available. This varies from site to site and if you use too many appliances at once, the supply will be terminated automatically by the site's trip switch system. Once you've been given this information on Amps, the guidance in Chapter Twelve explains which electrical appliances you'll be able to use.

As regards late arrival procedures, some sites have a small compound near the entrance where you can stay overnight, pending the re-opening of reception next morning. Most caravanners are unsympathetic with anyone who arrives on a pitch in the middle of the night. Even the most experienced owner is unable to position a caravan without generating noise.

So enquire when gates are closed or the barriers come down for the night. Ask when reception closes, too. If it's early, and there's no access barrier, the warden will often put your name and allotted pitch on the office noticeboard so you can 'help yourself' and then arrange to fill out the forms and pay the fee the following morning.

To prevent noise on a site in the evening, many sites have a 'late arrivals area'.

151

Chemical emptying points for toilets are sometimes built outdoors.

FINDING THE FACILITIES

Nature dictates that you'll probably seek out the toilet block first. Washrooms and showers will be located, too, along with fresh water taps, waste disposal points, chemical toilet emptying points, ironing rooms, washing/drying rooms, and so on. Some sites also have special washing-up rooms and vegetable preparation areas.

It is also wise to confirm where the fire points are situated. A few club caravanners place a fire bucket alongside their caravan although it's a practice that's seldom pursued now that more and more owners carry a fire extinguisher and a safety fire blanket.

If there's a swimming facility, check to see what safety precautions are in place. You won't always find a lifeguard on duty and some pools don't even advise which is the 'Deep end'. Some countries abroad are especially lax in these matters.

And the rest depends on you. Parents may want to locate the children's playground, and owners of dogs might want to locate a dog walk.

It's wise to check where fire points are located.

At a National Holiday weekend, the units here were sited far too closely together.

PITCH SPACING

With good sense and with safety in mind, the requirement on club pitches is that each resident's caravan should be a minimum distance from a neighbour. Although mainly a precautionary measure with regard to fire, it makes good sense where noise is concerned. For instance The Caravan Club makes the following statement:

'At the discretion of the Warden, caravan outfits may be positioned on the pitch in any way, provided that there is not less than six metres (20ft) spacing between facing walls of adjacent caravans and that there shall be left a minimum clear space of three metres (10ft) between adjoining outfits in any direction, in order to restrict the spread of fire. An 'outift' for this purpose comprises all mobile and other equipment brought on to the site by visitors.' Cited in The *Caravan Club Magazine*, March 2001, page 52.

No one likes too many rules and regulations, but the procedure given above makes good sense. It becomes even more apparent when you see some commercial sites on a public holiday weekend where the tight packing of caravans is neither safe nor satisfactory.

SETTING-UP PROCEDURE

When arriving at your pitch, the following tasks need to be carried out:

- Decide where you want to position the 'van, the car and perhaps an awning.
- Either reverse your caravan or drive it forward on to the pitch.
- Place a small spirit level or a part-filled translucent plastic water container on the floor. Try not to step inside since this puts considerable strain on the unsupported chassis members and may upset the reading.
- A side-to-side slope needs a remedy now. A few caravanners carry a special wheel-jacking accessory, but driving on to blocks is often easier.
  Angled plastic blocks are available from accessory shops and there's also a lifting bag which has to be pumped up.
- Apply the hand-brake on your caravan and if the pitch is sloping, chock the wheels. Chocks are most important accessories to carry.
- Unclip the breakaway cable, disconnect the 12V plugs from the tow car, lower the jockey wheel to the ground, tighten the clamp on the jockey wheel. Incidentally, if the ground's soft, put a small board under the jockey wheel as well.
- Lift the coupling head handle and hold it in the ball-release position while you turn the jockey wheel handle. When the coupling head clears the tow ball, it's time to drive the car away.
- If it's greasy, fit the tow ball cover before you get marks all over your trousers. Later, you'll want to remove the extension mirrors, of course.
- Use the spirit level or water container to check the level in the front-to-back line of inclination. Lifting or lowering the jockey wheel using its handle should find the correct position.

Wood blocks or purpose-made ramps allow you to level up from side-to-side.

153

Some owners use inflatable levelling aids instead of blocks.

Couplings are available for fitting into a rechargeable electric drill so that corner steadies can be operated quickly.

This type of TV aerial has to be set so that it points towards the nearest transmitter station.

Most caravanners fit a lightweight coupling lock or wheel clamp when stopping at a site.

- Once you're happy with the level of the caravan, lower the corner steadies. If they're not fitted with feet pads, use small blocks underneath each one to prevent them sinking into the ground. Some owners speed this process up by using a purpose-made socket that fits into a cordless drill.
- Position the step by the door and go inside. On the 12V fused distribution control panel, set the selection switch to 'caravan' as described in Chapter Thirteen.
- If you intend to use a mains hook-up, follow the strict coupling procedures given in Chapter Twelve and leave spare cable unravelled underneath the 'van.
- Turn on the supply gas cylinder and then get the refrigerator into operation as discussed in Chapter Eleven. If coupled to the mains, you have a choice whether to run the fridge on gas or 230V.
- Set-up the waste water container and couple the drain hoses accordingly as discussed in Chapter Ten.
- Top-up the fresh water container and couple to the caravan. If you've got a submersible pump system, lower the unit into the water barrel until it's submersed – then swing its hose so that it bumps against the sides. This helps to dislodge any air bubbles that may upset its operation.
- If the toilet hasn't been pre-prepared for use, add one litre of water followed by chemical to the waste tank, top up the flushing water and use a rinse-clean additive to help keep the bowl shiny and clean.
- If you're a TV enthusiast who uses a directional aerial, you'll need to get this pointing in the right direction to achieve the best possible signal.
- Most caravanners fit a portable security device while staying at a site; thefts have certainly become more prevalent in recent years.

CHOOSING AND USING A SITE

Notes

1. When setting up on a steep slope, the jockey wheel sometimes reaches the end of its travel before a level position is attained. Overcome this as follows:
- Lower the front corner steadies fully to support the 'van.
- Re-wind the handle on the jockey wheel to withdraw its tyre from contact with the ground, and complete plenty of further turns.
- Lower the jockey wheel again by releasing the locking clamp to lower the outer tube.
- Lock the clamp once more with the knowledge that you've now got more thread available on the lifting spindle to elevate your caravan even higher.
- Leave the corner steadies where they are (i.e. in a lowered position).
- You'll now need plenty of blocks under these if the caravan sits high above ground level due to an acutely sloping pitch.

2. Where do you place a spirit level to check the 'van is level? This leads to much debate amongst caravanners and here are the options often recommended:
- On the A-frame section of the chassis not far behind the coupling head.
- On the lower edge of the forward facing central window.
- On the bottom of a sink to ensure waste water runs down the outlet and doesn't collect at one edge.
- As far as a fridge is concerned, the shelf in its freezer section used to be seen as the point of reference, but now there are models without a freezer shelf.
- Probably the best place of reference for the caravan as a whole is on the floor directly above its axle. This presumes the floor hasn't sustained damage and that a fitted carpet or floor covering material hasn't puckered. On a twin-axle caravan you can take readings over both axles and make your own decision.

Blocks are needed under corner steadies, especially when the ground is soft.

On steeply sloping pitches, you may need a pile of blocks under the corner steadies.

DEPARTURE PROCEDURES

Once you've prepared the car with its towing mirrors, prepare the caravan for departure.

Inside

Get into a routine here and consider creating a check-list. This would include:

Close roof lights

Close windows

Secure cupboards

Clear the open shelves

Secure the fridge door

Select the 12V operation on the fridge's fascia controls

Turn off the fridge's gas operation controls

Turn the 12V panel switch to 'car' setting if you Owner's Handbook says this is necessary

Stow a packed awning centrally over the axle if possible

Secure a part-filled water container for picnic drinks

Stow the waste container, the step and other items

Make sure the toilet waste tank is emptied

Outside

TURN OFF THE GAS SUPPLY AT THE CYLINDER

Disconnect the mains supply as described in Chapter Twelve

Remove water containers and coupling hoses

Stow the mains hook-up cable

Retrieve any blocks of wood left under the corner steadies and wheels

To protect the rear of the car when coupling a caravan, this towing bracket has an over-run bump plate.

HITCHING UP

Be ready for the caravan to lurch slightly on a section of uneven ground. If it rolls forward a little the coupling head can sometimes make contact with the back of the tow car unexpectedly; in consequence, dents in the rear body work of a car are not unusual penalties. This is why some owners have an over-run bump plate fitted behind the tow ball.

LEAVING THE SITE

Some road safety advisers point out that road accidents often occur in the first few moments of a journey. Without doubt if the exit gate of a site takes you into a country lane which doesn't have any road markings, extra vigilance is needed – especially in countries which don't drive on the left. A surprising number of sleepy British drivers leaving a foreign camping site have a momentary lapse of concentration and take up their position on the wrong side of the highway.

CHAPTER **TEN**

WATER AND SANITATION SYSTEMS

In the 1950s, fresh water was often brought to a caravan in a white enamel jug which stood alongside the sink. Piped systems became popular in the 1960s with either foot or hand-operated pumps delivering water to the sink from a container left outside. Water heaters appeared in the 1970s and electrically operated pumps arrived around the same time. Shower rooms were also added and toilets became much more sophisticated.

Anyone who takes up caravanning after holidays spent in tents is often surprised by the sophistication of the sanitation systems. The provision of hot and cold water, a shower and a cleverly designed 'cassette toilet' means that you're pretty well self-contained. In fact, if you pull into a large lay-by during a journey you can step from your car into a well-equipped home.

This also means that you can stop at simple farm sites whose facilities comprise a cold water tap and a toilet emptying point. Self-contained independence undoubtedly has its advantages.

In spite of this, some caravanners still miss the simple arrangements of the past. Certainly, if you purchase an old 1970s 'van solely for summer touring and your intentions are to stop at well-equipped caravan sites, its lack of facilities is hardly a problem. Larger sites often have good showers, hair dryers, and washing-up sinks with hot and cold water.

Some sites provide taps to supply the occupants of individual pitches.

The fresh water supply has been coupled up and is ready for use.

Today, however, modern caravans are sold with every conceivable facility – whether you want them or not. Moreover, anyone purchasing a new caravan would expect to find a shower room in its layout, even though a large number of caravanners seldom use it and choose the site showers instead.

Anyway, things have changed a lot and this chapter includes the following matters:
• Recognising that many people start caravanning by purchasing an older caravan, earlier systems are described and their operation is explained.
• Facilities in the latest caravans are similarly discussed and brief explanations are given about the way things work.

Overall, the emphasis here is on getting things set-up and in operation. Repair and improvement modifications are not included because these are presented in a companion book, *The Caravan Manual*, published by Haynes.

LEAVING HOME

You'll probably want to travel with a small amount of water on-board in order to conduct a road-side picnic. In addition, a small supply of water may prove useful if the tow car's radiator or windscreen washers need topping-up. However, make sure you only partially fill the caravan's fresh water container because water adds considerable weight to the outfit.

Also make sure that any water-filled container is well secured. If a water container breaks free in a caravan, it might damage furniture and can cause serious stability problems while you're towing.

Note: Some caravanners suggest that surging water in a part-filled container can affect stability and braking. They prefer to carry travelling water in a small plastic bottle.

The Whale Aqua Source includes a pressure reducer so you can connect mains tap water directly into your caravan's supply system.

When coupled permanently to a tap, the Water Geezer ensures your water container is replenished automatically.

CONNECTING-UP ON ARRIVAL

Once your destination is reached and the caravan has been levelled-up on its pitch, you'll carry out these water-related tasks:

- Fill up the fresh water container and stand it near the caravan's fresh water inlet.
- Remove the screw cap from the waste water container; store this somewhere safe, and put the container near the waste outlet.
- Connect the fresh water coupling hose to the caravan's inlet – this might be fitted with a submersible pump on one end – as explained later. On the other hand, some 'vans just need a short length of hose because they've got a pump fitted inside.
- Couple the waste pipe from the caravan's outlet to the waste water container.
- Switch on the 12V system at the control panel if your caravan has an electric pump.
- Check that water is delivered to the sink and let the tap run for several seconds to clear any stale water that may have been left in the pipes.
- Put on the kettle for tea or coffee ... at least that's what many people do.

Technical tip

There are a few sites in Britain where you can connect up directly because every pitch has its own tap. However, to enjoy this facility you need either a product like the Water Geezer or a coupling hose that incorporates a pressure-reducing valve to protect the joints in the caravan's pipework. Direct coupling kits include:

1. The Carver Waterline, designed to couple with Carver Compact inlets.
2. The Whale Aqua Source which couples to the Whale Water-master socket or (with an adaptor) to a Carver Compact inlet.

The Wastemaster is a low-profile, wheeled, waste water container which can often be slid underneath a caravan.

WATER CONTAINERS

The procedures above presume, of course, that you've already purchased fresh and waste water containers. These are seldom supplied with a new or second-hand caravan and anyway, many people like a clean start.

It's a matter of choice whether you purchase an inexpensive plastic jerry can, a rolling water barrel like the Aquaroll, or a trolley-type water container such as the Wastemaster. However, as regards the waste container, this needs to be flat enough in design to lay close to the ground. That's because caravan waste water outlets are often fitted near the chassis so there's not much space to create a downward gradient on the coupling pipe.

Technical tips

1. If you drape a waste water hose so that it rests on the bottom of the receiving container, as soon as the container starts to fill, the discharge of water from sinks and wash basin will slow down significantly. You'll find that water runs much more quickly out of a caravan's pipes if the end of the connecting hose is positioned near the entry point to the waste container rather than on the bottom.

2. Ensure the top of the fresh water container is covered to keep out slugs, snails and other inquisitive creatures. Nylon shrouds are available from Gardner of Wakefield if your system doesn't have a plastic cap.

IN-BOARD TANKS

A few caravans, including models from Bessacarr and Vanroyce, are fitted with an in-board water tank. You shouldn't travel with this full, of course, because it would cause instability – and water takes up your valuable payload. So take a couple of plastic bottles of water for a road-side brew by all means, but make sure the tank's left empty until you arrive at a site.

The trouble with an in-board tank is the fact that if you occupy a pitch for several days, you'll have to tow your 'van to a site tap every now and again in order to replenish the tank. That's a nuisance, so many people carry a long hose or even take an additional plastic container and a funnel to top-up the tank. Perhaps an in-board tank isn't the best idea in a touring caravan.

Situated in a forward bed locker, this in-board water tank has been installed in a Bessacarr Cameo.

163

FRESH WATER AND WASTE PIPES

Moving inside a caravan, plumbing systems vary quite a lot. Caravans used to be fitted with a plastic hose which was coupled-up using clasp fittings such as Jubilee clips. This is a poor arrangement because hose can easily develop kinks over a period of time and this seriously restricts the flow of water. Curiously there are still a few well-known manufacturers who continue fitting flexible hose and clips.

Semi-rigid plastic pipe with push-fit couplings is very much better and this has been used domestically since the 1960s. But old habits die hard.

In the 1960s and '70s, clear plastic hose was specified but this lets the light penetrate, which in turn encourages algae to develop inside.

A disadvantage of plastic hose is the fact that kinks often form on sharp bends.

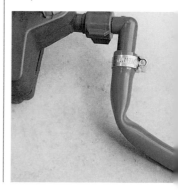

Ridges on convoluted waste water pipe, together with poor gradients, trap food and reduce flow rates.

Nowadays, an opaque red and blue plastic pipe is used for the hot and cold supplies respectively.

Without question, if you purchase an older caravan, the clear pipes will probably look dirty inside. It's not a healthy prospect, especially when recognising that this is the route taken by all your drinking water. Dealing with this is explained in the following section.

Then there's the waste water plumbing. Sadly, in many caravans, this is the most primitive example of plumbing you're ever likely to find. Far too many manufacturers fit a convoluted plastic hose which features reinforcing ridges. These ridges might add strength but on the inside they capture food remnants like rice, peas, meat and so on. Added to this is the fact that on some runs of waste pipe, a 'fall', or gradient, is scarcely discernible – which is one reason why caravan sinks empty so slowly. Sections of pipe might even travel uphill for short distances.

Look under the floor and you may find that a lack of support clips causes the waste pipe to hang like a Christmas garland. Hence food remnants and greasy washing-up water accumulate in each loop.

This criticism might sound harsh but in many caravans the waste water system hardly exemplifies state-of-the-art plumbing. Oddly enough, it's very easy to replace convoluted hose with rigid uPVC pipe which is fitted in our homes and is sold at builders' merchants. This easy up-grade is described in more detail in *The Caravan Manual*, published by Haynes.

KEEPING THINGS CLEAN

- **Fresh water system.** At the start of every season (at the very least) flush this through thoroughly with plenty of water and then sterilise the pipes and fresh water container using a product like Milton. This is the treatment used to sterilise babies' dummies, drinking bottles and so on.

- **Waste water system.** A product called Wastemaster SUPERCLEAN has recently been launched by F. L. Hitchman, manufacturer of the Aquaroll and Wastemaster. This is designed solely to clean waste water containers and tanks and must not be used on any of the fresh water components.

In addition, the waste system needs flushing out periodically and especially before a caravan is left in storage. One reason why a caravan interior smells unpleasant after a long winter break is the fact that odours from residual water trapped in the waste pipe creep up through the sink, basin and shower tray outlets.

Practical tip

If you purchase an older caravan and have doubts about the cleanliness of the supply and waste pipe, it may be wise to have these replaced. In some instances the original system can be improved as well, and tasks like this are discussed in *The Caravan Manual*, published by Haynes.

A grit filter is important for protecting the mechanism in a diaphragm pump.

FILTERS

Some caravans have filters fitted, but note that there are essentially three different types of filter fitted in caravans. These are:

1. A grit filter – one of these is needed if a caravan has a diaphragm pump as described later. A grit filter needs checking and cleaning periodically.
2. Taste filters – these can be easily fitted and are a great asset if you visit venues where tap water tastes ghastly. However, remember that a taste filter improves palatability but does not purify water.

The 'T'-shaped key used to remove this Carver water filter is no longer manufactured. However a short batten of wood with a slot cut in one end using a saw is just as effective.

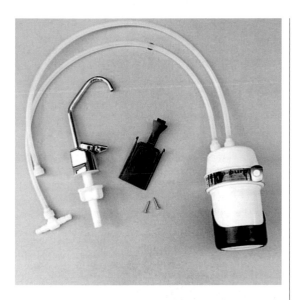

This water-treatment kit from General Ecology is one of the few products which will purify water as well as improve its taste.

3. Purifying filters – in this system, a filter achieves levels of purification and taste improvement that allow you to drink water coming from all kinds of uncertain sources. For instance, products like Nature Pure Ultrafine from General Ecology enable narrow boat owners to drink water taken directly from a canal

Needless to say, taste and purifying filters need changing periodically. Ignore this and the filter might even start to collect water-borne germs.

Strong finger nails are needed to remove this water cartridge which is fitted on recent Carver supply inlets.
On the rear of the Carver cartridge filter, the all-important 'O' rings ensure the inlets form a water-tight joint in the housing.

PUMPS AND TAPS

The final part of this section looks at water pumps and taps. By intention it takes account of older, non-electric systems as well as the very latest components.

On a simple cold-water system, coupling-up just needs a length of hose or a purpose-made plastic pipe.

NON-ELECTRIC SYSTEM

Caravans fitted with just a hand or foot-operated pump were only built to deliver **cold** water.

Advantages
- Simplicity: there's only one set of pipes for cold water.
- Pump: these are relatively inexpensive items and spares are still available for a surprising number of models – some of which have been around for twenty years or more.
- Battery: no need for a supplementary battery which is a requirement when an electric pump is installed.
- Switching: no need for a switching arrangement as required with an electric system.

Disadvantages
- Improvements: it's not possible to run a shower using a foot or hand pump! Hot water heaters cannot be added – they're designed to run in conjunction with an electric pump.
- Frost damage: some types are quite difficult to drain down prior to the onset of winter weather and it's often necessary to disconnect a pipe coupling to achieve this.

Operating procedures

To run the system you merely connect a length of freshwater hose to the caravan's inlet and hang this in the water container. Once you've pumped water up through the internal pipes to the sink you should find that the water won't drain back into the water vessel when you stop operating the pump. A loss of water every time the pump ceases to operate would be a distinct nuisance.

This retention of water in the pipes is sometimes helped by the pump itself but it's principally achieved because there's a non-return valve in the system. Normally this small component is fitted in the supply line close to the external coupling point.

Unfortunately, non-return valves do fail occasionally although a replacement isn't expensive. Incidentally, it's this component which causes water to remain in all your pipe runs after every caravan trip. Moreover, stale water held in the pipes during a winter lay-up isn't pleasant and it needs flushing through before your first trip away the following season.

This is why many owners will disconnect one of the low-level hose couplings situated 'upstream' of the non-return valve so as to drain off all the remnants of water. There ought to be a proper drain-down tap but few caravan manufacturers seem to fit these. This measure ensures there's no residual water left to freeze in the pipes. In reality, flexible plastic hose can cope surprisingly well with the expansion caused when ice starts to form, but pump casings can crack.

Technical tip

If your caravan has a foot-operated pump, the outlet at the sink is merely a shaped length of metal tubing, typically finished in chrome. If you check component specialists' catalogues, this is called a faucet rather than a tap. In this country, the term tap normally refers to an outlet which has a washer, closure system and a screw top or a lift-up lever to stem the flow of water.

In this hybrid system, the Whale foot pump on the left primes the in-line electric pump on the right.

COMBINED MANUAL AND ELECTRIC SYSTEMS

A few caravans built in the mid-1980s combined an in-board electric pump with a foot pump as well.

To couple-up one of these hybrid systems you first have to connect a plastic feed hose from the water supply container to the caravan's water inlet. Then you have to operate the foot pump for a short spell to draw water up into the caravan to fill the chambers of the electric pump. This is called pump priming and once the system is set-up, the electric pump subsequently does all the work.

Once established, the prime of the pump should continue until air gets sucked into the system – as it will when the water container is nearly empty. It also happens when you disconnect the coupling pipe in order to tow your 'van to the next site. Nevertheless, the pump priming task is hardly a chore.

Advantages

– Manual back-up: perhaps the main advantage of the dual system is the fact that you have a foot pump (e.g. a Whale GP51) to fall back on if the battery becomes discharged or the electric pump develops a fault. The type of electric pump installed – usually a Whale GP74 – permits water to be driven through its mechanism when it's not operating on its own account. This is not possible with a number of other electric pumps.

Disadvantages

– Priming: some caravanners don't want the bother of priming the system and when inexpensive submersible pumps appeared in the 1980s these became instantly popular. Strictly speaking, this type of pump does need priming, but a prime is achieved merely by immersing it in water.

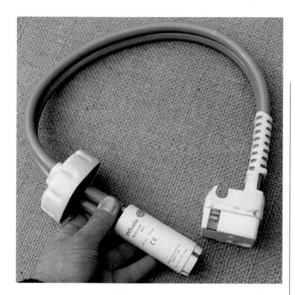

The Whale Water Master system here includes a Minisub 801 pump and the connector which couples with the Water Master wall socket.

ELECTRIC SUBMERSIBLE PUMP SYSTEMS

Most caravans are now supplied with a submersible pump which is a relatively cheap and reasonably efficient component.

On models built around 1990, you'll find that the pump, its supply pipe, and the coupling point to the 'van itself are permanently connected. The supply hose is simply folded flat when leaving camp, rolled up and stowed in a small external compartment. This was an early Carver Crystal water system and there are many examples still giving good service.

More recently, however, the pump, its connecting pipe and the electric feed cable are a separate and detachable assembly. So when arriving on site, you have to plug the assembled system into the caravan's wall inlet. This usually requires a firm and sustained push because there's an 'O' ring in place so that a water-tight seal is achieved, together with electrical contacts which have to mate tightly.

This Carver submersible pump is attached to roll-flat hose which is permanently connected to the caravan's inlet.

The coupling features both a water inlet and brass 12V connections for pump operation.

Once you've made the coupling, the pump is dropped into a full fresh-water container to activate the supply. However, check the Technical tip alongside, if the water doesn't start to flow.

A submersible pump system has both strengths and weaknesses. Certainly it's wise to carry a replacement pump because these units cannot be repaired. Equally, you're unlikely to find compatible units if you have a problem when touring abroad.

Advantages
- Cost: a submersible pump is far less expensive than the diaphragm pump described next.
- Self-priming: whilst this type of pump has to be primed before it starts working, it achieves this automatically as soon as it's dropped into water.
- Damage: the mechanism is merely a paddle wheel (or impeller) which is driven by a small motor. If grit or other water-borne debris gets into the mechanism, it is more likely to survive the intrusion than a diaphragm pump which is certain to suffer.

The 'O' ring on the water inlet nozzle ensures the coupling is water-tight but inserting the unit needs a sustained pressure.

On this Carver system, as soon as the connector is pushed fully home, two retaining lugs help to hold it in place.

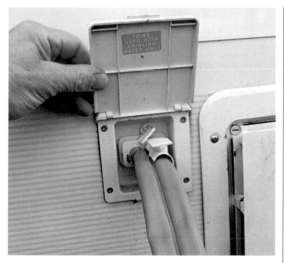

Coupling complete; the supply cable runs down one of the twin pipes and water will flow along the other.

Recent submersible pumps have an air release hole to ensure that air bubbles don't get trapped in the casing.

Disadvantages

– Repairs: these are throw-away items and if the casing splits and water gets into the motor mechanism, it is irreparable.
– Battery dependence: like all electric pumps, the submersible relies on having a 12V supply.

Technical tip

Until quite recently, submersible pumps didn't have an air release hole on the casing. This means that air bubbles can sometimes get trapped inside the unit – even when it's lowered into the water supply container. So whereas the motor might spring into life when a tap is turned on, water still isn't delivered to the sink.

If you have this problem, the answer is to swing the unit around by holding its connecting hose – ensuring it remains below the surface. Making the pump bump against the side of the water container below the surface also helps to dislodge the trapped air. Uncoupling the feed hose at the caravan connection point as well also provides a further escape route for trapped air. Having followed this routine, the water should then flow rapidly.

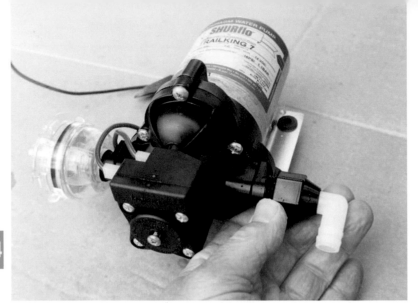

The Shurflo Trailking 7 is a good quality diaphragm pump.

ELECTRIC DIAPHRAGM PUMP SYSTEMS

More expensive models have what is referred to as a diaphragm pump which will be installed somewhere inside the 'van. On arrival at a site, you merely need to connect a length of hose from the coupling inlet to your water supply vessel and it's 'all systems go'. These pumps are well engineered but costly.

Advantages
– Output: these self-priming pumps usually achieve a notable flow rate.
– Repairs: most manufacturers and importers of these pumps offer a repair service.

Disadvantages
– Noise: diaphragm pumps can be noisy although this is often through a poor installation.
– Damage: grit soon damages the tiny pistons which create water flow and a special filter has to be checked and cleaned periodically.
– Cost: these items are considerably more expensive than submersible pumps although a diaphragm pump is likely to last much longer.
– Battery dependence: like all electric pumps, a diaphragm pump relies on having a 12V supply.

More information on grit filter cleaning, and installation checks is given in *The Caravan Manual*, published by Haynes.

PUMP SWITCHING

Like any electric motor, the unit in a water pump needs something to switch it into action. Most caravans have taps which embody a tiny switch which is fitted into the tap units themselves. As you turn the tap top, two things happen – first the water channel is opened up and secondly the tiny micro-switch is activated.

Unfortunately, micro-switches fail as soon as damp gets into their housing. On some taps, you then have to throw the whole lot away and get a replacement. That's a poor design feature although most tap assemblies are made so that a faulty micro-switch can be changed. Only the matter of access makes this a difficult operation. It certainly helps if you're a contortionist, slight of build, and able to see in the dark.

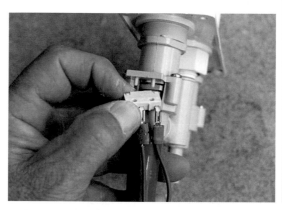

The micro-switch on this Whale Elegance mixer tap is fairly easy to change.

Handy tip

It's always wise to carry a spare micro-switch. Even if you have no intention of carrying out your own repair jobs, the spare can be given to a service specialist to fit. This is particularly appropriate if you're travelling abroad because the water systems and associated products are often different.

Whereas micro-switched systems are quite common, some caravans are fitted with a different switching system altogether. This involves a pressure-sensing switch which detects when a tap is opened and then it sets the pump into action. In fact, diaphragm pumps usually have a pressure sensing switch housed inside the casing.

The trouble is that pressure sensing devices have a nasty habit of switching on the pump when a tiny failure in a pipe joint causes an air leak. That's why there's an override pump switch on an electrical control panel and it's always wise to switch the pump off last thing at night. Forget this and you may awaken to hear the pump giving irregular pulses.

Pressure sensing can also be upset when the supply battery gets low so these switches usually have an adjuster control for fine-tuning.

To summarise, neither micro-switch nor pressure-sensing systems are the perfect answer. Some components work for years and years without a problem: others have a less impressive performance record.

Handy tip

Many caravans have a double tap system for the hot and cold water supply. If a micro-switch fails on one of the supplies – let's say it's the hot supply that cannot be switched into operation – you can sometimes solve this temporarily by 'cheating the system'. This is how you do it:

1. Open the hot tap a generous amount. Nothing will come out because we've established the micro-switch has failed.
2. Now very, very gently turn the neighbouring cold tap (or any other tap in the caravan for that matter) listening for a tiny click to indicate its switch is activated.
3. Don't open this tap any further – it just needs enough to trigger the microswitch.
4. Hey presto! The pump will be set in motion but the water will come from the hot tap which was opened a generous amount.

The bench-type cassette toilet from Thetford has been popular in caravans for more than 15 years.

177

WHICH PUMPING SYSTEM?

In the light of the points made above, anyone buying a new or pre-owned caravan would therefore be wise to ask:

1. What type of pump is fitted? And, in the case of a diaphragm type . . . where is it located?
2. Does pump switching rely on a micro-switch or a pressure-sensing device?
3. How is sensitivity of a pressure-sensing device (if fitted) adjusted?

TOILETS

It's a long time since the 'bucket and chuck it' toilet was used in caravans. Few modern caravanners would tolerate an open receptacle surmounted by a precarious seat. If using these toilets was primitive, caravanners' stories involving stumbling on the caravan's steps en route to the chemical emptying point with a full bucket were legendary, as you might imagine.

The portable flushing toilet with a connected holding tank was undoubtedly a great step forward in lavatorial luxury. Furthermore, these units could be transferred from caravan to caravan when you bought a newer model.

Chemical treatment fluid needs measuring out carefully and this cassette cap includes markings to make the task easier.

Granular treatments from Camco are sold in a container that features a measuring dispenser.

But now toilets are built-in and these so-called cassette loos have been fitted in most British 'vans for more than 15 years. Either way, the care, use and end-of-season servicing are much the same for portable flushers as they are for cassette types.

Equally, it doesn't make much difference between the bench-style cassette toilet or the version which features a swivelling bowl. Both need flush water, both need chemicals and both have a cassette that needs emptying when a gauge gives the warning.

Chemicals

The cassette or holding tank needs a chemical to break up the solids, and there are plenty of products on the market for this. Liquid or granular chemicals, and sachets are all available. Pay careful attention to the mixing levels of the liquid products and always remember to put a litre of water into the cassette first of all.

When purchasing chemicals, you'll find the blue type is usually based on formaldehyde. It certainly breaks down solid matter, but apparently it's detrimental to the environment. This has led to the introduction of 'environmentally friendly' green treatments as alternatives. However, in the last year or so, some camp site owners are now banning the use of green treatments because they are believed to cause drain blockages. No doubt there will be chemists looking into this.

Handy tips

- When adding a chemical, avoid spilling it on your caravan carpet at all costs. The marks are virtually impossible to remove.
- It's best to introduce liquid chemical directly into a holding tank rather than via the toilet bowl. If neat chemical gets on to the rubber seal that keeps the open/close blade water-tight, it can cause damage.
- Flushing water additive really does keep a toilet bowl shiny; it's not merely sales talk.

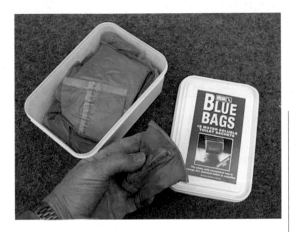

Elsan Blue Bag sachets are another convenient product used to treat the contents of a toilet waste tank.

User advice

Explaining to adult readers how to use a cassette toilet might seem demeaning and vulgar. But, if the job isn't explained here, how will you learn an all-important fact of caravanning life? It certainly never gets mentioned in other caravan handbooks. So here goes.

Many caravanners have 'house rules' that dictate that their toilet is only used for liquid waste. On most sites that's fine, but not when you stop at ill-equipped farm sites where you have to be fully self-contained. The rule also ignores the fact of the 'human emergency'.

So the time-honoured trick is to precede a 'performance' by flushing a small amount of water into the pan. Then a few pieces of toilet paper are carefully placed to float on the water like flower petals, making sure they make brief surface contact around the pan as well. This origami exercise may sound bizarre but it brings its rewards.

Once the 'performance' is complete, you find that as soon as the toilet emptying blade is swung open, the solids drop unhindered into the holding tank below and the paper encloses them completely with gift-wrapping panache. This means that no stains are left on the pan – or more importantly – on the blade and its sealing rubber ring. Don't forget that you see this rubber sealing ring every time the cassette is taken for emptying, so you don't want soil marks. If this all sounds unseemly, I promise you, it works!

The addition of Thetford's Aqua Rinse in the flush water helps to keep the plastic toilet bowl clean and shiny.

Depressing the air release button while tipping a holding tank calls for dexterity, which comes with practice.

There's always a plastic catch to hold a cassette holding tank in place.

Put the cassette screw cap in a safe place so that it cannot get knocked into the emptying point.

Emptying advice

There's a certain knack in emptying a cassette and it doesn't help to learn by using a brim-full container. Some points to bear in mind:

- When removing the screw cap, place it well away from the emptying bowl. Site owners are not happy if they have to try to fish out lost screw caps for butter-fingered caravanners.

- As you point the cassette's outlet to the receiving pan, you need to press the air release button. This can sometimes be difficult to reach, depending how you hold the cassette. However, if you ignore the button, the contents tend to glug into the pan and you're more likely to get splashed.

- Add some fresh water to swill the last remnants of paper out, but don't replace the screw cap and swirl the water around too vigorously. This has been known to damage the internal float mechanism which warns when a cassette is ready for emptying. Do it gently.

- Finally, it might not be a bad idea to do your first-ever emptying with a cassette full of fresh water rather than effluent. The operation isn't quite as straightforward as you might imagine.

The cassette is removed and emptied first of all.

Lay-up procedure

Obviously it's catastrophic to leave a toilet unemptied even though the cassette is built with a pressure-relief valve. But you won't make that mistake if you always remember to leave the blade in its open position prior to a lay up. Apart from acting as a reminder, this prevents the blade sticking to the rubber valve – which can happen over an extended storage period.

Even better is to lubricate the valve prior to this. Do this as follows:

1. Clean the rubber seal using Thetford Bathroom Cleaner or a luke warm diluted solution of washing-up liquid; never use a household cleaner which can damage the seal.
2. Dry thoroughly then spray with Thetford's Toilet Seal lubricant or use olive oil. Never use Vaseline or any other form of grease or lubricant.
3. Leave the blade open during the period of storage.

Thetford bathroom cleaner is used to remove deposits from the toilet seal.

The seal is treated with olive oil, after which, the blade should be left open.

An alternative to olive oil is Thetford's maintenance spray for toilet seals.

CHAPTER ELEVEN

USING A
REFRIGERATOR

A refrigerator is one of the most useful appliances in a modern caravan. However, it is different from the fridges we've got at home and to get the best from one, it helps to have a rough idea how it works. For example, unlike household refrigerators, the appliances fitted in modern caravans operate on one of three sources of power. First, they can work on gas, secondly, they operate on 12V electricity while the caravan is being towed, and thirdly, they can work using a 230V mains supply.

A modern refrigerator is one of the most useful appliances in a caravan.

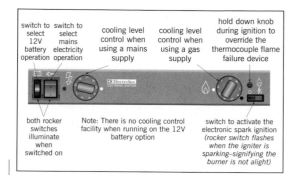

switch to select 12V battery operation / switch to select mains electricity operation / cooling level control when using a mains supply / cooling level control when using a gas supply / hold down knob during ignition to override the thermocouple flame failure device

both rocker switches illuminate when switched on / Note: There is no cooling control facility when running on the 12V battery option / switch to activate the electronic spark ignition (rocker switch flashes when the igniter is sparking–signifying the burner is not alight)

Example of controls and their functions on a late 1980s and early 1990s electronic ignition fridge.

Handy tip

In almost all caravan appliances the refrigerants are circulated by heat. This is called the 'absorption' process. However, in your refrigerator at home the chemicals are circulated by a compressor pump and you can often hear the hum of its motor when a thermostat brings it into operation.

The noise from a compressor fridge is seldom a problem in a large kitchen but the intermittent hum can be a nuisance in a caravan – especially at night. Nevertheless, a few compressor fridges are now being fitted in leisure vehicles and this alternative approach to refrigeration might gain ground in the future. Time will tell.

GETTING THE BEST FROM A REFRIGERATOR

When you want to operate your caravan refrigerator, it's simply a matter of choosing what you want it to run from – gas or electricity – and selecting the operating mode on the fascia control panel.

Unfortunately, a variety of fascia panels have been fitted over the years and if you've purchased a second-hand caravan and the handbook is missing, this may pose a problem. So the accompanying drawings show two of the more popular designs. Guidance about the function of the switches and selectors is shown on the drawing and you should remember that if you want to run a refrigerator on gas, the burner will need igniting.

However, with three supply sources on offer, which one should you use ... and why?

Example of controls and their functions on a mid and late 1990s electronic ignition fridge.

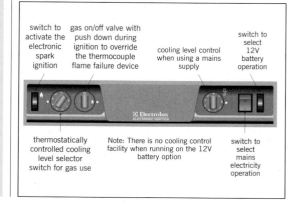

switch to activate the electronic spark ignition / gas on/off valve with push down during ignition to override the thermocouple flame failure device / cooling level control when using a mains supply / switch to select 12V battery operation

thermostatically controlled cooling level selector switch for gas use / Note: There is no cooling control facility when running on the 12V battery option / switch to select mains electricity operation

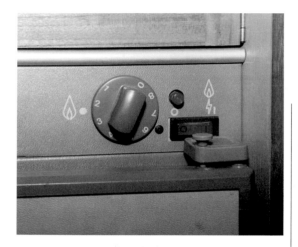

When a fridge is running on gas, you can adjust the level of cooling using a gas control knob.

THREE-WAY OPERATION

Refrigerator manufacturers talk about three-way operation in recognition of the fact that three power sources can be used to run one of these appliances. Each has its merits and there's good reason for giving caravanners three alternatives.

Whichever option you choose, the supply is used to heat the refrigerant chemicals stored in the cooling unit at the back of the casing. Once heat has been applied, the refrigerant starts to circulate around a complex route of pipes. During the circulation, the refrigerant chemicals change to a gas and then back to a liquid – a process which is instrumental in drawing heat out of the food compartment. That's all you need to know about fridge chemistry – although the Tip box explains how this differs from the system employed in the home appliance.

Operation on gas

Applying heat from a small burner is particularly effective. Whilst this is located low down at the back of the unit, you can alter the degree of cooling by adjusting a selector knob on the front panel. The control is exclusively for use when working from gas and it raises or lowers the height of the flame. Incidentally a fridge is made to run

Note

Ignition systems only work if the spark gap is correctly set at the burner. Additionally, soot is created when a fridge runs on gas and this coats the burner assembly which can also upset igniter efficiency. It's most important to have a caravan fridge serviced regularly as explained later in the chapter and one of the tasks is cleaning the system and realigning the electrode where the spark takes place.

on either butane or propane gas without any need for alteration.

To ignite the gas burner, several different systems have been fitted. When caravan fridges first became popular around thirty years ago, you had to light the burner with a match. That was most inconvenient and has long been superseded. To begin with a spark ignition was developed using a Piezo crystal. Plenty of fridges in use continue to use this system and the red push button on the fascia is a familiar sight. However, an electronic system is much more convenient. Provided the appliance is switched on at the fascia, the electronic circuits will generate a spark automatically whenever the burner isn't alight.

Operation on 12V

It is very unwise to run your fridge on gas when the caravan is being towed and it is also illegal to enter a filling station forecourt with an exposed gas flame. To avoid a potentially dangerous situation, fridge manufacturers fit a heating element that runs on 12 volts as an alternative heat source. This means you can keep your fridge working while you're towing without using the gas system.

Unfortunately, however, a refrigerator takes a lot of current to heat the refrigerants (around 8 amps) and the demand would discharge a 12V battery very quickly. So it is entirely impracticable to run this appliance from a caravan leisure battery when you're at the site. Accordingly the caravan's wiring does not include a supply which links the fridge with its inboard battery.

Nevertheless, as long as your tow-car has been correctly wired, a refrigerator is able to operate when you're towing and the engine is running. Current for the 12V heating element is drawn from the vehicle by taking advantage of its alternator charging system. In other words the alternator keeps the car battery charged even though there's a power-hungry appliance calling for current.

Note

When you've set the selector switch to obtain operation on the 12V supply, you will not be able to control the cooling level as you can when the appliance is running on either gas or a 230V supply. On a 12V supply the refrigerator runs at a steady level and neither of the cooling controls on the fascia will make any difference whatever. However, don't be misled into thinking that 12V operation is any less efficient than it is when running on gas or mains electricity. This is not the case.

USING A REFRIGERATOR

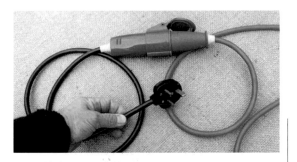

An adaptor is needed to connect a caravan mains lead to a domestic 13 amp socket.

Operation on 230V

If you select the mains option, another heating element comes into use for circulating the chemicals. Equally there's a different control knob with setting numbers for altering the level of cooling.

This operating mode is not only useful on a caravan site. It is also useful if the caravan is parked on your drive and you're packing it up ready for a holiday. It allows you to pre-cool the fridge before setting off without having to use your gas supply.

If you choose this option, make sure you run the fridge using your normal caravan hook-up lead so that the RCD safety protection devices in the 'van are being used. This safety element is described in Chapter Twelve. Of course, you'll need a plug adaptor if you want to connect the hook-up lead to a domestic 13 amp socket.

When you stop at caravan sites whose pitches have hook-ups, you'll probably prefer the 230V option if you've paid to use a mains supply.

Note

On some crowded sites in summer, particularly in certain European countries, the draw on the mains system is considerable. This is especially acute in hot weather when fridges and air conditioning units are running 'flat out'. In some instances, the level of use causes the supply to fall and reports suggest that it can even drop below 195V. If this happens your fridge operation can be badly affected. The tip is that if you cannot get satisfactory cooling when running on mains, switch over to gas operation. This is likely to improve the performance, especially if you're on a busy site.

Handy tip

If you accidentally run your caravan fridge on more than one supply at once, it can damage the system. On pre-1992 models, this can occur by accident when you've been running the appliance on gas and then select the 12V option. In addition you turn the gas temperature control knob to its lowest setting – presuming that this will extinguish the flame.

Unfortunately on these earlier models the gas burner remains alight because the control knob only selects the cooling level; it doesn't extinguish the flame. The only way to do this is to switch off the gas supply at the cylinder. In point of fact, you are always advised to switch off cylinders before taking to the road – but it can get overlooked. On more recent refrigerators the control knob does incorporate a gas shut-off valve – so this problem doesn't arise with models made since 1992.

Handy tip
In the event of continuing problems consult your caravan dealer. Note that there is also a nationwide network of Electrolux service specialists. It is usually possible to obtain advice from the manufacturer by telephoning: 01582 494111.

POSSIBLE PROBLEMS AND SOLUTIONS

As a rule, a refrigerator which is serviced regularly and installed correctly will be notably trouble-free. The following tips may be useful, however, if you're experiencing problems when trying to get it started:

If you find the refrigerator doesn't work on gas, check:
a) The gas cylinder isn't empty.
b) The gas valve for the refrigerator is open.
c) If you can't ignite the burner after repeated attempts, arrange to have the appliance serviced.
d) If the flame doesn't stay alight when releasing the gas control knob, the flame failure device needs attention.

If you find the refrigerator doesn't work on 12V, check:
a) The 12S plug is connected to the tow car.
b) The fuse for the refrigerator on the 12V supply panel is intact.
c) The 12V selector switch is in the correct position on the refrigerator fascia.
d) The tow car engine is running – the 12V option is for use when towing only and is not available when the engine is switched off.

If you find the refrigerator doesn't work on 230V, check:
a) The 230V fascia switch is on.
b) If the fridge is coupled to the caravan mains system by a 13 amp plug; check the fuse in the plug is intact.
c) Check that the miniature circuit breaker which controls the fridge supply hasn't tripped out on the 230V consumer unit.

A fridge can hold a lot of food, but don't pack it too tightly or the contents cannot cool effectively.

FOOD STORAGE ADVICE

To get the best from a caravan refrigerator there are also a number of tips relating to food storage:

Pre-cooling

Before setting out from home, refrigerator manufacturers recommend that whenever possible, it will help if you start operating the appliance for around three hours before the final departure. During this period, a few non-perishable items should be placed in the food compartment – for example, bottles of water or some cans of drink.

Adding foodstuffs

When packing for a holiday, try to delay putting perishable foods in your refrigerator until its cabinet temperature has dropped considerably. If you are able to transfer items from your kitchen fridge which are already cool, so much the better.

Loading-up

Avoid packing food tightly in the fridge and try to position items so that air can circulate around the cabinet. This is important because the cooling process is based on the principle of withdrawing heat from the food cabinet.

Cooling efficiency is greatly reduced if a pack of drinks is placed directly over the heat extractor fins.

Cooling fins

Heat withdrawal is carried out via a bank of silver fins at the rear of the food compartment. So it is important not to cover these completely. Quite often poor cooling occurs when a caravanner pushes a shrink-wrapped pack of drink cans hard against the cooling fins.

Covering food

Remember to pack strong-smelling commodities like pungent cheese or onions in a sealed plastic bag. Similarly pack any damp vegetables in a bag – such as freshly washed lettuce. Failure to do this will lead to the formation of water droplets or frost on the silver cooling fins, and this impairs performance.

Heat from the food compartment is drawn out via silver heat extractor fins.

Door catches

Get into a fixed routine of checking that the door security catch is engaged before taking to the road. Many caravanners have the dreadful experience of finding the refrigerator's contents strewn across the floor on arrival at the destination. But you only make this mistake once!

Wet lettuce must be wrapped in a sealed bag before storing it in a fridge.

PRACTICAL OPERATING ADVICE

Igniting the gas burner

If you haven't used your caravan for some time, it may take several attempts to get the burner to light. This usually means there's air in the gas supply pipe and it may take repeated ignition attempts while the air is being purged. Where this becomes a regular problem it usually means the spark is weak, the electrodes are dirty or the spark gap is incorrect because the electrodes need realignment. These are all signs that it's time to have the appliance serviced.

Checking the flame

On many models, there's a small inspection port in the bottom left-hand side of the food compartment. This will have a clear plastic cover and it may be necessary to move some of the contents to see the glow of the flame. On a refrigerator with electronic ignition, you will hear the unit clicking when it detects the flame has been extinguished which signifies it is attempting to re-light it. You will also note a flashing red switch on the fascia which also confirms the burner isn't alight and that the igniter is trying to resolve this.

Flame failure devices (FFDs)

Like most gas appliances a refrigerator has a flame failure device (FFD). This means that if the flame blows out in a wind, the gas supply to the burner will be shut off automatically. The FFD uses a probe (called a thermocouple) which is angled into the gas flame; when it gets hot it creates a small electric current which in turn keeps a gas valve open in the supply line. However, when you start the fridge from cold, you have to hold down the main control for several seconds to manually open

Many refrigerators have an inspection port in the bottom of the food compartment through which you can check the gas flame.

the gas valve while the probe is getting warmed up. If you find the flame goes out as soon as you release the control knob, the FFD probably needs attention – and that's one of the jobs included in an annual service. Don't be tempted to jam the control knob open since you will over-ride the all-important flame-failure facility.

Handy Tip

For refrigerant chemicals to circulate correctly, it's important that your caravan is set up in a level plane. Indeed if your caravan was built before 1986, this is critical and a refrigerator fitted at the time is unlikely to achieve cooling if it is 2–3° from level.

Since that date, Electrolux refrigerators are described as being 'tilt tolerant'. In practice this means:

• Models like the RM122 and RM4206 will operate correctly as long as the degree of tilt doesn't exceed 3°.
• Models like the RM4217, RM4237 and RM4271 will operate at angles up to 6° from a level plane.

Note: *When you're on the road, the pitch and toss of towing isn't a problem for fridge operation. As long as the refrigerator passes through a level plane every now and again, the cooling unit will remain in operation.*

Efficiency

As long as a refrigerator has been correctly installed by the caravan manufacturer and provided the user-recommendations are followed, an Electrolux refrigerator operates efficiently in air temperatures as high as 38°C (100°F). Unfortunately, however, a number of caravan manufacturers take short cuts in the installation and this often prevents an appliance from achieving its full potential.

USING A REFRIGERATOR

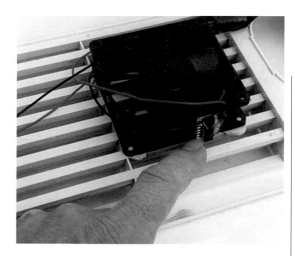

Some owners mount a 12V fan on the rear of the upper ventilator to improve the cooling.

Ventilation

The external vents are important contributors to the cooling process and you should make sure that they don't get covered up. Occasionally the sections of an awning can obscure a ventilator and if this happens, the fabric should be modified so that a clear airway is created. On some models, the caravan's door opens directly across the vents and this doesn't help either. Make sure a gap is maintained of at least 50mm (2in) when the door is held back, especially when the weather's warm.

Note: If you buy a pre-owned caravan and find there's a small electric fan fitted on the inside face of the upper fridge ventilator, this is a modification to improve the flow of air across the cooling unit. This may improve cooling although Electrolux maintains that a fan is not necessary if the appliance has been installed correctly.

Door

In very hot weather, try to open the door on the fridge as little as possible. The wisdom of this is self-evident but young children may not appreciate that cooled air falls from the food compartment quite readily in an upright fridge and disciplined use of the door pays dividends.

In very hot conditions try to open your fridge door as briefly as possible.

Covers for use in winter are available from several manufacturers.

COLD WEATHER CARAVANNING

Most caravanners take their holidays in summer and poor cooling is often a matter of concern. On the other hand if you use your 'van when outside temperatures are low, you can experience the opposite problem: over-cooling. It partly depends on the model fitted in your caravan.

Models prone to over-cooling

This problem is only likely on Electrolux models fitted with a gas valve such as the RM212, RM4206, RM4230 and RM4200. It doesn't normally happen on models fitted with a gas thermostat like the RM2260, RM4237 or the RM4271 models.

Winter covers

Aware of the over-cooling problem, the manufacturers introduced an accessory referred to as 'winter covers'. If your caravan has Electrolux ventilators, you can purchase compatible winter covers from your dealer. These covers are designed to restrict the flow of air across the rear of the appliance and you're recommended to clip these on to the ventilators whenever outside temperatures fall below 10°C (50°F).

Unfortunately, some of the cheaper vents often used on caravans are of a different pattern and you can't buy covers that fit. As a rough and ready alternative some owners attach a piece of silver cooking foil over a small part of the upper ventilator. However, don't cover the lower ventilator because on some refrigerator installations this also acts as a gas escape point in the event of a leak in the supply pipe.

USING A REFRIGERATOR

Some caravanners resort to a makeshift way of reducing ventilation levels during winter by covering part of the upper ventilator with kitchen foil.

Draughts

If a refrigerator has been installed in accordance with the Electrolux instructions, the section at the rear of the appliance will be completely sealed-off from the caravan living quarters. In other words if a strong wind blows towards the external ventilators, it cannot reach the occupants inside the 'van.

It is a matter of considerable regret that a number of caravan manufacturers fail to seal off the rear section as required. Not only does this impair the cooling performance in summer: it also leads to draughtiness in cold, windy weather. Some owners wrongly presume that winter covers are intended to overcome this. In practice they might ease the problem but winter covers were not designed to act as draught excluders.

On the latest Electrolux ventilators, the grill section can be removed independently from its frame below.

CHECKING AN INSTALLATION

If you're buying a caravan – whether brand-new or second-hand – it is often possible to establish if the rear has been sealed off correctly. For instance if you look through the external ventilators you should not be able to see into the living space. In fact on the latest ventilators you can remove the grill using a coin to undo the retention catch and this makes it especially easy to see if there's a likelihood of a draught problem.

Alternatively if you remove drawers in the kitchen adjacent to a fridge and peer outwards towards the vents, you shouldn't be able to see any light from outside. Indeed you shouldn't even be able to see the ventilator from the inside.

At least one manufacturer tries to seal off the top part of the refrigerator by placing a length of sponge on top of the casing. This is poor practice which is not recommended by Electrolux since the sponge can compress and get dislodged. Moreover, a piece of sponge offers poor sealing efficiency when the wind is strong.

USING A REFRIGERATOR

If a draining board gets hot when a fridge is running, the installation is unlikely to have followed the Electrolux guidelines.

A further test to confirm if the cooling unit at the back of a fridge has been correctly sealed-off from the interior is possible when the appliance is operating on gas. If there's a work top or draining board directly over the top of the appliance, put your hand on it. If it is warm, it's almost certain that the installation is unsatisfactory.

If you carry out these checks and find that the installation is unsatisfactory in terms of ventilation provision, don't presume there's any danger involved. This is nothing to do with the flue system which does have safety implications but this is entirely separate from the ventilation requirement. On the other hand, be prepared for disappointing cooling in hot conditions and draughtiness in windy weather. Hundreds of caravanners have learnt to live with these shortcomings.

*Most refrigerators have a
catch that allows the door
to be locked slightly ajar
during periods of storage.*

CLEANING AND LAYING-UP

To provide you with satisfactory service, a
refrigerator needs to be kept clean inside and free
of mould.

- To clean the food compartment, use a mixture
  made up with a teaspoonful of bicarbonate of
  soda dissolved in a litre of warm water.
- Do not use other cleaners; some brands react
  with the plastic lining material of refrigerators
  although the damage might not become
  apparent for many months.
- To remove a food stain on the plastic lining of
  the cabinet, a very fine wire wool pad can be
  used together with a liberal lubrication of water
  in order to reduce its abrasiveness.
- Leave the door ajar using its security catch in
  the storage position. If the catch is broken or the
  'van has a false wooden door to hide the fridge,
  rig up a system which will ensure the refrigerator
  door is held slightly open without being able to
  swing free if the caravan is moved during
  storage.

One of the most demanding parts of a refrigerator service can often be the business of withdrawing the appliance in the first place.

REFRIGERATOR SERVICING

To ensure that a caravan refrigerator gives good service, Electrolux recommends that their appliances are serviced every 12–18 months depending on the frequency of use. However, don't be misled into thinking that a fridge need not be serviced if the caravan remains stored for a couple of years. Rust will form in the flue and this can easily dislodge and fall on to the burner. Moths and spiders can also upset the fine operation of a gas appliance.

One of the oddities, however, is the fact that if you book your caravan for its annual service, very little work is done on the refrigerator. Cooling is usually checked and the appearance of the gas flame might be inspected by a gas engineer. But little else.

This is regrettable and a full fridge service is usually regarded by caravan servicing specialists as an additional, optional task. It is not an expensive operation although one of the more time-consuming jobs is removing the appliance from the caravan. Several service jobs are virtually impossible to complete if the appliance is left in situ.

One of the tasks carried out by a service engineer is cleaning the flue and burner assembly.

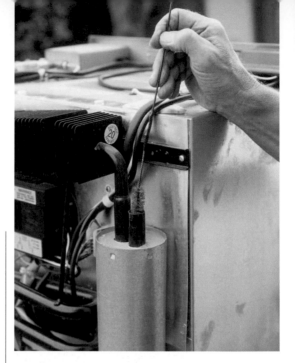

Service jobs include:

- fitting a new jet
- cleaning the burner, flue, FFD probe and ignition assembly
- checking distances and realigning the ignition probe
- checking the operation of the flame failure system

The work must be entrusted to a qualified engineer and more detailed information on servicing, refrigerator operation and installation are given in *The Caravan Manual*, published by Haynes.

The burner assembly needs periodic attention but this is a job for a trained service engineer.

PORTABLE REFRIGERATORS

If you buy a very old caravan which hasn't been fitted with a fridge, it might be possible to have one installed. However, this can be a costly option and alterations to the kitchen will probably be needed. A better alternative might be to purchase a portable refrigerator.

Don't get these mixed up with 'cool boxes' which have a similar look. Portable units are manufactured by several specialists and many owners buy them to provide a further cooling facility in an awning.

These appliances normally offer three-way operation and it is important to read the instructions most carefully when putting one into commission. Operation from gas, for example, must follow all safety procedures.

Otherwise all the points about food packing, pre-cooling and so on mentioned already are equally applicable to these appliances as well. And of course, if you decide to buy a more recent caravan, you can always transfer a portable cooler.

CHAPTER **TWELVE**

USING MAINS ELECTRICITY

Being able to use mains lighting and 230V appliances in your caravan is extremely convenient. Indeed, in the last 25 years, more and more sites have been offering mains connection points – called 'hook-ups'. However, two matters must be recognised. First it's essential to observe safety procedures; mains electricity can cause fatality. Secondly you won't be able to operate some of the power-hungry appliances that you're used to using at home.

In this chapter a number of key issues are discussed. The following points are dealt with:

- If you've purchased a second-hand caravan and the handbook is missing, a full description is given here of a mains installation. Each important item is described so that you can identify it.
- The correct procedure for connecting up to a site supply is set out in step-by-step stages.
- Details are given about hook-up pillars in the UK and abroad – together with the use of adaptors.
- The issue of 'reverse polarity' is explained. This refers to a situation where there are 'crossed wires' in the site's supply system.
- You'll need to establish what appliances you can and can't run. This varies from site to site and the procedure for finding out how to avoid over-loading the site's supply is explained.
- A way to provide a safe 230V supply in an awning is described – as well as issues concerning the use of a portable generator or an inverter.

203

This supply pillar on an Ardèche holiday site offers a two-pin French socket on the left and two British-style sockets on the front.

Note

Having your system checked periodically by a qualified electrician and obtaining a signed certificate confirming its safe condition is strongly recommended.

CARAVAN INSTALLATION

Virtually all caravans now manufactured in Britain are fitted with a mains electricity supply system as standard. In addition, older models that were not originally equipped with a wiring supply for 230-volt appliances can have a mains system installed retrospectively. Work can be carried out at a caravan workshop or by a qualified electrician who has a knowledge of the special wiring arrangement needed in a caravan.

On this Belgian site, the hook-ups offer 220 volts.

Technical Tip

In Britain, a mains supply is traditionally provided at 240 volts AC. The accompanying photograph taken a few years ago on a Belgian caravan site indicates that the supply in that country is 220 volts.

As part of European standardisation, reference is now made to 230 volts AC and agreements include a permitted variation of +10% or −6%. More recent information suggests that the permitted variation from 2003 will be a tolerance of +10% or −10%.

Throughout this book, reference is always made to a 230V supply in recognition of the standardised situation. At the same time, it appears that the actual voltages available can be very different. Apparently on very busy caravan sites, particularly abroad, a high demand for mains electricity sometimes means that hook-up pillars might only yield 190 volts – which is one reason why a refrigerator sometimes runs poorly on its mains setting as described in the previous chapter.

USING MAINS ELECTRICITY

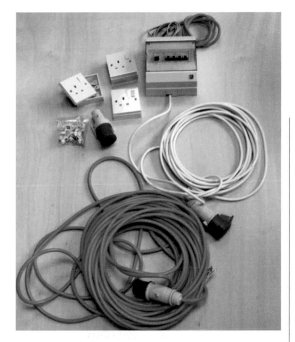

A kit from Powerpart provides all the items needed to use a mains supply.

In addition, DIY installation kits are sold and these are ideal for owners who have the skill and knowledge to carry out the conversion work themselves. An approved kit is strongly recommended because the way that a caravan has to be wired-up is quite different from the way our homes are wired. Moreover you may find a kit – like the one from Powerpart – in which the mains consumer unit is already pre-wired. This means it's supplied with lengths of pre-connected cables extending from its casing. So most of the fitting operation involves basic carpentry and general practical skill rather than difficult electrical work.

With a supply system in place, all you need to connect up your caravan to the supply pillar (or hook-up point, as it's often called) is a length of approved hook-up cable. Under no circumstances should you use any other type of flex, cable or coupling wire.

However, before describing the sequence of operations needed to make the connection, it's necessary to identify all the parts involved and to understand their function.

The consumer unit in a Powerpart kit is already pre-wired.

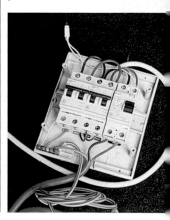

This consumer unit mounted in a locker offers two MCBs and the RCD.

In some caravans the consumer unit is housed in an external locker.

Some consumer units are fitted alongside other controls – here it's on the extreme right.

PARTS NEEDED IN AN INSTALLATION

Irrespective of the age of your caravan, look for the following items:

A) FIXED PARTS
These include:
- The consumer unit
- A safety earth cable
- The input socket
- The internal cables and 13-amp sockets

Consumer unit

The most important part of a mains supply system in a caravan is referred to as 'the consumer unit'. This key control and safety item can be fitted in a variety of places and it is important to find where the manufacturer located it. Sometimes it is fitted in a wardrobe or a cupboard. Occasionally it's fitted in an external locker that has been deliberately designed to store electrical accessories like the hook-up cable and adaptor couplings. There are also manufacturers who build this all-important item into a panel which includes other electrical controls and switches. The accompanying illustrations show examples of these alternatives.

The function of the consumer unit and an explanation of the control switches which you need to use are covered later. See the section entitled, Switches on a Consumer Unit.

USING MAINS ELECTRICITY

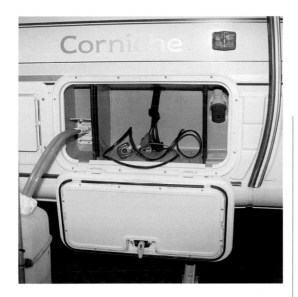

The hook-up inlet on this Swift Corniche is mounted inside the battery box compartment.

Bonded safety earth cable

For safety, the consumer unit has to have a thick earthing cable which is bolted on to the caravan's chassis. This is normally covered with a yellow and green insulation sheath. Near the chassis connection there should be a warning label and this will bear words such as: 'SAFETY ELECTRICAL CONNECTION – DO NOT REMOVE'. If your caravan has a metal sink or wash basin, this should also be bonded with an earthing cable and fitted with a label.

Input socket

A hook-up cable, described later, will have to be connected to a mains input socket on your caravan. This socket must be an industrial type which will be robustly made. At one time sockets were often fitted on the underside of the floor. The trouble with this location is that grit and rainwater can get into the connection when the 'van is being towed. It's possible, of course, to fit a protecting cap, but on balance it is better still if the socket is mounted inside an external locker and it's sometimes fitted in a special box designed to hold the leisure battery. Lastly there are also purpose-made flush-fitting wall boxes which have a hinged cover flap.

The earth cable from a consumer unit has to be connected to the chassis together with a warning label.

SAFETY ELECTRICAL CONNECTION DO NOT REMOVE

Note

Any professionally built British caravan which displays a National Caravan Council badge of approval would have been wired to British and European Standards. However, if you have bought a second-hand caravan, you are strongly recommended to get a dealer or qualified electrician who is knowledgeable about caravan installations to:

1. Check the installation
2. Verify that it is safe
3. Make any necessary alterations
4. Issue a dated certificate as explained in the Safety Tip box opposite.

Some DIY installations are wholly unsatisfactory.

Internal cables and 13-amp sockets

Inside the caravan, you are likely to find two or three 13-amp sockets fitted at convenient points. Truthfully I often wish that more sockets were fitted in a standard installation.

There may be a mains-operated 230V lamp, too, although most lighting is provided by 12V units which run from the caravan's battery. Additionally the refrigerator and a built-in battery charger are usually connected up directly to the mains system as well. Wiring inside a caravan should consist of flexible three core cable which is clipped permanently in place at frequent intervals. You should not find the relatively inflexible 'twin and earth' flat PVC sheathed cable which is used for wiring in our homes and the reason for this is explained in the accompanying Technical Tip box.

Technical Tip

Flexible three-core cable

For the technically-minded, the individual cores in each of the three cables should be $1.5mm^2$ and made up of thin copper filaments as opposed to a solid copper strand; it is this construction which provides the flexibility. The choice of a flexible product is needed in a caravan installation to cope with the vigorous 'shake-up' experienced during towing. The grey solid core cable used for fixed wiring in our homes is not suitable in a caravan context. Solid core rigid cable is more likely to become accidentally disconnected at fittings on account of the relentless movements on the road. So have a look at the internal cable if you've purchased a second-hand caravan; many well-meaning DIY installers do not realise that caravans are wired differently from household installations.

USING MAINS ELECTRICITY

Safety Tip

When considering the purchase of a pre-owned caravan, ask if there's a signed Inspection and Completion Certificate to confirm that the mains installation meets the requirements set out in BS7671.

If a certificate is missing, or if the date on the certificate shows the inspection wasn't recent, arrange for one of the specialists below to check the system:

Either
• an approved contractor of the National Inspection Council for Electrical Installation Contracting (NICEIC),

or
• a member of either the Electrical Contractors Association (ECA) or the Electrical Contractors Association of Scotland.

If an inspection certificate isn't included with a caravan's documents, it is strongly recommended to arrange for the caravan to be inspected before the mains provision is put into service. Telephone 0171 582 7746 to find out your nearest NICEIC specialist or 0171 229 1266 to find your nearest ECA member.

B) ADDITIONAL PARTS NEEDED

You will also need the following items and may have to purchase them from a caravan dealership:

• An approved hook-up cable
• Adaptors if you want to couple-up to hook-up pillars abroad
• An adaptor if you want to couple-up to a 13-amp socket at home.

This short adaptor lead allows a British caravanner to couple up to a French supply pillar.

Hook-up cable

A hook-up cable of 25 metres (+ or − 2 metres) is now supplied as standard equipment with every new caravan. But that's a comparatively recent requirement so connection leads are also sold at caravan accessory shops. Regulations are very precise about the hook-up lead and it should be a heavy duty flexible three-core cable which meets the standard explained in the Technical Tip box opposite.

Note

It is a matter of some concern that less-sturdy cable is sometimes sold for hook-up purposes. Thinner cable should NOT be used. If you see a lead being sold at an unusually low price, it might be sub-standard. It is strongly recommended that you purchase a coupling lead marketed by a well-established caravan specialist such as Powerpart.

USING MAINS ELECTRICITY

Technical Tip

Hook-up cable

The girth of the required cable is quite considerable and for the technically minded, each of its three individual cables in the cover sheath should have a cross sectional area of 2.5mm². This is covered by BS EN 60309-2. On the ends, pre-fitted industrial connections are employed to meet this specification – one with brass pins and the other with deeply recessed brass tubes. It appears that some cut-price suppliers are selling cable in which the individual cables are 2.0mm². An orange outer insulation can make a lower-rated cable look deceptively similar to the required 2.5mm² cable.

Adaptors

As regards adaptors, these are often needed if you travel abroad. It's appropriate to point out, however, that the industrial-style couplings used in Britain are now being fitted on new installations in many European countries. In fact on some sites you may even see both types fitted on the hook-up pillars. But for the most part, you are likely to need an adaptor to suit the supply sockets used in the country you are visiting. It will be many years before a universal standard is established throughout Europe.

In addition, you may want to couple-up your caravan to a supply at home. In the previous chapter, for example, it was recommended that a refrigerator is pre-cooled before leaving for a holiday and most owners like to do this using mains electricity. By purchasing an adaptor to suit a 13-amp domestic socket, this option is then available.

This test button on the RCD allows you to test the operation of the safety switching in the consumer unit.

Technical Tip

How the RCD identifies a fault

When a safe supply system is in operation, there will be a balance in both the live and neutral cables. However, if you accidentally touched a live component or if there was a short circuit caused by a fault, electrical current is able to take a 'short cut to earth'. In milliseconds, this imbalance in the live and neutral cables is detected by the RCD and the main supply switch trips out automatically. This instantaneous termination of the supply can prevent a fatality, even though a very brief shock may still be experienced.

SWITCHES ON A CONSUMER UNIT

Irrespective of whether you purchase a new or second-hand caravan, you should understand the function of the switches on the consumer unit. Moreover, you will be advised to operate one of these switches during the coupling-up procedure described later.

Consumer units may look different externally and you'll come across both larger and smaller types according to the model of caravan and the extent of its mains supply. However, the accompanying photographs show the key points to check.

• The RCD

Firstly look for the switch connected to the residual current device or RCD. This is effectively the 'life saver'. If you want to know how it operates, check the Technical Tip box.

The switch forming part of the RCD unit operates in one of three ways:

1) You can switch off the supply manually.
2 The supply will switch off automatically in milliseconds if there's a fault.
3) There's a test button which will cause the switch to disengage instantly when depressed – just as if a real fault had occurred.

Provided the unit is in full working order, any of these actions will disconnect the mains supply.

USING MAINS ELECTRICITY

The two switches on the left inside this consumer unit are miniature circuit breakers or MCBs.

• The MCBs

Miniature circuit breakers or MCBs are the modern equivalent of rewirable fuses. In the installations in older houses, a fuse 'blows' when a fault develops in an appliance. However, in caravans, like recently built houses, there are 'trip switches' instead and these are shown in the accompanying photograph. The devices are properly referred to as miniature circuit breakers and in appearance they look much the same as the RCD trip switch.

However, the MCB has a different purpose and it shouldn't be confused with the similar looking switch fitted to the RCD. Put in very simple terms, the principal function of the RCD is to prevent fatality. The purpose for having MCBs is to prevent serious consequences e.g. a fire, when there's a short circuit in the system.

Most caravan consumer units have either two or three MCBs and their respective functions will be explained in the caravan's Owner's Manual. If there are two MCBs, one is usually assigned to the fridge; the other serves the 13 amp sockets. In both cases you can either operate the switches manually or they will come into automatic operation when a fault is detected.

Terminology

Whilst the term 'residual current device' has been adopted for several years, you will often see it referred to by its earlier names. For instance, in the past it has been referred to as an 'earth leakage circuit breaker' (ELCB) and also as a 'residual current circuit breaker' (RCCB). Some caravan handbooks have even used the terms interchangeably – which doesn't help with clarity or consistency. Officially, we should all be calling this life-saving automatic cut-off device an RCD.

If you feel uneasy about old hook-up pillars and a multitude of questionable cables, it may be safer not to use the supply.

COUPLING-UP PROCEDURES

Once the caravan owner knows the location and purpose of the RCD and MCB switches, the sequence of operations involved when coupling a caravan to a mains supply is easier to follow. The routine should follow these procedures:

1. Have a look at the site hook-up pillar nearest to your caravan. Most pillars have several couplings and these will be shared by caravanners on nearby pitches. More recent ones even have a meter and a few include a credit card swipe facility so that you can pay as you go. But that's unusual. Incidentally if you find a multitude of dodgy-looking cables all around the hook-up, or have any doubts about the safety of the supply itself, you might wisely decide not to couple-up your caravan.

2. Check that all appliances in the caravan are switched off and as a precautionary measure, move the RCD switch to its 'Off' position.

3. Presuming the hook-up point looks sound, unravel the hook-up cable and do not be tempted to leave this tightly coiled on its drum. If left on the drum there's a risk it might overheat when high-consumption appliances are in use. In severe cases, the insulation might even start to melt. Place the unravelled hook-up lead in loose coils underneath your caravan away from rain or puddles.

4. Insert the female connector into the caravan inlet. That's the one on the lead which has the recessed brass tubes.

This supply pillar even has a credit card swipe facility so you can pay for your electricity as you use it.

Always make the connection with the caravan before coupling-up at the hook-up pillar.

5. Now insert the male coupling into the socket on the hook-up pillar. This coupling on the lead has three brass pins moulded casing.

6. On some systems, the connection has now been completed. However, on others, the power doesn't start to flow until you rotate the coupling clockwise and hear a click. On couplings where this rotation is necessary, you'll also see a red button. This is part of a retention system which locks the plug in place and prevents it from being pulled out accidentally.

7. Check that the cable is laid out in a tidy fashion between the supply point and your caravan. Projecting loops could might cause passers-by to trip over.

8. Now go to the main consumer unit (described earlier) and move the RCD main control switch to its 'On' position. Check as well that the MCB switches are in the 'On' position.

9. That's the job completed, but it's always useful at this point to confirm that the RCD is in full working order. So press in the small check button to confirm that the emergency trip switch comes into operation instantaneously. Once this is confirmed, reset the RCD switch to its 'On' position, secure in the knowledge that this all-important safety device is operating correctly.

Note

There may be a label as well which explains this coupling-up procedure – although in many instances you'll find that instructions on the label have been bleached out in the sun.

On this hook-up, the socket has to be twisted clockwise after it has been inserted to activate the supply.

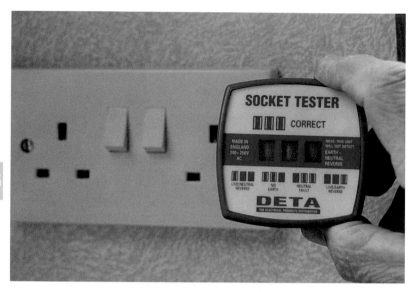

 is placed above.

A tester available from a caravan accessory shop will confirm if the polarity of the site's supply is reversed.

10. Check a lamp unit or an appliance to confirm that the mains supply is live.

Note

Now you should check the polarity of the supply using the explanation and advice in the next section.

REVERSE POLARITY

As a further safety check, you should establish that the live (+) and neutral (−) supply wires on the site supply system are not reversed. This is a fairly common occurrence on the Continent and when this happens it presents a potentially dangerous situation. The reasons for this are described in the Technical Tip box on the opposite page.

To show when the live and neutral feeds are reversed, some consumer units have a red warning light. If you're unit doesn't have one, you are advised to buy a polarity tester. Simply push this into one of your 13 amp sockets and then put the socket switch to its 'On' position. The tester has three small lights and these illuminate in various combinations to indicate the situation. If all three lights glow simultaneously, all is well.

However, if the light sequence on the tester reveals reversed polarity, you have several options:

USING MAINS ELECTRICITY

- Most caravanners acknowledge the potential danger and decide not to use the mains supply.
- Some caravanners recognise the fact that polarity-sensitive appliances may receive damage and that appliances remain live, even when switched off – but choose to use the supply in spite of the risks involved.
- A few caravanners carry a polarity conversion adaptor which has been specially made-up using a short length of hook-up cable and whose live and neutral connections are wired in reverse. When fitted into the site pillar socket and the normal hook-up cable is connected next, the reversed polarity supply is rectified long before it reaches your caravan.

Technical Tip

Reverse polarity

In Britain, switches on all mains appliances or lights are fitted on the live cable. This means that when an appliance is switched off, power doesn't reach the appliance. That's why you can safely change a light bulb without switching off the supply to the entire house. However, in a supply where the live and neutral cables are reversed, the switch would now control the supply on its way out of an appliance. In other words, the appliance or socket would remain live, even when switched off. This could be dangerous.

In mainland Europe, the usual practice is to fit switches which operate on both the live and neutral cables. These are referred to as 'double-pole' switches. In this instance, safety remains assured even if the live and neutral supply is reversed. Accordingly, installations abroad quite often offer reverse polarity whereas it is extremely unusual to come across this problem in Britain.

Note

Caravans manufactured since 1994 now have a double-pole switched RCD and double-pole MCBs – so the level of protection is improved. It is a pity that 13-amp double-pole switched sockets are seldom installed, even though they are available in Britain. This would add the final protection to the caravanner when staying at a site where the supply is reversed.

On this type of hook-up pillar, the coupling plug can only be withdrawn when a red button is depressed.

DISCONNECTING THE SUPPLY

When you want to leave your pitch, the disconnection procedure is mainly a reversal of the above sequence. In particular, it involves:

1. Switching off all appliances and the RCD switch on your consumer unit.
2. Withdrawing the plug at the site pillar to terminate the supply. Normally this involves a sustained pull, but on pillars whose sockets have red locking buttons, you have to depress the button to release your connecting plug.
3. Withdrawing the plug from the caravan input socket. Once again some of the coupling points on caravans have a small tag which has to be depressed before the input socket can be withdrawn.

Needless to say, it helps to dry off the cable on damp mornings before coiling it up.

MAINS
ELECTRIC
INLET

A small blue lever on this caravan input socket has to be depressed in order to withdraw the hook-up plug.

USING MAINS ELECTRICITY

Some caravans are fitted with an external socket so that items like this portable fridge can be operated in an awning.

The mobile supply unit from Powerpart includes a fully equipped consumer unit and three 13-amp sockets for use in an awning.

Technical Tip

If you want to run mains appliances in an awning, there are two options. Some caravans are manufactured with an external 13 amp socket which is housed in a weather-proof box. One of these can sometimes be fitted later by a caravan dealer.

Alternatively, a mobile supply unit manufactured by Powerpart is available through caravan dealers. This features a compact consumer unit with RCD and MCBs, three 13-amp sockets and a 25-metre length of hook-up cable. The advantage with this product is that it can also be used at home when working outdoors with DIY power tools and gardening equipment.

A few hook-up pillars have a re-setting device that the caravanner can operate if the supply disconnects through over-load.

CALCULATING WHICH APPLIANCES WILL OPERATE

When arriving at a site reception, always enquire what output is available from the hook-up pillars. This will be expressed in amps which refers to the amount of current available. Some sites offer as little as 4 amps; a few offer as much as 16 amps. But what does this mean in practical terms?

To establish what appliances you can and can't run on the pitch, you have to find out the wattage of all your appliances. For instance a light bulb might be rated at 60 or 100 watts. A small colour TV might be 50 watts and a normal domestic electric kettle might be 2,500 watts (often described as 2.5kW).

Now consider the amp output available at the site and multiply this by 230 – which is the nominal voltage for a mains supply. This produces the yield in watts. Hence on a site offering 4 amps, you have 920 watts available (4 x 230). Alternatively on a site offering 16 amps, there will be 3,680 watts available (16 x 230). In other words, if you want to run a domestic 2,500-watt kettle, it simply wouldn't work on the site offering 4 amps and you would 'trip out' the supply switch at the bollard. Nothing would be available until the site warden has been brought over to reset the overload device – and you might be unpopular if he or she was having dinner when help was summoned.

Note: A few sites' pillars have the reset system mounted externally so that the RCD and MCBs can be easily reached.

USING MAINS ELECTRICITY

Many caravanners take a special low-wattage electric kettle for use in their caravan.

Obviously this is an over-simple explanation since you normally operate more than one appliance at a time. For example you might be running your fridge on mains (typically 125 watts) and the battery charger might be permanently left on (typically 100 watts). Add the lighting, a fan-assisted gas heater and a colour TV and it's surprising how quickly you approach the limit of the supply.

This underlines why domestic appliances like toasters, high-speed kettles, deep fat friers and fan heaters usually have to be left at home. Equally you'll see why caravanners buy low-wattage electric kettles which are less demanding on the system – and merely take a bit longer to boil the water. As regards microwave ovens, these are perhaps the most confusing items of all. For instance, the wattage rating quoted usually indicates the oven's output rather than the appliance's required input. To get the all-important figure for site use, you have to double the quoted output and then deduct 10%. Hence a small microwave oven rated at 500 watts will have a consumption of 900 watts (500 x 2, minus 10%).

Note: On cold, dark, winter nights, a site's supply will be placed under heavy pressure when all pitches equipped with hook-ups are in use at once. Whereas one pitch might be able to provide a 16 amp maximum supply, the site's wiring isn't rated high enough for all the pitches to be providing 16 amps at the same time. Accordingly you are asked by the owner to be as careful in your use of electricity as possible in order to avoid plunging the site into darkness.

The Honda EX650 leisure generator performs remarkably quietly – but you need an adaptor to couple-up to the domestic-type 13-amp socket on its casing.

POWER FROM GENERATORS AND INVERTERS

Leisure generators

The modern portable generator is smartly designed, compact in size and remarkably peaceful in performance. On the other hand, it is surprisingly heavy, relatively costly to buy, and there are other disadvantages, too.

The output from this type of generator is modest and offers considerably less than an average hook-up point. It's perfectly true that you can build a generator with a large enough output to illuminate a fairground. But the higher the output the bigger the machine and the greater the noise it creates.

So the portable leisure machines are seldom going to produce more than a 1,000 watts (called 1kW) and a more usual output is around 650 watts. Note that these generators have two settings – 60Hz and 50Hz. Hence to achieve a 650-watt output you have to select the 60Hz setting which provides a less stable supply and its fluctuations are not suitable for sensitive appliances.

Another point to remember concerns the micro-wave oven. It is explained on the previous page that to run a 500-watt oven, you'll need a supply able to produce a 900-watt output at the very least.

A final warning. As appliances in the caravan are switched on and off, the generator engine usually alters its note – which often leads to brief irregularity in the output. Moreover, a short surge can create a problem. If you use the mains outlet of the generator to run the caravan battery charger, and if it's a modern switch-mode type of charger, fluctuation in the supply will often damage its electronic circuits. Older, heavier chargers built using a transformer are less likely to

When switched to a 50Hz setting, this Honda generator will provide a more stable supply – although the output is reduced slightly.

USING MAINS ELECTRICITY

To charge your caravan battery, use some connecting cable to couple-up directly to the generator's DC charging outlet.

be affected, but these have long been replaced by lighter, electronic products. So if you want to recharge your caravan battery using a generator, run heavy duty cables direct to the battery from the 12-volt outlet terminals on the generator ... presuming it has got them.

If that sounds all rather negative, I would hasten to add that in some circumstances, a generator is most useful to own. But you do need to realise its limitations.

Inverters

Like portable generators, an inverter is a clever device. When these compact boxes are connected up to a 12V battery they convert the 12V DC input to a 230V AC output. Without question these can be extremely useful additions and even the lower rated models will allow you to run a mains light from a 12V battery.

However, the more you run through the inverter, the sooner your leisure battery will reach a state of total discharge. To give an example of this, if you were to buy a 250-watt inverter and ran it to its limit, you would draw more than 20 amps from the leisure battery in an hour. In other words a typical 60 amp hour caravan battery would be 'flat' in under three hours.

Of course, it's true that a larger 90 amp hour battery would work for longer between recharges, and the situation is much better if you run an appliance intermittently. So if a compact mains colour TV was just needed to see a half hour episode of a favourite serial, an inverter could be the answer on sites without hook-ups. On the other hand, long evenings of TV watching are simply beyond the current state of the art.

The Xcell inverter from Driftgate 2000 is an example of a well-made product that can be coupled up to a caravan's leisure battery.

CHAPTER THIRTEEN

USING 12 VOLT ELECTRICITY

225

Around 30 years ago, caravans were fitted with gas lamps. However, this changed when an Essex electronic specialist found a way to run a fluorescent light from a 12V battery. At first, the tow car's battery was used as the power supply. A few years later owners then wanted to use this supply to run TV sets, stereo systems, heat distribution fans and extra reading lamps. It immediately became clear that a caravan would need its own 12V battery. Over-using a car battery means you might not be able to get the engine started.

In modern caravans, putting a 12V supply system into operation is easy. Provided you have a charged 12V battery connected up in its special compartment, you simply go to a control panel in the van and flick on a few switches. Normally you'll find:

- A battery selection switch. These use a rocker-type switch which can be set in one of three positions. In the middle, the 12V supply is switched 'Off'. The two side positions allow you to draw current from either the caravan battery or the car battery (presuming that you're still coupled up to the towing vehicle). In practice, it's best to regard the towing vehicle's battery as an emergency supply – only putting it to use for short spells.
- Individual controls. On most 12V control panels you'll also find switches which control individual accessories. So you merely switch these to the 'On' position. These operate items like the water pump, the lights and auxiliary 12V accessories such as a TV set.

Wind generators send a trickle charge to a 12V battery – provided there's enough wind, of course.

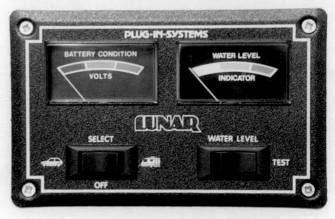

In this Lunar caravan, the 12V source selection switch and battery condition indicator are matched with fresh water tank indicators.

In reality, control panels vary in design and appearance quite a lot and on very old caravans there's not a panel at all. That's because there may only be a couple of lights to run and the 12V supply for these is usually taken from the tow car.

To illustrate how 12V control panels differ, the accompanying photographs show some examples. A few caravans even have their own built-in water tanks so a control panel might include a water level indicator. You will also find panels with a bank of fuses to protect individual accessory supplies.

And controlling the 12V system is as simple as that! Well almost. Owners also need to know something about caravan batteries because these are never supplied when you buy a caravan. Similarly, it helps to know about recharging a caravan battery – so different kinds of charging device are also described.

The all-embracing panel in this caravan from the Swift Group includes the mains consumer unit and a security device as well as 12V switches and fuses.

This simple control panel has separate switches for the external awning light, pump and other auxiliary circuits – together with fuses.

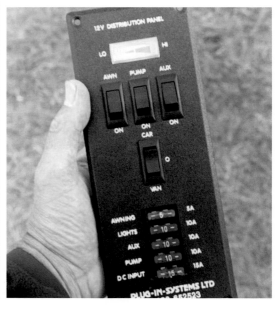

USING 12 VOLT ELECTRICITY

CARAVAN BATTERIES

A battery designed for use in a caravan, motorcaravan or boat is usually referred to as a 'leisure battery'. This is because it's made differently from the automotive batteries fitted in cars. Whereas both products comprise a polypropylene case which houses lead plates and an electrolyte of dilute sulphuric acid, they have to do very different jobs. Moreover, they don't do each other's jobs particularly well.

For instance, a car battery has to provide a large amount of current to start an engine, but then it immediately gets recharged by the vehicle's alternator. In contrast, a leisure battery has to keep low current appliances running for extended periods – often without any likelihood of getting a recharge.

If you use a car battery in a caravan, it will soon need replacing. That's because its lead plates are soon damaged if it has to supply sustained power until it's nearly 'flat' and then has to undergo a long recharge. A leisure battery on the other hand, can cope with these repeated discharge/recharge cycles because its lead plates are constructed differently. For this reason, it's sometimes referred to as a deep cycling battery.

When you compare leisure batteries, you will also notice that they differ in size and have a rating marked on the side in amp hours (Ah). The higher the Ah figure, the longer a leisure battery will supply power before it needs recharging.

This ABI caravan includes a digital clock along with individual switches for the pump, lights, external awning light, and heating fan.

Most modern caravans have a dedicated battery box with an external access door.

CARAVAN BATTERY LOCATIONS

The Safety Tip panel on page 230 explains that a battery often gives off an explosive gas when it's being charged. This is why modern caravans have a purpose-built box with an outlet so that gas can escape – although outlets are often discreetly located to achieve protection from the weather. There should also be security straps so that a battery doesn't topple over and spill its corrosive acid.

There was a time in the 1980s when some caravan manufacturers provided a storage location for a battery in the gas locker compartment. However, this is potentially dangerous because gas control valves occasionally develop a leak. Equally when you couple a connection to a battery terminal, you sometimes create a small spark. So a small accumulation of leaking gas could conceivably be ignited by a spark from the battery. Nowadays, caravans have separate external lockers so that gas cylinders and batteries are always stored apart.

The problem of sparks at battery terminals is another reason why clamping devices are better for making a connection than crocodile clips. They are less likely to create a spark if nudged accidentally and seldom spring off unexpectedly.

Clip-on terminals sold at caravan accessory shops are much more suitable than crocodile clips.

USING 12 VOLT ELECTRICITY

The TP2 battery box was designed to hold the battery as well as a specially made mains charger mounted at one end.

A few owners keep their caravan battery in a blanket box under a bed or in the bottom of a wardrobe. However, if it's not secured carefully it can easily fall over in transit; and then there's the important matter of ventilation. There is rarely an outside ventilator in a wardrobe or bed box so a plastic ventilator tube is essential here. It's even better to buy a purpose-made battery box with sealed lid to screw down in a wardrobe, and create an outlet hole through the floor of the caravan to accommodate the flexible gas escape tube.

As a further point of interest, a few readers might purchase a second-hand caravan which is sold complete with a TP2 battery box. This product is no longer manufactured because it fails to comply with European safety regulations. The TP2 was a plastic carrying box for a battery which also had a purpose-designed battery charger mounted at one end.

This was a thoughtful arrangement and the battery box could be coupled up in the back of a tow car in order to get a good charge from the vehicle's alternator whenever travelling around. The carrying strap also made it easy to transfer the unit to a workbench at home so that its built-in charger could be connected up to a mains socket. The TP2 was a clever idea – provided safety points were observed during charging. However, as soon as caravans were built with purpose-designed battery lockers and fitted with fixed mains chargers, the TP2 box became obsolete.

This Elecsol battery is fitted up with a gas escape tube before being installed in a caravan.

Safety tip
Emission of an explosive gas

When a battery is charged at a high rate, it creates an explosive gas. Hence if you are smoking when you disconnect a charger there's a possibility that the battery casing will explode. When this happens, there's a risk that acid might be thrown in your face. A similar thing can happen if there's a flame nearby – such as a pilot light.

It is most important, therefore, to ensure there are no naked flames near a battery when it's being charged, or the cells are being checked.

The gas given off is lighter than air – so if a battery is in a closed compartment, there must be a high-level ventilator so that escaping gas can discharge to the outside. Alternatively, there's usually an outlet at the end of a leisure battery where a connecting elbow and gas escape tube can be coupled-up. These are usually supplied at the time of purchase.

Provided the coupling and flexible plastic tube fit tightly, any gas created can then be directed externally. In fact, when a tube is used, the gas can even be forced downwards through the floor on account of the captive pressure. However, in the absence of a sealed coupling pipe, escaping gas will rise.

LIFE BETWEEN CHARGES

The period of use between recharges is determined by the Amp hour (Ah) rating of a battery. You should also recognise the difference in demand between caravanning in summer with its light evenings compared with winter caravanning when evenings are often spent clustered around a TV with a fan blowing warm air and the generous use of lights.

When used thoughtfully, a 60Ah battery meets most caravanners' needs for a full weekend in summer. However, a 75Ah battery gives more scope, especially in spring or autumn. Even better is a 90Ah battery; but these tend to be notably larger and are too big for some caravan battery compartments. They are also more expensive.

None of this matters one jot if you are likely to always use a pitch with a mains hook-up. You must always have a battery fitted in a modern caravan, of course, but most built-in battery chargers can be left permanently running. This means that when you are using battery-operated appliances, the battery's output is matched by a charger input. However, a few chargers are best switched off when a battery has achieved a full charge and that's something that should be checked either with a dealer or with the charger manufacturer direct.

In contrast, if you seldom stop at sites which have mains hook-ups, you'll be entirely reliant on the battery for a supply of electricity. However, calculating a battery's likely performance period before needing a recharge can be quite complex because temperature plays a part and so does the age of the battery. More detailed technical guidance on the subject is provided in *The Caravan Manual,* published by Haynes.

Note

Battery manufacturers strongly advise that you never run a leisure battery until it is absolutely flat. So, as soon as the control panel in a caravan indicates the battery is low, endeavour to get it recharged at the earliest opportunity. Some caravan site owners even run an overnight battery charging service.

ASSESSING BATTERY CONDITION

The control panel in modern caravans provides information about a battery's charge condition.

To get a true picture, however, bear in mind that if the battery has just been receiving a charge – either when you've been towing or when a mains charger has been coupled – it should be left to settle for at least four hours before the reading is taken. Certainly after a long charge on a work bench, a truer picture is obtained if you wait 12 or even 24 hours. This is because older batteries look misleadingly good when the charger is first disconnected – but they subsequently lose their charge quite quickly even without being put to use.

Notwithstanding the use of warning light systems often fitted on caravan control panels, a much more accurate assessment of condition is achieved by putting a voltmeter across a battery's terminals. The readings from a voltmeter are interpreted in the accompanying panel. Suffice it to say, a product that we refer to as a 12V battery carries a rather inaccurate title. If a voltmeter registers 12V, the battery is discharged. In a fully charged state, it should read 12.7V.

Note

1. Some electrical specialists point out that this information should only be taken as an approximate guide.
2. Remember the advice about letting a battery rest for four hours or more after a charging period in order to get a more accurate reading.
3. Make sure every 12V appliance is 'Off' when taking a reading. This should include a clock which sometimes gets overlooked.

Approximate indication of a battery's state of charge

Voltmeter reading	Approx. charge state
12.7V or over	100%
12.5V	75%
12.4V	50%
12.2V	25%
12V or under	Discharged

If the level of the electrolyte falls below the top of the lead plates, top this up using de-ionised water sold at car accessory shops.

LOOKING AFTER A LEISURE BATTERY

In view of the cost of a leisure battery, it's wise to take heed of the manufacturer's advice. Here are some of the ways to get the best from a battery:

1. A battery's electrolyte should be checked periodically. This involves removing the caps over each cell and checking the level of acid inside. The electrolyte, as it's called, should just cover the lead plates which you can see in each cell. If the level has fallen in one or more cells, top up where necessary with de-ionised water. This is sold at car accessory shops. Do not smoke when carrying this out.

2. If a lead acid battery is left in a discharged state for a day or more, it will often be irreparably damaged. Attempts to recharge it may prove fruitless.

3. Avoid running a battery until it is completely flat. You should always start recharging a battery when the control panel indicates that it's in a low state rather than using it to the point of exhaustion.

4. When you want to remove a battery from its locker, always disconnect the negative terminal first. Equally, when you're installing a battery, connect the negative terminal last.

5. Sometimes you find that the terminals on a battery get covered with a white powdery substance. To prevent this forming, lightly smear the terminals with grease or petroleum jelly (Vaseline).

To prevent a deposit forming on the battery terminals, coat them with a thin film of Vaseline or grease.

The Zig DCU-3 mains charger was fitted into many caravans in the early 1990s.

CHARGING A LEISURE BATTERY

a) Using the tow car

When you're towing a caravan, some of the charge from the tow vehicle's alternator should make a small input into the leisure battery. Since this isn't a particularly high input, it's referred to as a trickle charge.

In some caravans, the wiring is such that you have to put the battery selection switch on the control panel to the 'car' position in order to receive a trickle charge from the car. Guidance on this should be given in the caravan owner's manual. Failing this, tow your caravan to a service centre and get an electrician to put a voltmeter on the battery's terminals. When the engine is started there should be a distinctly higher reading – say 13.8V – at the battery. This increase from the resting voltage of the battery (12.7V if it's fully charged) indicates that the alternator's replenishing charge is reaching the battery.

If the battery remains at 12.7V or lower, then alter the position of the selection switch, restart the engine and ask the electrician to take another reading. One way or the other there should be a clear rise in voltage when the engine is running. If this is not the case, an electrician would then take a reading at the 12S socket at the back of the car to confirm that the tow-bar has been wired up correctly. Sometimes the fault is in the car rather than the caravan.

This book is not concerned with trouble-shooting and repair work; further information is given in *The Caravan Manual* (published by Haynes), Chapter 3, Tow car preparation.

USING 12 VOLT ELECTRICITY

Many portable generators have 12V DC outlets for sending a charge directly to a battery's terminals.

b) Using a hook-up on a site

If you use a mains hook-up, the caravan's built-in charger will keep the battery in a good state of charge. As mentioned already, some chargers can be left on all the time and electronic circuits prevent them from over-charging a battery.

c) Using a portable generator

These products are compact and useful but they are also heavy and rather costly. Unfortunately they often give an irregular output and fluctuations can damage the circuits in 'switched-mode' electronic chargers which are fitted in the latest caravans. This can prove an expensive mistake. So the recommended procedure is to disconnect the battery from the caravan and to couple it up directly to the 12V output terminals which are fitted on most portable generators. This eliminates the caravan's charger altogether and gets a 12V supply to the battery direct.

d) Using wind generators and solar panels

Both of these devices give a trickle charge to a battery. Whilst the idea of getting 'something for nothing' is attractive, neither are cheap commodities to buy in the first place. One, of course, is wholly dependent on a good wind; the other requires light – but not sunshine as its name implies. In fact, solar generators are usually more efficient under cold clear skies in winter weather than in the hazy heat of a Mediterranean seaside resort. Whilst these devices may helpfully provide a trickle charge to a battery, few caravanners use them.

Before laying-up a caravan for an extended spell, it's usually best to remove the battery so that it can be checked and kept on charge at home.

END OF SEASON

If there are long periods when your caravan remains unused, you should still arrange to keep the leisure battery charged. In most cases, owners take it out of the caravan and put it on a bench at home near a charger. However, this means that if your caravan has an electronic alarm powered by the battery, it will then be disarmed. When bench charging at home, again ensure that no-one is smoking near the battery and ensure there are no naked flames (e.g. a pilot light) nearby.

a) Trickle chargers used by owners of classic cars are sometimes left permanently coupled to a battery throughout the winter. Now their use for keeping a caravan battery in a good state of charge is also recognised. Electronic circuitry switches them 'On' and 'Off' automatically and models from Airflow and Carcoon are especially effective.

b) Standard car chargers are not recommended for leisure batteries which require a different charging regime. However, a few car chargers are now sold with a selection switch to suit the different needs of leisure batteries.

Some chargers sold at accessory shops like Halfords have a switch which selects a charging regime more suitable for leisure batteries.

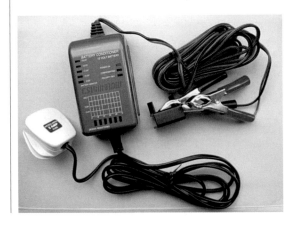

Products like the Airflow battery monitor and charger can be left permanently connected to a battery during a lay-up period.

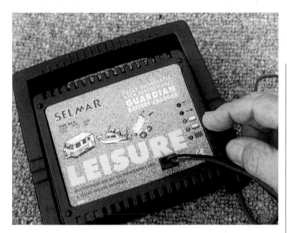

The Guardian Leisure charger from Selmar starts with a boost charge which subsequently tapers off automatically as the battery recovers.

c) Stage chargers like the Selmar Guardian are specially designed for leisure batteries and they provide a variable output. They commence with a high output 'boost charge' to overcome an internal resistance often found in a discharged battery. Then, as the battery revives, the rate of charge progressively drops until the output becomes a trickle charge. This is all done automatically.

CONCLUSION

Older caravans were far more simple and a lot less sophisticated. For use in warm places in the summer when the evenings are light, it is hard to justify the expense of having an elaborate 12V supply system coupled to a costly leisure battery.

On the other hand, today's modern caravans can be used all year round and offer all sorts of comfort features. Few owners could do without electric water pumps, halogen spot lights, fluorescent ceiling lamps, a TV supply socket and a warm air distribution system. But this means you're hugely dependent on a good 12V supply so the leisure battery needs to be kept in a good state of charge, and looked after thoughtfully throughout the year.

CALOR Gas It's here when you need it.

CHAPTER FOURTEEN

UNDER-STANDING GAS

Cooking, space heating and water heating appliances in caravans normally run on liquefied petroleum gas – or LPG as it's usually called. This is a good fuel although it needs to be treated with care, respect and understanding.

LPG is available in portable cylinders which are sold throughout Britain and mainland Europe. However, there has been little standardisation in caravan gas installations and this prompted the introduction of two British Standards/European Norms which were published in 2001 and 2002.

A gas cylinder is one of several important items that's not included when you purchase a new caravan. Equally a gas regulator used not to be included with a new caravan either, although that ceased to be the case when new standards were implemented by UK manufacturers from 1st September 2003 – i.e. on 2004 models. Either way, once a cylinder and a regulator are coupled-up correctly and the owner understands safety procedures, LPG is certainly a very convenient product to use.

Strict safety regulations apply to the storage of gas cylinders on caravan sites.

Note

A large part of this chapter is devoted to the supply system that has traditionally been used in British caravans for the last few decades.

However, with more owners touring abroad and the increasing importation and exportation of European-built caravans, it became clear that greater standardisation in products, practices and procedures would be mutually beneficial.

To achieve this, two new standards relating to gas systems were introduced. (BS EN 1949:2002 and BS EN 12864:2001) As a result, UK caravans built after 1st September 2003 adopt a number of different gas supply features which are discussed in this chapter as well.

Once the new gas standards came into effect, connecting hoses were made to fit the couplings on cylinders used in many countries throughout Europe. However, these carry the same coupling on the other end since the new 30mbar regulators all have a universal fitting.

SAFETY FIRST

The fact that LPG has the potential to create explosions has contributed to its development as an alternative to petrol. In fact, more and more cars are currently being converted to run on LPG.

This feature more than any other helps to emphasise why it has to be used with the greatest of care. It also confirms why a caravanner is strongly advised to know something about LPG's characteristics and the way it can be put to use in complete safety. Let's start with some terminology.

TERMINOLOGY

1. The term LPG does not stand for 'liquid petroleum gas' as many people wrongly state; a gas engineer will correctly refer to it as liquefied petroleum gas.
2. Lemonade and milk are sold in 'bottles', but not gas. The correct word to use is 'cylinders' and newcomers to caravanning are often puzzled by what is meant by gas 'bottles'.

This may sound rather pedantic but terms which are ambiguous or inaccurate should be avoided when dealing with LPG.

FACTS ABOUT LIQUEFIED PETROLEUM GAS (LPG)

- In its natural state, LPG is not poisonous.
- LPG does not have a smell – in its natural state leaks wouldn't be noticed.

UNDERSTANDING GAS

- Distributors add what is called a stenching agent – to warn of a leak.
- LPG is heavier than air, so if a leak occurs the gas sinks to the lowest point.
- The crucial gas escape outlets in a caravan are called drop-out holes.
- Caravanners use two distinct types of LPG – butane and propane.
- Appliances fitted in British caravans run on either butane or propane without needing adjustment.

On account of the product's explosive potential, it is extremely important to follow all warnings applicable to its use. Storage is a case in point.

STORAGE

• On site
A caravan site owner has to follow the strictest rules when storing LPG cylinders. Mesh cages are often used so that if the valve on a cylinder develops a leak (and it does happen), the escaping gas can disperse.

• In caravans
In your caravan, the gas locker should have low level drop-out holes and a battery should never be stored in the same compartment as gas cylinders. This is mentioned because a few caravans made in the 1980s had a large gas cylinder locker which also provided a mounting point for a 12V battery. That was a bad design element because gas cylinder valves do leak occasionally and equally, sparks can sometimes occur when you're clipping on a battery connector. So today the storage compartments are completely separate.

Note
Most gas lockers are situated centrally at the front of a caravan and they mustn't be over-loaded since this creates excessive nose weight. A few manufacturers construct a gas cylinder locker along one of the sides and close to the axle. This position has its merits, too, but can create too much weight on one side of the 'van.

A gas cylinder storage locker must have a drop-out escape outlet at its lowest point.

On caravans built after 1st September, 2003, an owner has to purchase a HIGH pressure hose with factory-fitted couplings to suit the type of cylinder preferred. Low pressure hose with clips must NOT be used.

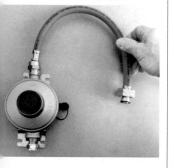

Caravans manufactured before the new standards were implemented need a LOW pressure hose for connecting a cylinder-mounted regulator to the main supply. Good quality clips are essential to prevent hose damage.

• At home

There's a further potential for problems if you remove the gas cylinders from your caravan during a lay-up period. It could be extremely dangerous to keep them in your house. The very worst place of all is in a cellar. If the valve develops a leak, the heavier-than-air gas has nowhere to escape so it accumulates around the lowest parts of the floor.

Garages are not particularly safe places either, especially if that's where you keep a car, store a petrol can, or charge your caravan battery. A garden shed with low-level ventilation is much more suitable, provided, of course, it doesn't have a heater with an exposed flame.

Safety tip
Always keep a cylinder in its upright position
The valve on a cylinder can develop a leak. For instance if a tiny piece of grit gets caught in the spring-loaded ball bearing that seals a Campingaz cylinder, the obstruction may lead to a slow loss of gas. Sometimes you can even hear a faint hiss. The problem is usually solved by taking a Campingaz cylinder outdoors, checking that there's no flame nearby and depressing the ball very briefly with a small screwdriver. The sharp blast of escaping gas, which happens instantaneously, usually dislodges the obstruction and the ball bearing then re-seats itself correctly.

Having acknowledged that leaks can occur, the extreme danger of resting a cylinder on its side is now self evident. Even if the tiniest drop of liquefied gas were to trickle out from a cylinder resting on its side, it would multiply in volume many, many times as it converts from its liquefied form into a gas. That would be extremely dangerous.

UNDERSTANDING GAS

Red propane cylinders are a common sight in cold winter weather.

TYPES OF LPG

Now that some of the key safety issues have been introduced, you need to decide which type of LPG is best suited to your caravanning activities. There are two distinct types of LPG used by caravanners in Britain – one is called butane; the other is propane. Their characteristics are as follows:

Butane
The main points about butane are:
– It is widely sold in cylinders suitable for use in a caravan and there are many distributing specialists throughout Europe.
– It has a higher calorific value than propane and burns at a slightly slower rate so it's a more efficient heat producer. When conditions are suitable, it's the preferred choice of most caravanners.
– It presents problems, however, in extremely cold conditions because it doesn't change from its liquefied state to a gas vapour. This happens when temperatures are lower than 0°C (32°F) at atmospheric pressure. You'll find the liquefied gas freezes in its cylinder so butane is not the preferred gas if you plan to visit a cold region, or caravan in the winter.
– It is heavier than propane. For instance, in the smallest cylinder sold by Calor Gas, the propane version holds 3.9kg (8.6lb) whereas an identically-sized cylinder filled with butane holds 4.5kg (10lb) of butane.

In Britain, butane is usually sold in blue cylinders.

Technical tip
When the temperature falls, the rate at which butane changes from liquid to gas decreases progressively. So, even though the temperature in a gas cylinder locker might still be above freezing point, a significant reduction in the output of gas might become apparent if you're cooking a meal and trying to run a space heater and a water heater at the same time. On noting a lower-than-normal flame on the hob, many caravanners wrongly presume that the cylinder is nearly empty and prepare to get a replacement.

Many caravanners who travel in Britain irrespective of season use propane gas all the time.

On caravans built before 1st September, 2003, you have to buy a butane regulator to use with a butane cylinder and a propane regulator to use with a propane cylinder.

Propane

The main points about propane are:

- It's the preferred winter fuel because it changes from a liquefied state into a gas in temperatures as low as minus 40°C.
- It is seldom sold in portable cylinders outside the United Kingdom although it is used commercially abroad. However, some processing companies are believed to add a small amount of propane to their butane cylinders in order to improve cold weather performance.
- It has a vapour pressure around five times that of butane and for the majority of caravans in use, you need to fit a gas-specific regulator. The function of a regulator is to standardise the pressure of gas reaching your caravan's appliances. To ensure you use the right type of regulator for your chosen gas, the couplings on butane and propane cylinders are different. *Note: On caravans built since 1st September 2003, this is no longer the case. A universal 30mbar regulator is supplied which has been specially made to operate using either butane or propane.*
- It is lighter than butane in its liquefied state. This is why in two cylinders of identical size, you'll see from the markings on the side that the propane one holds less in weight than a butane cylinder.

In Britain, propane is usually sold in red cylinders.

WHICH GAS SHOULD YOU USE?

Taking note of the differences between butane and propane, caravanners who only go away in the summer usually keep to butane. In contrast many year-round caravanners use propane all the time. Others run both types of gas and have different regulators to suit the different couplings – unless it's

UNDERSTANDING GAS

This adaptor, with a red tap, is available from specialists like Gaslow International so that a threaded Calor cap nut connector can be used in conjunction with a Campingaz cylinder.

a post-September 2003 caravan fitted with a universal 30mbar regulator.

In this country, Calor is the most popular gas supplier for caravanners and there is a choice of cylinder sizes; you also have a choice of butane or propane. Many dealers even allow you to trade in an empty butane cylinder for a full propane one, and vice versa. It's not like this on the Continent.

In many European countries you are most unlikely to find propane sold in portable cylinders even though it is used extensively for industrial purposes. You cannot obtain Calor Gas cylinders or Calor-approved refills abroad either. The most universal product in Europe is Campingaz, which is butane, and once again, the cylinders are painted blue.

That aside, it is generally believed that Campingaz cylinders contain a very small quantity of propane mixed with the butane so the product is reasonably satisfactory if you visit a cold place like the Alps in winter. Equally, if you don't want to buy a purpose-made regulator to fit the unique Campingaz coupling, you can buy adaptors in Britain. These match the Campingaz cylinder and have a turn-tap on the top; their outlet connection, however, has a thread which accepts the screw nut coupling used on regulators made for Calor's 4.5kg butane cylinders.

This coupling-up versatility is fine, but there's still the disadvantage that the largest Campingaz cylinder (Type 907) only holds 2.72kg (6lb) of butane. This is a very modest amount compared with Calor cylinders' capacities as the table on page 247 shows.

In response to the situation, many British tourists take a full Calor cylinder abroad (even though it can't be replaced on the Continent) and a Campingaz 907 unit as well. But that doesn't solve all the problems. Whereas Campingaz is quite widely available abroad, there are some European countries where even Campingaz is unobtainable.

Only the large 907 cylinder in the Campingaz range, shown on the left, is suitable to supply the gas demands of a modern caravan.

Handy tips

In Finland, Norway and Sweden, Campingaz cylinders are unavailable even though disposable camping cartridges are occasionally sold. If you visit these countries for longer than the normal output life of your Calor cylinders, you would need to switch to the countries' own suppliers and purchase the appropriate regulators as well.

To find the list of countries where Campingaz, is available, contact Coleman UK Inc. (See Campingaz in Appendix.)

Obtaining gas cylinders

If you decide to use Campingaz, you start by purchasing a cylinder full of gas. When it's empty, your exchange it for another and merely pay the price for the LPG. The charges are reasonable and in Spain the costs are remarkably cheap because the product is government-subsidised. In the case of Campingaz use, you own the cylinder. The situation is different if you want to use Calor Gas in your caravan. To obtain a cylinder of gas you have to enter into a cylinder-hire arrangement which entails completing a form and leaving a small sum of money. So when you exchange an empty cylinder for a full one, you only pay for the LPG. Strictly speaking you never have ownership of the cylinder, even if you caravan for years and years. In fact, if you cease caravanning, you can get back the deposit by taking your Calor cylinders to an approved specialist as long as you can produce the original hire contract papers. Finding them can be quite difficult . . .

UNDERSTANDING GAS

Cylinder sizes

Calor products

3.9kg (8.6lb) propane   Same external
4.5kg (10lb) butane   size of cylinder

6kg (13.2lb) propane   Same external
7kg (15.4lb) butane   size of cylinder

13kg (28.7lb) propane   Same external
15kg (33lb) butane   size of cylinder

19kg (41.9lb) propane

Calor Gas butane cylinders are painted blue.
Calor Gas propane cylinders are painted red.

Note: The larger cylinders, notably 13kg propane, 15kg butane and 19kg propane will often be found in use on permanent pitches but these are normally too large for safe transport. Caravan locker compartments are not designed to accommodate cylinders of these sizes and it has already been emphasised that a cylinder should never be transported on its side.

Campingaz products

0.45kg (1lb) butane
1.81kg (4lb) butane
2.72 kg (6lb) butane
Campingaz cylinders are painted blue.

Note: Only the Type 907 Campingaz 2.72kg butane cylinder is a practical proposition for the caravanner. The two smaller cylinders are really intended for camping use only.

USING LARGER CYLINDERS

It is critically important that a cylinder is always kept in an upright position for the reasons given earlier. However, if you stop on a site for a long spell in winter, it is tempting to exchange a small cylinder for a much larger one. The gas works out very much cheaper this way, so you can keep your central heater going without counting the pennies. It's certainly tempting to change a small Calor cylinder for a large 19kg sausage-shaped cylinder if you're on a winter sports holiday at a UK venue. However, three problems arise if you're tempted to do this:

1. On account of its size the cylinder has to be sited outside the gas locker. In this case, it must be secured so there's no chance that it could fall over. That's not always easy and a 19kg cylinder is a heavy item which could be a hazard when children are playing near the caravan.

2. When your holiday comes to an end, you usually find there's still a large amount of unused gas and there's no way you can transport one of the tall cylinders home in it's upright position (unless you tow with a large van or lorry fitted with a low-level ventilation drop-out hole).

3. Using a cylinder outside of a locker or covered area means that the regulator is now exposed to the weather. In consequence, dust can accumulate in the regulator's all-important breather hole – and damp as well. If rainwater seeps into the breather hole and freezes when it's cold, the regulator is unlikely to function correctly and you might get a situation of 'over-gassing'. When this occurs, the flame on a hob burner can reach a height of around 300mm (a foot) or more.

UNDERSTANDING GAS

Large cylinders will not fit inside a touring caravan's locker and using one of these as a free-standing unit is not recommended.

So the moral here is clear. Don't try to save money by using large cylinders intended for holiday homes or domestic installations. It's not practical and it could be hazardous

How full is the cylinder?

This is the caravanner's perennial problem and several products are available to indicate the 'state of fill' of a cylinder. For instance, Gaslow gauges are helpful but will only tell you the cylinder's condition when an appliance is actually in operation – i.e. when gas is being drawn from the supply.

The Sonatic system from Truma uses ultrasonics to check a cylinder's state of fill and the findings are relayed to a liquid crystal display mounted inside the caravan. At present, however, the Sonatic is only available for operation with 7kg butane or 6kg propane cylinders.

A simple but effective alternative is to weigh a freshly purchased cylinder on your bathroom scales in order to establish the combined weight of both the cylinder and its gas contents. Since the weight of gas in a new cylinder is marked on the side, you can then calculate what part of the total weight is represented by the cylinder itself. In addition, whenever you recheck the total weight after some of the gas has been drawn off, it's easy to work out how much gas is remaining.

Note

Products like Calor Gas are not available outside the United Kingdom. However, the advantage of having a 30mbar wall-mounted dual gas regulator is the fact that during trips abroad, gas cylinders sold in the countries you are visiting can be used. You merely need to purchase a connecting hose with the appropriate couplings – or in some instances – an adaptor. The benefits are clear and yet many post 2003 German-built caravans are supplied with non-fixed regulators designed for direct cylinder mounting. These adhere to the dual-gas specification, conform with the new 30m bar pressure requirement but don't offer the versatility of a wall-mounted regulator system.

REGULATORS

Until the latest gas standards were put into effect in caravans built after 1st September, 2003, a caravanner was required to purchase either a 28m bar regulator made specifically for butane gas or a 37mbar regulator made specifically to suit propane. Normally these gas-specific regulators are connected directly to the valve coupling on top of the cylinder.

However, under the new standards, a fixed 30mbar regulator (which is able to accept both butane AND propane) is normally mounted on the side of a gas supply locker. All you have to purchase from your caravan dealer is a length of high pressure hose with factory-fitted couplings in order to connect the regulator up with the cylinder.

Irrespective of whether you own a caravan with the old or new systems, a regulator's purpose is to ensure that butane and propane gases which leave cylinders at dissimilar pressures finally enter a caravan's supply pipes at the SAME pressure. In addition, a regulator will smooth out irregularities in the flow of gas. In other words, it shouldn't matter if your cylinder is brim full or nearing exhaustion; a regulator ensures that gas reaching an appliance achieves a consistent pressure as long as the supply is adequate.

In spite of its importance in a supply system, a regulator cannot be serviced and the casing is purposely sealed by its manufacturer. Repairs are not possible either and if a regulator fails it must be replaced at once. However, when used solely inside a gas locker, these devices usually last for many seasons. Some specialists suggest it's wise to replace a regulator every five years although others advise that replacement is only needed every ten years. These recommendations presume, of course, that the item looks sound and functions as expected.

REGULATOR COUPLINGS

The sealing washer on the type of regulator needed for a Calor 4.5kg butane cylinder must be changed periodically.

Recognising that on pre 1st September 2003 caravans a different regulator is needed for propane compared with butane, the couplings are purposely different. This is a sensible feature because it ensures that a butane regulator isn't accidentally connected up to a propane cylinder or vice versa.

Rather less sensible is the fact that there are three different types of coupling found on butane regulators. To begin with, Calor couplings are different from Campingaz ones – which is probably not surprising since these are rival companies. Less logical is the fact that in the Calor range there are screw-on couplings for the company's smallest cylinders (4.5kg butane and 3.9kg propane) and clip-on versions complete with their own tap for all the other Calor propane units.

This adds up to four different types of coupling in total to suit all the butane, propane, Calor and Campingaz combinations that you'll come across in Britain.

Don't be misled into thinking that the red washer in the cap supplied with a Calor 4.5kg cylinder can be re-used in the cap nut connection; the compound isn't suitable.

Note

On all Calor propane cylinders and on the Calor 4.5kg butane cylinder, the screw couplings have a left-hand thread. So when looking at the connecting cap nut from the back i.e. the flexible hose side:
– Turning it clockwise loosens it and disconnects the nut from the cylinder.
– Turning it anti-clockwise tightens it, as when connecting it up to a cylinder.

An inexpensive spanner is sold at caravan dealers to suit Calor propane and Calor 4.5kg butane coupling nuts.

Technical tip

Neither propane screw couplings nor Calor clip-on couplings have sealing washers. However, if you use one of the screw-on butane regulators to suit Calor's 4.5kg butane cylinder, it has a sealing washer which must be changed regularly. A packet of three washers costs pennies rather than pounds so it's not a major outlay, and yet some caravanners think they can re-use the washer in the screw-on cap that comes with a re-filled 4.5kg cylinder. Wrong! It's not made of the correct compound and will soon be the source of a leak.

Regulator spanner

Coupling a regulator to a Campingaz cylinder doesn't need a spanner and the clip-on regulator used for Calor's system doesn't require any special tools either. However, if you use any of Calor's propane cylinders or the small 4.5kg butane cylinder, a spanner is needed to tighten the coupling cap nut. So most caravanners purchase the inexpensive open-ended spanner sold at caravan accessory shops.

But be warned. If someone has coupled up your regulator using a plumber's wrench and unnecessary, over-zealous muscle action, the poor little Calor spanner won't be robust enough to loosen it when the cylinder needs changing. Curiously, you always find out about this when the gas runs out on dark, stormy evenings.

Changeover systems

At the very least, you should always carry a back-up gas cylinder. Furthermore, to avoid the bother of having to change a regulator from an empty cylinder to a full one, there are several changeover devices on the market. Some switch from one supply cylinder to the other automatically; others incorporate a manual switch-over tap. Both Gaslow and Truma supply these devices.

Coupling hose

After the regulator you'll notice there's a short length of flexible hose. It's made of a special composition which is not rubber – so never use anything other than the correct product.

Unfortunately, even the correct type of hose will eventually become corroded by LPG so it has to be changed at least every five years – or earlier if there are signs of stretching at couplings or any other evidence of deterioration.

It is now a requirement to have a date

UNDERSTANDING GAS

The diaphragm inside a gas regulator can only work properly if a breather hole in the casing is completely unobstructed.

Automatic gas change-over systems are growing in popularity and this is a standard fitting in models like the Bailey Senator Montana 2002.

displayed on approved coupling hose, but unfortunately this only denotes when it originally left the factory – not when it was fitted to your caravan. So it's wise to keep a note of when it was installed.

Safety tip

Safety when fitting and removing gas cylinders

When changing a cylinder, make sure there are no sources of gas ignition anywhere nearby. An electric heater, a gas water heater, pilot lights on an instantaneous water heater, an outside barbecue, a gas-operated portable awning lamp and so on should be extinguished if their proximity could lead to ignition. Equally, no-one should be smoking nearby.

SWITCH OFF THE CYLINDER YOU WANT TO CHANGE. If you have an approved twin-cylinder coupling device with a manual or automatic changeover valve, it IS permissible to let the active supplying cylinder remain switched on. But still turn off the cylinder you want to change – there may be a small amount of gas still remaining, even if it's not sufficient to run the caravan's appliances properly.

Technical tip

The all-important breather hole on the casing of a regulator must never get blocked. The problem of water getting into the hole and freezing has been already mentioned. In fact if you ever get a frightening tall flame on a stove burner, this is 'over-gassing' which is usually caused by a faulty regulator.

The First Alert gas alarm uses a 12V supply to run an electronic smell-detector and alarm system.

Leak detectors

As a safety precaution many owners have a leak detector fitted in their caravan. There are several types on the market and the Gaslow gauge is a product installed near the supply cylinder. Leaks are revealed on a dial. In contrast the Alde detector is fitted in the supply gas line. If any bubbles are noted in its glass inspection chamber when all appliances are switched off, it shows there's a leak somewhere in the system. Alternatively, the First Alert Gas Alarm reacts to gas smell and an audible alarm is activated when there's a leak. This device has to be connected to a caravan's 12V supply to run its detection circuit. In addition carbon monoxide detectors are now being fitted in caravans and these are on sale at DIY stores.

A leak detector is undoubtedly a worthwhile consideration, but it's never a substitute for the periodic servicing check test by a gas engineer. This is mentioned in Chapter Sixteen.

To conclude, the benefits of LPG are legion. But never take risks; gas accidents can lead to fatality.

The gauges from Gaslow indicate the amount of gas remaining in a cylinder – but only when appliances are being used.

Some caravanners have an Alde leak detector fitted in a gas supply pipe.

Technical tips

Procedure when fitting and removing gas cylinders

1. Campingaz cylinders

Since there's a screw thread on top of a Campingaz cylinder, it means that when the regulator or adaptor is finally becoming detached from the coupling, a very small quantity of gas usually hisses out while the ball bearing valve reseats itself. So act promptly to complete the disconnection.

The same thing occurs very briefly when connecting a new cylinder. In view of this brief moment when there's a small leakage, it's best to carry out the work with a Campingaz cylinder on the ground rather than left inside a locker. It also helps to hold the regulator and to rotate the cylinder itself – rather than the other way round which merely twists up the connecting hose.

2. Screw-thread Calor cylinders

a) When connecting and disconnecting a cylinder, always make sure first of all that the cylinder's handwheel is 'off' – i.e. turned fully clockwise (this has a conventional right-hand thread).

b) When a new butane cylinder is supplied, it has a small black cap over the threaded outlet. Prior to coupling to your caravan, remove this by turning it clockwise as you look at it. (The coupling has a left-hand thread.)

c) When a new propane cylinder is supplied, it has a small black plug in the coupling. Remove this with a large slotted screwdriver, turning it clockwise when looking at the slot. (The coupling has a left-hand thread).

d) Check the connection surfaces (whether it's a butane or propane cylinder) to confirm they're clean and unobstructed. Then offer-up the threaded coupling, hand tighten it first of all, turning it anti-clockwise, and complete the job using an open-ended spanner. Since they don't have a washer, propane couplings have to be especially tight.

e) Turn on the gas at the hand-wheel and confirm there's no hiss to indicate an unsatisfactory connection.

f) When returning a cylinder to a supplier, it's preferred that the plastic cap (butane) or plastic plug (propane) are re-fitted to the empty unit.

3. Clip-on Calor cylinder connections

Note: No tools are needed to connect or disconnect this type of cylinder. Remember, too, that there's no 'on/off' turn-wheel on these gas cylinders; the 'on/off' control now forms an integral part of the regulator. You will also come across variations in the regulator design although the one shown here is quite a common pattern. Detail aside, all types embody a feature whereby the regulator's coupling lever will not operate if you have forgotten to turn off the tap.

256 FEATURES OF THE CALOR CLIP-ON PROCEDURES

a) Preparing a new cylinder

Rotate the orange cap so that its arrow points towards the opening in the cylinder shroud. Now remove the orange cap by pulling on the plastic strap and lifting as you do this. (On an exhausted cylinder the cap is merely pushed back on to the coupling.)

b) Attaching a clip-on regulator

The retaining collar is lifted up with the thumb while the regulator is pushed down on to the cylinder connection.

c) Switching on the gas

Once the regulator is seated properly and the retaining collar has been lowered, you can now rotate the operating tap to the vertical 'on' position.

d) Disconnecting a clip-on regulator

Notice that on this 'clip-on' type of regulator, the design ensures that the release collar can only be pushed upwards when the operating tap is in its 'off' position.

Notes on the supply system fitted on caravans built after 1st September, 2003.

■ Technical literature distributed by Calor Gas Ltd and supported by the National Caravan Council states that combined butane/propane regulators should NOT be installed retrospectively in pre-1st September 2003 caravans i.e. those models fitted with the former supply system. The Company reported: "The gas pressures of the new regulator and your existing installation are NOT compatible". (Leaflet published February 2003 *New Requirements for LPG in Caravans*).

■ Whereas the previous gas-specific regulators were rated at 28mbar (butane) and 37 mbar (propane), the new regulator which operates in conjunction with both butane and propane delivers gas at a standard pressure of 30 mbar.

■ The gas appliances installed in caravans fitted with the revised system have to be manufactured to run at a standard pressure of 30mbar. This has to be clearly shown on a label affixed to the product.

■ The hose which connects a wall-mounted regulator to the supply cylinder MUST: a) carry a High Pressure rating, b) be marked accordingly on the side, and c) be supplied with factory-fitted couplings on both ends. Under no circumstances should low pressure hose and conventional hose clips be used on the revised system; the unregulated gas being drawn from the cylinder is emitted at a high pressure.

■ The overall length of the new coupling hose must not exceed 450mm (about 18in) and many different versions are sold so that a caravanner can purchase one to suit the connections on cylinders sold in the European country being visited. (Longer hose up to a maximum length of 750mm is permitted where cylinders are mounted on a pull-out tray arrangement).

■ It has been decided not to sell coupling hoses to suit every type of cylinder and sometimes an adaptor is needed. For instance, there are adaptors to suit the clip-on couplings used on Calor 7kg and 15kg butane cylinders.

■ The specification of flexible hose has to be stamped on its side. It is NOT rubber; it is a special compound resistant to damage by LPG and its colour does NOT signify its high or low pressure rating. For instance there are examples of black Low Pressure hose and black High Pressure hose – hence the importance of checking the markings on the side.

■ Under the post 2003 system, a factory-fitted regulator now forms part of a supplied caravan's fixtures and fittings. It therefore receives a manufacturer's soundness check together with the rest of the installation before it leaves the factory.

CHAPTER FIFTEEN

GAS APPLIANCES

Having looked at the gas supply system in the previous chapter, we now look more closely at gas appliances. Much has changed over recent years and if you buy an older caravan, its simple heater might now be considered dangerous. So matters of safety are explained, together with the all-important subject of servicing.

At one time, LPG was merely used to run a small hob and a couple of wall-mounted gas lights. With only two burners on the hob, the preparation of a meal called for some forethought – but few caravanners complained. It would have been unthinkable to envisage the level of provision that's commonplace some 30 years later.

However, when the number of gas-operated appliances increased, caravan designers realised that the supply system had to adopt practices similar to those used for electrical wiring. In this arrangement a main trunk route comes from the source which subsequently sub-divides into branches to provide individual supplies to individual appliances. Then you need to be able to isolate the different gas appliances.

The smart cooker on this Lunar Gemini offers all sorts of cooking possibilities; but not all caravanners need this elaborate provision.

To achieve this, today's caravans have a series of gas isolation valves which will control the flow serving each of the branches. Banks of isolation valves are usually well labelled and the information is reproduced in the Owner's Manual, too. If this is missing, you can often follow the route of the pipes, albeit on your knees, with a torch and maybe a mirror as well. There's not a lot of space in caravan kitchen units. Having established the layout, you can then ignite appliances one at a time and finally add your own labels to mark each isolation valve.

Now let's look at the all-important subject of Safety.

SAFETY

When you buy a new caravan, its gas appliances will have been installed in accordance with the latest regulations applicable to LPG appliances in leisure vehicles. Documents provided with the purchase will verify their compliance and the fact that a qualified gas engineer will have inspected the installation.

Things are seldom as straightforward when you purchase a second-hand caravan. Ideally, a pre-owned caravan will be supplied with a recently signed and dated certificate to confirm the integrity of the supply system and its appliances. A good service centre can arrange for this to be carried out prior to the sale and signed/dated documents will give the purchaser assurance that the gas system is in safe working order.

That's the 'ideal world'. In reality it's not unusual to find that this certification is missing and then it's up to you to have the checks carried out before putting the newly acquired caravan into commission. It only needs something like the gas and air mixture to be wrong on a hob and there's

On the Avondale Landranger 6400, the gas isolation valves are clearly labelled.

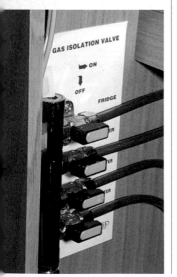

a risk that carbon monoxide is emitted – with possibly disastrous consequences. This is one of the reasons why appliances must be checked and serviced regularly.

When a caravan is built, the manufacturer also has to make a provision for a possible gas leak – either in the supply pipes or perhaps in an appliance itself. So under gas appliances and at other appropriate locations you will find low-level vents. Since the gas used in caravans is heavier than air, these ventilators are needed so that leaking gas can escape to the outside.

Unfortunately, some owners find these 'drop out' ventilators a source of draughts so they cover them up, which is obviously a big mistake. If gas escape vents do lead to uncomfortable draughts, it's usually possible to fit a simple deflector arrangement below the floor. This should shield the ventilator but it mustn't affect the purpose of the vent or reduce its all-important outlet area.

Now let's look at individual appliances.

HOBS AND GRILLS

Whereas hobs have been fitted in British caravans for a long time, the latest products have features like a flame-failure device (FFD) and automatic spark ignition. Hence you don't need matches.

Nowadays, an FFD is an obligatory item on new models and its function is to ensure that the gas supply to the burners is automatically cut off if one of the flames gets blown out. To achieve this, a small probe is angled into the path of the flames and when this gets hot it automatically holds open the gas supply. However, its operation means that when you initially light a burner, you have to depress the control knob for around ten seconds to over-ride the control mechanism. This gives the probe a chance to heat up.

If gas isolation valves bear no markings, it's advisable to label them yourself.

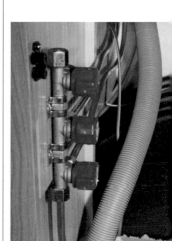

Never cover or restrict the opening of a low-level gas escape vent – which is often called a drop-out hole.

The small probe indicated here is part of the flame-failure device; to the left is a spark igniter.

As regards grills, these are normally only fitted to British caravans. Few Continental manufacturers fit a hob that's coupled with a grill and it seems that caravanners from other European countries see no use for them. We can only presume they haven't discovered the pleasure of toast.

In recognition of our expectations, some importers of foreign models fit a grill system as soon as every caravan is delivered to Britain. Others insist the manufacturer abroad makes special export models to suit British needs.

Finally, please read the Safety Panel opposite on 'Heating and hobs'. It is most important.

Technical tip

Flame-failure device operation

So how does a flame-failure device work? In simple terms, the metals used for the probe respond to heat, interact and create a small electrical current. This is conveyed to the gas control itself and the supply is powerful enough to open an electro-magnetic valve. Hence:

- When the probe is hot, gas flows to the burner.
- When the probe is cold, a spring shuts off the valve and stops gas flowing to the burner.
- If a burner blows out, the flow of gas is cut-off automatically as soon as the probe starts cooling.
- Pushing in the control knob when you're lighting the burner merely over-rides the electro-magnet and holds the valve open, thereby allowing the probe of the FFD to get hot.

If an FFD fails, get the appliance checked by a qualified gas engineer. Never prop open the control with a stick or peg.

OVENS

Whether owners need an oven is a personal matter, but in modern caravans you nearly always have one, whether you want it or not. Some of the full-size cookers are smart, efficient, and often unnecessary. These are heavy appliances that take up a significant part of the potential payload.

If you bake cakes or like to cook a traditional Sunday lunch on holiday, an oven is obviously important. Whether it's worth having one just to heat a meat pie or to re-heat fish and chips is arguable.

That said, if you buy a caravan fitted with a gas oven, please note the points mentioned already about safety and servicing.

SPACE HEATERS

The term gas fire has long been superseded for good reason. Moreover, the word heater is insufficient because modern caravans are fitted with two completely different heaters: one's a water heater whereas the other heats the living space.

Gas fires

In the early 1970s, many owners had an optional gas fire installed. Even in the 1980s, some caravans were equipped with a gas outlet mounted on the floor. Portable gas fires were also sold for coupling up to these gas points using a flexible hose – this was simply pushed on to the ribbed nozzle of the outlet and clipped in place.

Many fires were lit using a match and the problem of carbon monoxide emission – described above with regard to hobs – was potentially a source of danger. So these products are no longer fitted for safety reasons

263

Safety tip
Heating and hobs
Never use a hob to act as a space heater. There are some kitchen designs where the heat rising from a burner that hasn't been covered by a pan or kettle is sufficient to cause damage to a locker or shelf above.

Also, if the gas/air mix on a hob is slightly out of adjustment, there's a possibility that small quantities of carbon monoxide are present in the products of combustion. If you find that the undersides of cooking implements become badly covered with soot, this indicates that the flame is incorrect. Get the hob checked by a qualified gas engineer at once.

Leaving a hob running for a prolonged period to act as a heater can be extremely dangerous and two people who did this overnight recently both lost their lives.

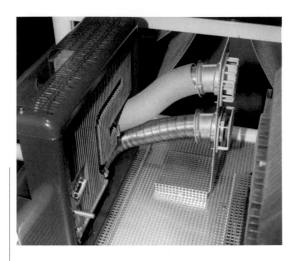

This display of a room-sealed heater shows how both the air intake and flue are coupled-up to an outside wall.

Room-sealed space heaters

A room-sealed heater has the following features:
- The modern space heater in caravans is permanently installed; it is never a free-standing, movable unit.
- Its gas burner is situated within a sealed enclosure.
- A feed duct or specially constructed inlet draws oxygen into the enclosure from outside the caravan.
- All products of combustion are returned directly outside via a flue system.
- As the sealed enclosure gets hot, it warms up the air around it.
- The enclosure is designed to release its heat efficiently and is referred to as a heat exchanger. Fins on an exchanger look reminiscent of air-cooled motorcycle engines and release heat with notable efficiency.
- Normally a room-sealed heater can be left in operation all night. However, confirm this is the case first by checking the Owner's Manual, or seek the advice of a dealer.

From this description you will note that the entire burning process is completely sealed off from the interior living area of your caravan. However, it stands to reason that a fully enclosed heating appliance needs an efficient and reliable ignition system. You cannot light the burner using a match because there's no point of access. On the other hand, as long as you have the heater serviced regularly, neither Piezo igniters nor electronic ignition systems are likely to give a problem.

Safety tip
Exposed-flame gas fires
If you buy an older caravan fitted with a gas fire that has exposed flames and no permanently installed flue, get it removed and scrapped at once. It really could cause a fatality, and if it hasn't been checked by a qualified gas engineer, do not use it.

Below the removable front on this Carver space heater you can see the finned heat exchanger which releases heat from the burners to the living area.

Fan assistance

The use of a fan to help distribute warm air from a space heater was developed in the 1980s. Usually, the air is sent along ducts and this enables you to heat a shower room and to control temperatures in other zones where heat is needed.

In most instances there are two main ducts emerging from the rear of heaters and these usually serve the opposite ends of a caravan. However, on occasions you find that one end of a caravan stays rather cool whereas the other end seems to get hot very easily. To adjust the balance, some Carver and Truma heaters have an output adjuster mounted on the back of the fan. The lever which alters air distribution is often below the fan unit and it's surprising how many caravan owners are not aware of its existence. This is partly because it's usually out of sight and rather difficult to reach.

After the introduction of ducted systems and the idea of mounting a 12V fan on the rear of space heaters, manufacturers then decided that it would increase an owner's options by fitting a 230V mains heating element within the fan casing as well. The Carver Fanmaster introduced in 1994 is well-known and means that you can provide mild heat to your caravan without using gas – as long as you're coupled to a mains hook-up. On models like the Mk 1 Fanmaster, however, you must not use gas and mains heating at the same time.

Then another strategy was followed in which heating elements were fitted adjacent to the heat exchanger – and inside the space heater cabinet itself. This system was followed in the Carver 4000 Fanmaster heater and also in the Truma Ultraheat appliance.

Useful tip
Spare parts
Two of the main manufacturers of efficient space heaters in the past have been Carver and Truma. In the mid-1980s the German company, Truma, supplied many components to Carver which was based in Warwickshire. Later, however, this joint venture was terminated and the companies then worked as two separate manufacturers. However, in the late 1990s, Truma took over the Carver product and created a UK base in Staffordshire.

The supply of spare parts for Carver heaters was also taken over by Truma.

The Truma Ultraheat appliance has an electrical heating element which can be operated at different levels and thermostatically controlled by a dial.

The additional sophistication means that in the case of a Truma Ultraheat unit, you can even use gas and mains heating at once.

Note

Chapter Twelve explains that hook-ups on sites can only provide a limited mains supply. So a Fanmaster fitted with both 1kW and 2kW heating elements which draw 8.3 amps and 4.2 amps respectively, can easily exceed the hook-up capabilities of many sites. That's even without running any other mains appliances in your caravan.

Technical tip

Fan cut-out and reset switch

With the Carver Fanmaster model where an electric element is mounted inside the casing of the fan unit, it's essential that at least one duct is left fully open whenever the heater is in operation. But even though one duct is usually installed without a closing device, it's still possible for this to be accidentally obscured, e.g. by a blanket that has fallen from a bed. So Carver fitted a safety cut-out switch on the fan casing to deal with over-heating situations.

When this comes into operation, many owners presume that the heating system has broken. In reality you only need to carry out the following procedures:

1. Wait until the appliance has cooled down.
2. Open all the outlets.
3. Disconnect the mains supply at the consumer unit (see Chapter Twelve).
4. Reset the trip button by depressing the push switch on the side of the casing.

The accompanying photograph shows the re-set switch which is sometimes hard to locate. The fact that it's at the rear of the heater and often situated in the bottom part of a wardrobe can lead to some fumbling in the dark.

More recent models feature an automatic reset. So check the handbook and if this is missing either seek the help at a caravan workshop or telephone the customer help-line at Truma (UK).

On the Carver Fanmaster, where the electrical element is situated in the fan housing, there's a reset button which is part of the over-heating safety cut-out.

Wet heating systems

A few of the more expensive caravans are fitted with a central heating system that uses radiators. The efficient 3000 Compact Alde system, for example, is highly regarded and is fitted in top specification caravans including models from Avondale, Bessacarr, Buccaneer and Vanmaster.

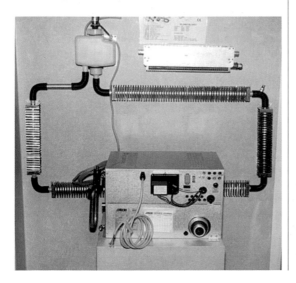

This display shows the Alder 3000 Compact heating system which uses radiators.

After the arrival of room-sealed gas appliances, products like instantaneous water heaters were no longer fitted in touring caravans.

WATER HEATERS

A water heater is certainly a luxury item. Few complained about boiling a kettle for washing-up water in the 'old days' and it was only the advent of caravan showers which changed things for ever. Water heaters became commonplace and followed a similar evolutionary pathway as space heaters.

For example, any heater with exposed flames was deemed unacceptable more than a decade ago, so instantaneous water heaters, like the Paloma or the Rinnai, ceased to be fitted by British manufacturers. Appliances with a hot water storage tank became the norm.

Then it was decided to fit a 230V immersion heater element in the tank so that both gas and mains could be used – either as alternative fuels or together to speed-up the heating time when starting from cold.

Apart from the inbuilt facilities in an integrated central heating system like the Alde 3000 compact, or the Truma Combi, three makes of independent storage water heaters have been prominent in Britain:
1. The Carver Cascade (several versions since its debut in the mid-1980s).
2. The Maxol Malaga (also made bearing the Belling badge).
3. The Truma Ultrastore.

After its appearance, the Carver Cascade underwent a number of improvements. For instance, the original model had a very slow drain-down time due to air locks and it might approach an hour before the last drops of water were emptied. The Cascade 2 Plus featured an air release point as well, and this resolved the problem.

GAS APPLIANCES

You can always travel with the storage water heater empty if you're close to the limit of your permitted payload.

In addition, the Cascade 2 Plus GE features a 660W mains heating element whereas the Cascade Rapide has an 830W heating element together with an overheat reset button situated behind a cover flap.

Technical tip

Draining down the water

With the onset of frosty weather, it is absolutely essential that you drain off the water from a heater. This is explained in Chapter Seventeen. But of course, you can drain it down at any time.

Few caravanners drain down their water before taking to the road but remember that water is heavy and takes up part of an all-important payload. For instance, a Carver Cascade holds 9 litres (2 gallons) thereby taking up 9kg (20lb) of your payload potential. You can certainly travel with a storage water heater empty which is wise if your 'van is loaded close to its payload limit. However, it means you cannot use your water supply system during a roadside picnic.

A Belling water heater is fitted to some caravans such as the Bailey Hunter Lite which was made in the late 1990s.

Since the demise of Carver, virtually all caravans are now fitted with a Truma water heater.

Even a spider's web or other obstruction at a flue outlet can upset heater ignition. Periodic servicing by a qualified gas engineer is essential.

Many British caravans have been fitted with Carver Cascade water heaters and it has proved an excellent product. On the other hand, the Maxol Malaga and the Malaga E (with 230V heating element) have also been fitted into a number of caravans including models in Fleetwood's 1995 range. Water heaters bearing the later name of the Belling Malaga were fitted in the Bailey Hunter Lite range from 1997 onwards.

Now the Truma Ultrastore is prominent and, like the Cascade and Malaga units, it is usually situated in a bed box with its intake and flue mounted on a side wall.

To operate these products check the manufacturer's instructions which are usually repeated in the owner's handbook. Like any other gas appliance in a caravan, they must be serviced at least once a year.

Servicing

The fact that caravan gas appliances are not used regularly throughout the year presents a problem. During storage periods it's not unusual for insects, moths and the common spider to get into the air intakes or flues. In some instances this can upset the delicate air/gas balance; it can also interfere with the ignition process. It's not unusual for a pilot flame to ignite on a space heater whereas the main burner subsequently fails to fire-up. This is usually caused by obstructions and even a spider's web spun around the cowl on a roof-mounted flue has been known to upset a heater's ignition process.

This is one of several reasons why routine and regular servicing of these appliances is essential.

A number of caravans have external outlets for electrical and gas appliances. The red gas coupling on the left is for a barbecue.

BARBECUES

As a final comment, a few caravans have been manufactured with external gas connections mounted on a side wall. These are intended for gas-operated barbecues which are permitted on many (though not all) caravan sites. Here is another pleasure of the caravanning experience although once again, all the vigilance mentioned earlier about individual appliances should be noted.

Thanks to gas couplings on some caravan walls, we can often enjoy the pleasures of al fresco meals.

CHAPTER SIXTEEN

CARAVAN
SERVICING

Whereas car owners recognise that vehicles need servicing on a regular basis, caravan owners are often surprised to learn that a caravan needs servicing, too. Yet it is a matter of safety that the brakes are adjusted periodically; and an owner's failure to keep an eye on tyre condition might lead to a conviction. Then there are issues like routine checks of gas appliances, gas pipes and the electricity supply systems.

All-in-all, a full service involves a lot of areas of attention. On one hand, the work ensures that a caravan is kept in good working order as a leisure home: on the other it's a way to ensure that it's safe to use on the road. So how often does servicing work need to be carried out?

SERVICE INTERVALS

With no mileometer gauge in a caravan, there's no easy way of registering the miles it travels. Nor is it feasible to record the hours that a fridge or cooker is in operation. So although it is normally recommended that a caravan is serviced at least every 12 months, this is really only a guide.

Many workshops have elevating ramps to enable a service technician to have good access to brakes and running gear.

Some service jobs can be tackled by a practical and experienced owner, but many operations require formal qualifications and the use of specialist tools.

Lubricating the over-run assembly that moves with the coupling head can be done regularly by a DIY enthusiast.

This recommendation means, of course, that a caravan will have been through a year of seasonal weather. Certainly the extremes of heat in summer and frost or snow in winter both take their toll. In addition, a problem that doesn't help the life of a caravan is the fact that it often stands unused for prolonged spells. For many mechanical components, remaining stationary is the worst thing possible. Even tyres deteriorate surprisingly quickly if the same part of the sidewalls remains flexed when a caravan stays parked and unmoved. Yet it's a reality that most caravans spend more time parked than being towed along the road.

At the other extreme, a few owners spend a year or more touring around – particularly in mainland Europe. This is becoming increasingly popular – especially among caravan owners who have taken early retirement from their work. In this instance, it stands to reason that the recommendation of having a caravan serviced once a year is clearly insufficient. Without doubt, all-important items like the brakes are going to need checking and adjusting on a much more regular basis.

Suffice it to say, that whereas it is generally recommended to have a caravan serviced annually, it's the owner who ultimately has to decide whether more regular attention is needed.

The next question which newcomers usually ask is: 'What jobs should be included in a routine service operation?'

SERVICING JOBS

In a full service, around 50 jobs need to be carried out. Broadly speaking, these fall into the following areas of attention:

1. The chassis and running gear – which includes things like brake adjustment, wheel bearing checks, tyre checks, corner steady lubrication.

CARAVAN SERVICING

On recent caravans, the type of torque wrench needed to tighten the one-shot nut holding a brake drum in place costs a three-figure sum.

2. Gas system and appliance checks – this would include a check for leaks in the supply system, cleaning gas burners on space heaters, water heaters and so on.

3. Electrical check – to include road light operation, the safety of the mains supply system, operation of interior lights, etc.

Since the early 1990s, a brake drum is held in place with a one-shot nut; once it has been removed, a new one must always be fitted in its place.

During a standard service, a new one shot nut holding the drum in place is marked with a security paint to guard against tampering.

In this standard service, the burners in a Carver Cascade water heater are cleaned and checked.

Many owners have a socket tester for checking a mains system; this is work included in a normal service.

4. Water system check – flushing through with purifying cleaner, checking operation of the water pump, filter changing and tasks like lubricating the valve seal on a toilet.

5. Refrigerator operation check and service – a full service of this appliance includes replacing the gas jet, re-aligning the igniter and cleaning the gas burner and flue. To carry this out, a fridge normally has to be taken out of a caravan and transferred to a work bench – so a full fridge service is often regarded as an optional extra. In the standard service there's only a check to see that the refrigerator is working on its three sources of power.

6. Bodywork and general condition – this important checking operation should include: a damp test, a visual inspection of sealant condition, a window operation check and so on.

To check for damp in a caravan, an electrical meter is used and there are 30 to 40 points around the interior where a specialist will take readings.

7. Fire warning system check – to make certain that a smoke alarm is working and that a fire extinguisher is within its stated date life.

SERVICE SCHEDULE

To find out more about all the jobs involved, a full service schedule is given in *The Caravan Manual*, published by Haynes. Working to a strict job list is very important and when arranging to have your 'van serviced, you must ask to see the centre's service schedule before confirming the booking.

Not only is it desirable to know the scope of the operation, when the work is completed you should then be given a copy of the schedule duly signed, stamped and dated. This document should include remarks on the amount of wear on brake shoes, the tread left on the tyres, and so on.

This point is emphasised because there are still so-called 'service specialists' who provide customers with no documentation at all about the work they've carried out. There are no statements made about brakes, tyres and so on and no form of certification to verify the condition of gas and electrical systems. Not only might you have doubts about the thoroughness of their work; you have no written evidence to state that servicing work has been undertaken. Needless to say, this kind of documentation is always useful to have when you finally decide to sell a caravan.

PART SERVICING

When considering the servicing operation as a whole, there's a distinct difference between absolutely essential tasks, highly desirable work, and recommended jobs. For instance, keeping a caravan's brakes, tyres, suspension and road lights in good order is absolutely essential.

Elements like verifying the condition of a gas supply system and the safety of gas appliances is a further matter of extreme importance. So, too, is electrical safety.

Rather less 'life-threatening' are issues like checking a water pump, and cleaning its grit filter. It might even be suggested that conducting a damp test on a caravan is not exactly a health and safety issue – although any serious caravanner wouldn't ignore this inspection. Then there are less important matters like repairing faulty cupboard catches, lubricating door hinges, adjusting spring mechanisms on roller blinds and so on.

On account of these differences, a number of service centres offer gold, silver and bronze services (or similar worded operations). Many will also offer a damp test on its own which is very beneficial if you suspect a leak has developed unexpectedly.

Then there's the matter of receiving signed and dated certificates by:
1. A qualified electrician
2. A qualified gas specialist

Such documents verify the integrity of these respective supply systems thus providing peace of mind. In addition, these certificates help when you decide to sell a caravan. In practice, many caravan workshops have to bring in qualified specialists to make these checks and to issue approval certificates. So this is often an 'optional addition' to the standard service, and a small fee will be payable.

CARAVAN SERVICING

Technical tip

Qualifications deemed necessary for verifying the integrity of mains electricity and gas supply systems.

1. Mains Electricity

To establish that a mains installation in a caravan meets current technical requirements, an inspection should be carried out by one of the following specialists:

Either

- An approved contractor of the National Inspection Council for Electrical Installation Contracting (NICEIC),

or

- a member of either the Electrical Contractors Association (ECA), or the Electrical Contractors Association of Scotland.

If there is no inspection certificate accompanying a pre-owned caravan, it is in the purchaser's interests to arrange for the 'van to be inspected before the mains system is put into service. To find out your nearest NICEIC specialist telephone 0207 582 7746, or to find an ECA member, telephone 0207 229 1266.

2. Gas

The inspection of a gas supply system and the verification of its integrity should be carried out by a CORGI qualified person who has successfully completed a course which embraces training in LPG installations in leisure vehicles. Note: CORGI stands for Council for Registered Gas Installers. Registration is a requirement for those who install and maintain LPG installations as laid down in the Gas Safety (Installation & Use) Regulations 1994.

To carry out a full refrigerator service in accordance with its manufacturer's instructions, the appliance normally needs to be removed from the caravan.

REFRIGERATOR SERVICE

Quite a number of centres only check that a refrigerator achieves cooling within the standard schedule, even though Electrolux recommends a full annual service as described above. Again, the extent of this is shown in *The Caravan Manual,* published by Haynes. Without doubt there's nothing more inconvenient than a fridge letting you down in the middle of a holiday spent in a warm location. So the task should be carried out even though many owners find their fridge works well for years and years without attention. Then it fails in the middle of a Mediterranean heat wave.

MINOR REPAIRS AND AUTHORISATIONS

When a service is carried out, it's not unusual for the technician to find items at fault. Perhaps one of the interior lights needs a new bulb or a replacement fluorescent tube. Many centres will replace small items like this – as long as there's time to do the job within the allotted period for the service work. The cost of the component, however, has to be charged to the customer.

This is another question to ask when arranging a service. Similarly you should get the dealer's assurance that a technician is not going to embark on more costly repairs without gaining your permission first. You might even agree a cost limit, but also ask the receptionist what procedure is followed when something serious emerges during the service operation.

Many workshops have elevating ramps to enable a service technician to have good access to brakes and running gear.

CHOOSING A RELIABLE SERVICE SPECIALIST

If you own a caravan which is still under warranty, manufacturers require that it is serviced in accordance with information given in the Owner's Manual. Failure to do this is likely to invalidate the warranty. To be absolutely sure that your local caravan service specialist is authorised to carry out the work, a call to the Customer Helpline of the caravan manufacturer is strongly recommended. Get them to give their approval of your chosen service provider before going further.

Recognising that there have been examples of poor servicing, a recent initiative by:
The Camping and Caravanning Club,
The Caravan Club and
The National Caravan Council
has established a nationwide chain of Approved Service Centres. You can find your nearest centre by contacting one of the above agencies and a high standard of work and general customer care is assured.

Before being accepted into the scheme, service centre applicants have to undergo a lengthy and elaborate inspection by an independent agency. The currently appointed inspection company, Jones Vening, also publishes a list of approved centres on its Internet web site: www.jones-vening.co.uk. But it doesn't end there; a re-examination inspection is also conducted annually.

Useful tip

Having your caravan serviced regularly is thus very important. But there's a problem caused by primroses, daffodils and that delightful 'rustle of Spring'. As Easter approaches, many eager owners plan their first post-winter holiday break – only to find that the local service centre is fully booked for weeks and weeks. Be ever-mindful of the seasonal nature of this leisure pursuit and take steps to book the caravan for servicing, well in advance of your first trip of the year.

CHAPTER SEVENTEEN

WINTER LAY-UP AND SPRING PREPARATION

Modern caravans are so well heated and insulated that they can be used in any month of the year. However, circumstances might necessitate that your caravan is laid-up for the winter, in which case there will be some important pre-storage tasks. Equally, when you want to re-commence your travels the following spring, there will be pre-season matters to attend to as well. This chapter looks at some of the jobs involved.

In Chapter Four, the subject of storage was discussed in detail. Now for the jobs you need to carry out before turning the key in the door, fitting your anti-theft devices and leaving your caravan to hibernate.

A good wash is usually needed at the end of the season, and a high-pressure hose will remove dirt and grime very effectively.

SPARE PARTS AND SERVICING

- **Spare parts:** Make a list of anything that was damaged during the season. If replacement items are needed, order them now. Anything from awning repairs to a light bulb should be arranged before the run-down to Christmas. Leave it until the spring and you may have to wait for weeks to receive the parts you need.
- **Servicing:** Book a service for next spring – even if it's still only October. The 'silly season' at dealerships starts in earnest in February or March. Servicing 'slots' are soon filled and it's 'first come, first served'. So think ahead and book ahead.

PRE LAY-UP JOBS

Indoor cleaning

- Start with a good clean-up using either a 12V vacuum cleaner or arrange to run a domestic machine via your caravan's 230V supply system. If there's room in your house to store caravan cushions and mattresses in a dry place, so much the better. Finding a caravan with its upholstery missing is also a deterrent to a thief.

A compact vacuum cleaner can be stored in the caravan and is then available when required.

Tip box

Fluff removal

In spite of work with a vacuum cleaner, fluff often remains around the perimeter of carpeted areas. Complete the job by putting on a rubber glove and wiping your finger around the places that the vacuum cleaner didn't reach. The glove grips the fluff and pulls it away from the carpet pile.

WINTER LAY-UP AND SPRING PREPARATION

Care needs to be taken when cleaning the stove-enamel surfaces of hobs and ovens.

- Use proprietary cleaners on the stove-enamel surfaces of your hob and oven. On plastic sinks and drainers, however, use the cleaning products recommended by the caravan manufacturer so you don't abrade the surface.

- Put plugs in the sink, the wash basin and the shower tray outlet to prevent smells from any stagnant water that might be held in the waste pipe infiltrating the living space.

- Clean out the inside of the refrigerator following the advice given in Chapter Eleven.

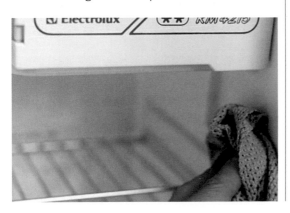

Be careful what you use to clean a refrigerator food compartment. Refer to Chapter Eleven for details.

A crank-handled brush will help when cleaning less accessible areas.

Outdoor cleaning

- It's best to clean the whole of a caravan at the end of a season. But busy owners and dark evenings mean that it often gets unceremoniously left. However, at the very least, find time to remove the black streaks that form under external fittings. Products like Autoglym Caravan Cleaner do this with ease.

- For a quick application of cleaner to some of the less accessible parts prior to a winter lay-up, get one of the crank-handled brushes used for painting the back of domestic radiators. Paint merchants sell these.

- A quick smarten-up of those hard-to-reach parts which harbour squashed flies and road dirt is easily achieved with a radiator brush and a proprietary caravan cleaning product.

A proprietary caravan cleansing product will help to remove road dirt.

Useful tip

Caravan covers

If you suspect that damp is creeping in around the awning rail or through a skylight, covering the roof with a large polythene sheet or plastic 'tarpaulin' is a logical emergency measure. But these materials will retain the damp and condensation often develops on the underside of the cover. In strong winds flapping plastic can also damage paintwork and acrylic window surfaces.

Purpose-made caravan covers manufactured using a breathable fabric are much better. However, it's not unusual for rainwater to penetrate via their stitched seams. So regard these products as a way of keeping a caravan clean from green algae and bird droppings rather than as a temporary cure for suspected leaks. Some covers are costly, too, and can be quite a struggle to fit and remove – especially on a large 'van with projecting roof fittings.

Useful tip

Avoiding frost damage

When water freezes in a pipe its volume increases by around 8.79 per cent. If all the outlets are sealed – for instance if none of the taps are left open – freezing water creates a serious pressure build-up in the pipe sections which have not been completely emptied. Whilst flexible plastic hose can sometimes cope with this without splitting, couplings and water-operated devices certainly can't. Nor can water heating devices.

Moreover, with the increasing popularity of lever mixer taps, it has been found that if the lever is left open for only the hot supply, the sealed cold supply may get damaged – and vice versa. So if your caravan is fitted with this type of tap, make sure the lever is lifted and left in its mid-way position during the lay-up so that both hot and cold feed pipes are open.

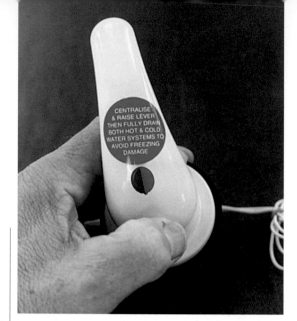

On lever-operated mixer-taps keep the lever central so that both hot and cold feeds are opened up.

If your caravan has a drain-down tap, open it to drain off water and leave it open.

The air release stopper in a Carver water heater.

Protecting a water system against frost

- Before draining down a fresh water system, open all the taps and leave them open throughout the lay-up period. On lever-operated mixer taps like the Whale Elite models, it's most important to keep the lever central so that both hot and cold feeds are opened up.

- A few caravans are fitted with a drain-down tap. Open this to drain off water left in the pipes and leave it open. If there isn't a drain-down tap, you may have to disconnect one of the hose or pipe connections in order to drain residual water into a receptacle.

- After opening all the taps, drain down a Carver water heater by releasing the bottom stopper. It's meant to hang in place but if it comes out completely, leave it in your sink as a reminder. Note that on the early heaters it can take an hour or more to release all the water from the unit.

- Later Carver water heaters have an air release stopper on the top left-hand side of the casing. When this is undone, the drain down operation proceeds much more rapidly.

- Since the demise of Carver gas products, Truma water heaters are now being fitted and these must also be drained down before the frosts arrive.

WINTER LAY-UP AND SPRING PREPARATION

The lift-up water release valve on a Truma water heater.

- If you've got a Truma water heater, look for the yellow lift-up water release valve that drains off water from the unit.

- A few caravans were fitted with Paloma or Rinnai instantaneous water heaters. The drain point is usually just below the casing. Whilst these appliances don't store water inside, there's always a lot of residual water that will ruin the unit if it isn't drained off before the frosts start.

- Submersible water pumps sometimes retain a small quantity of water. It's recommended to shake this out as well.

Draining residual water from a Rinnai water heater.

Shaking the water from a submersible water pump.

The flush water indicator tube on a Thetford bench-type cassette toilet.

- Cassette toilets hold flushing water in their casing and the bench-type Thetford units have a flush water indicator tube. You unclip this and angle it down into a bucket to drain off the flushing water. However, in a Thetford swivel-bowl version, you empty the water by repeated flushing, followed by a collection of the last cupful or two by unplugging a rubber drain plug.

Unplugging the rubber drain plug from a Thetford swivel-bowl toilet.

- The filling reservoir on a Thetford bench-type cassette toilet also holds a small quantity of water. The reservoir has its own plastic screw-cap for releasing the contents.

Draining the filling reservoir on a Thetford bench-type cassette toilet.

- To avoid the drain-down rigmarole, American RV (Recreational Vehicle) owners usually add potable anti-freeze to their motorhome fresh water supply system. This is poured into a container, pumped into the system and left during the lay-up period. The product is not poisonous – although you wouldn't want to drink it. Now the idea is catching-on in Britain and many motorcaravan owners are using Camco Potable Anti-freeze imported by Alde International (UK). The water additive can also be used in stored caravans although some water appliance manufacturers e.g. Carver, have not officially approved the use of anti-freeze in their appliances.

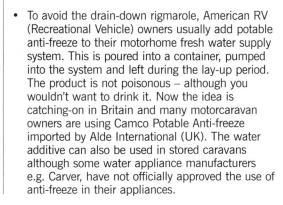

- Put cap covers over both your waste and fresh water inlets. Ignoring this means you are giving an open invitation to homeless spiders.

Plug and socket protection

- The 12N and 12S plugs on a caravan and the equivalent sockets on a tow car need spraying with a water-repellent product that cannot damage the plastic casing. Some sprays do cause damage. A particularly effective product is Tri-flow which contains Teflon and keeps the brass pins clean and shiny for a long period after each application. The product is distributed nationally to many retail outlets by WYKO Industrial Services.

Spray the plugs and sockets with a water-repellent product.

Gas cylinders

The wisdom of transferring gas cylinders to a safe, ventilated place was discussed in Chapter Fourteen. It's also wise to tie a linen bag over the regulators to make sure no spiders can get into the system. If regulators are removed, be certain to cover the open end of the gas hose.

Battery removal and charging

- It is most important to keep a caravan's leisure battery charged during an extended lay-up period. The subject of charging is discussed in Chapter Thirteen.

Tyres, suspension and brakes

- Don't forget the comments made earlier in this book about tyre wall damage through lack of use. Fastidious owners will mount the caravan on robust axle stands and remove the wheels. This will also relieve the suspension as well. Alternatively you can use 'Winter wheels' which are angle steel structures fitted in place of the normal wheels. These 'square wheels' act as security devices and the fact that you can then store your caravan's wheels in a garage means the tyres are rested and kept away from sunlight. However, 'Winter wheels' don't relieve the suspension – you need a pair of axle stands to achieve this. Note: The original 'Winter Wheels' are sold by PGR products. Similar examples are sold by Safe and Secure products.

  Provided a caravan is parked on level ground and not at risk of running away, it's best to leave the hand-brake completely OFF. This means that any developing rust won't lock the brakes well and truly on.

Useful tip
Extending tyre life

If you do have to leave your caravan parked for a long period without putting it on axle stands, arrange to move it a foot or so (300mm) one way or the other every couple of months. This ensures that different parts of the tyre's side-walls are placed under stress during the lay-up period.

WINTER LAY-UP AND SPRING PREPARATION

Other jobs may be listed in your caravan owner's manual. Check this with care because some of its appliances might be different from those discussed in this chapter.

PRE-SEASON JOBS

Before setting off after a winter lay-up, you need to get everything working again.

- When parked near trees, caravans often get covered with green vegetation. Don't be too distressed if you go to collect a caravan from a storage centre and find it stained and dirty.

- A good wash is usually needed and some owners do this using a high-pressure hose. But be careful. On its more powerful setting and used too close to the caravan, a pressure hose can blast away sealant from the panel junctions, damage the windows and break brittle plastic decals.

This staining may look awful but can be removed with careful cleaning.

Over-enthusiastic use of a high-pressure hose can damage brittle plastic decals.

Brush around trim strips with a soft brush.

- A soft hand brush is useful for removing spiders and their webs.

- A concerted effort to polish-up a caravan is a sure way to start things in style. If the acrylic windows sustained scratches through windy weather and nearby branches, Caravan Pride from Farecla can reinstate their condition very successfully.

Cleaning prior to the start of a new caravanning season.

- Products like Mer polish will soon smarten up dull GRP ('fibre-glass') body panels.

A good polish will smarten up GRP body panels.

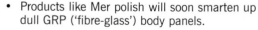

WINTER LAY-UP AND SPRING PREPARATION

Loosening up an under-floor spare wheel carrier.

- Before re-installing your leisure battery, give it a top-up with de-ionised water as discussed in Chapter Thirteen.

- Under-floor spare wheel carriers often get rusted up and it's regrettable that a carrier's telescopic tubing is seldom checked during a caravan service. This photograph shows pre-season loosening-up – a job that might need plenty of wire brushing to remove rust, penetrating oil and a quantity of grease to reinstate seized-up tubing.

- Fit a new water filter. This one is being removed using a hardwood batten with a saw cut made in the end to grip the 'turn plate' on the cartridge. Trying to unscrew a cartridge manually by holding on to this plate takes the finger strength of an Olympic wrestler.

Then you'll want to set up the water system and try it out before leaving home. Equally you'll want to check fridge operation, the gas cooker and so on, especially if you couldn't get your caravan serviced because the local dealer was busy. Add to this a tyre pressure check – not forgetting the spare – and you're well on the way. In fact you're back to many of the points I listed in Chapter Eight.

So as the summer season approaches once again, every best wish with your continuing caravanning adventures!

Removing a water filter using a hardwood batten.

APPENDIX

A   The national clubs for caravanners

The two principal caravan clubs have very large memberships and a long history. When they were formed around a hundred years ago, their activities and objectives were very different, but nowadays the services to members are much the same.

Membership benefits are wide-ranging and both clubs own and run some excellent sites. Some are for members only, whereas others admit non-members albeit with an additional surcharge. In addition, both clubs provide excellent guidebooks to sites of all sizes, including hundreds of small venues licensed to accept no more than 5 caravans at a time.

Insurance schemes, holiday booking services, monthly magazines, technical advice, and popular towing and caravan ownership courses are offered by both clubs. Equally there are regional groups whose committees arrange local functions to supplement the clubs' national events.

So send for literature and decide if you'd prefer to join The Camping & Caravanning Club or The Caravan Club. Some owners cannot make up their mind so join both! The clubs' addresses are given in the accompanying list.

B   Owners' clubs

At the time of writing, there are around 50 clubs devoted to particular makes of caravan, together with specialist associations like the Historic Caravan Club and other formally constituted bodies catering for particular groups of people. Addresses of club secretaries are often published in magazines and the list which currently appears periodically in Caravan Magazine is especially comprehensive.

Needless to say, clubs catering for owners of particular makes of caravan are extremely valuable if you want spare parts and your 'van is no longer being manufactured. Members show great brand loyalty and usually arrange a programme of social events. Moreover, it's not unusual to find representatives occupying small stands provided by existing manufacturers at major indoor caravan exhibitions such as The Boat, Caravan and Outdoor Leisure Show held every February at the National Exhibition Centre.

C   The National Caravan Council

The NCC, to use its well-known acronym is, '…the representative trade body for businesses trading in the UK caravan industry.' (Annual Report & Accounts, 2000, P1.) Thus it represents the four sectors of the UK industry, namely: Touring Caravans, Motor Caravans, Caravan Holiday-Homes and Residential Park Homes. Whilst its main reason for existence is to serve its fee-paying trade members, the NCC runs many schemes which help individual caravanners.

In particular the NCC Approval Badge displayed on most UK-manufactured caravans confirms that the product complies with the relevant British or European Standards or Industry Code of Practice, together with UK laws. Other initiatives include The Approved Caravan Workshop Scheme, CRiS (Caravan Registration and Identification Scheme), *The Towing Code* booklet, and the site guide entitled, *NCC Quality Graded Touring Parks*.

Information leaflets are available free of charge either from the NCC stands at major indoor exhibitions, or direct from the Association's headquarters. (See Address list.)

D   Continental travel booking agencies

This handbook provides detailed guidance about using a caravan and when read in conjunction with, *Driving Abroad* by Robert Davies (published by Haynes), it is immediately apparent that there's no reason why you should restrict your touring to the UK. In fact, taking your caravan around Europe is not as daunting as many imagine. Nevertheless, many caravanners find that to reduce the amount of pre-holiday 'paper-work', it's worthwhile entrusting the booking arrangements to one of the specialist agencies.

Both the national clubs run ferry and site booking services, as well as specialists like: Eurocamp Independent,

Select Sites Reservations, and The Alan Rogers' Booking Service.

These booking specialists provide most helpful guidance as well as making ferry reservations and site bookings. Taking Select Sites Reservations as an example, this Company's Travel Pack includes a 48 page *Holiday Guidebook*, a booklet on sites recommended for overnight stop-overs, a guide to your destination region, leaflets giving full information on your selected sites, Michelin Maps covering areas around your booked sites, and GB car and caravan stickers. It really does make the whole process so easy.

If you decide to travel in Europe during the low season, there are also schemes whereby you can pre-purchase vouchers for use at participating sites at a considerable discount on the normal overnight fees. The Camping Cheque service is probably the best known of these off-season voucher discount schemes.

E   Address list of key accessory suppliers

Please note: This address list was correct at the time of going to press. It includes specialist suppliers and manufacturers whose products and services have been mentioned in this book. Several of the firms have web sites and these are easy to locate using search engines.

Abbey Caravans - See *The Swift Group*

A.B. Butt Ltd,
Frog Island,
Leicester,
LE3 5AZ
Tel: 0116 251 3344
(Solar Systems and inverters)

ABI Caravans Ltd,
(ABI ceased manufacturing touring caravans in summer 2001. Information or supply of parts and warranty repairs currently unavailable)

ABP Accessories,
27 Nether End,
Great Dalby,
Leicestershire,
LE14 2EY
Tel: 08700 115111
(Importer of Camco products)

A.C. Holdings,
4, Breckland Business Park,
Watton,
Norfolk,
IP25 6UP
Tel: 01953 884999
(Mail Order for 'A' Glaze Caravan Total Surface Protection)

Adria Concessionaires Ltd,
Hall Street,
Long Melford,
Sudbury,
Suffolk,
CO10 9JP
Tel: 01787 378705
(Importers of Adria caravans)

Airflow (UK) Ltd,
Crown House,
Faraday Road,
Newbury,
Berkshire RG14 2AB
Tel: 01635 569569
(Airflow trickle battery charger)

Air Muscle Ltd,
(Flexator leveller and Rolljack)
At time of reprint, the Company appears to have ceased trading.

Alde International (UK) Ltd,
A3 Regent Park,
Booth Drive,
Park Farm South,
Wellingborough,
Northamptonshire,
NN8 6GR
Tel: 01933 677765
(Central heating systems, Gas leak detector, Kitchen systems)

Al-Ko Kober Ltd,
South Warwickshire Business Park,
Kineton Road,
Southam,
Warwickshire CV47 0AL
Tel: 01926 818500
(Chassis, running gear, stabilisers, wheel carriers)

Apollo Repair Chemicals,
Leisure Plus,
Unit 3,
Airfield Industrial Estate,
Hixon,
Staffordshire ST18 0PF
Tel: 01889 271692
(Wholesaler distributing Apollo delamination kits)

Ashley Banks Ltd,
5 King Street,
Langtoft,
Peterborough,
PE6 9NF
Tel: 01778 560651
(Supplier of tow car spring assisters, MAD systems, Monroe)

Assembled Supplies (Electrical) Ltd,
Albany Road,
East Gateshead Industrial Estate,
Tyne and Wear,
NE8 3AT
Tel: 0191 477 3518
(Manufacturer of electronic wiring systems)

Auto Glym,
Works Road,
Letchworth,
Hertfordshire,
SG6 1LU
Tel: 01462-677766
(Caravan and car interior and exterior cleaning products)

Autovan Services Ltd,
32 Canford Bottom,
Wimborne,
Dorset BH21 2HD
Tel: 01202 848414
(Major body repair and rebuilding work)

Avondale Coachcraft Ltd,
Carlyon Road,
Atherstone,
Warwickshire CV9 1JE
Tel: 01827 715231
(Manufacturers of Avondale caravans)

Awning World,
Barron Group Ltd,
Chapel Lane,
Coppull,
Chorley,
Lancashire PR7 4NE
Tel: 01257 793008
(Display and sale of awnings)

Bailey Caravans Ltd,
South Liberty Lane,
Bristol BS3 2SS
Tel: 0117 966 5967
(Manufacturers of Bailey caravans)

Bailey & White Ltd,
2 Corn Kiln Close,
Cogenhoe,
Northampton,
NN7 1NX
Tel: 01604 890686
(Centinel Security Devices)

A. Baldassarre,
Upholsterer and Coachtrimmer,
103, Coventry Road,
Queens Park,
Bedford,
MK40 4ES
Tel: 01234 359277
(All types of upholstery work and soft furnishings, foam supplied to order. Edge finishing of removable carpet pieces)

BCA Leisure Ltd,
Unit H8,
Premier Way,
Lowfields Business Park,
Elland,
North Yorkshire HX5 9HF
Tel: 01422 376977
(Manufacturers of Powerpart mains kits, the Power Centre & Powerpart Mobile)

Belling Appliances,
Talbot Road,
Mexborough,
South Yorkshire S64 8AJ
Tel: 01709 579902
(Belling cookers, hobs and water heaters)

Bessacarr Caravans – See The Swift Group

Blue Diamond Products,
Unit 13,
Bottoms Mill,
Rouse Mill Lane,
Batley,
Yorkshire WF17 5QB
Tel: 01924 420048
(Spares and accessories)

BPW Ltd,
Legion Way,
Meridian Business Park,
Leicester LE3 2UZ
Tel: 0116 281 6100
(BPW chassis and Winterhoff stabilizers)

Bradleys,
Old Station Yard,
Marlesford,
Suffolk IP13 0AG
Tel: 01728 747900
(Mail Order supply of ABS repair kits and paint products for plastic)

Brink UK Ltd,
Unit 7,
Centrovell Industrial Estate,
Caldwell Road,
Nuneaton,
Warwickshire CV11 4NG
Tel: 01203 352353
(Towbars)

British Car Auctions Ltd,
Sales & Marketing Department,
Expedier House,
Portsmouth Road,
Hindhead,
Surrey GU26 6TJ
Tel: 01428 607440

British Rubber Manufacturers' Association Ltd,
6 Bath Place,
Rivington Street,
London,
EC2A 3JE
Tel: 020 7457 5040
(Trade Association for the tyre industry)

BRK Brands Europe Ltd,
Fountain House,
Canal View Road,
Newbury,
Berkshire RG14 5XF
Tel: 01635 528080
(First Alert smell-sensitive gas alarm)

Buccaneer Caravans - See The Explorer Group

Bulldog Security Products Ltd,
Units 2, 3, & 4,
Stretton Road,
Much Wenlock,
Shropshire,
TF13 6DH
Tel: 01952-728171/3
(Bulldog stabilisers, SSK stabiliser importer, security devices and posts)

C.A.K. Tanks,
Caravan Accessories (Kenilworth) Ltd,
10 Princes Drive,
Kenilworth,
Warwickshire,
CV8 2FD
Tel: 01926 854271
(Water and electrical accessories, appliances, furniture fittings)

Calor Gas Ltd,
Athena Drive,
Tachbrook Park,
Warwick CV34 6RL
Tel: 0800 626626
(Supplier of butane, propane and LPG appliances)

Calver's Caravan Storage,
Woodlands Park,
Bedford Road,
Clapham,
Bedford MK41 6EJ
Tel: 01234 359584
(Indoor and outdoor storage specialist)

Camco Products - See ABP Accessories

The Camping & Caravanning Club,
Greenfields House,
Westwood Way,
Coventry CV4 8JH
Tel: 0845 130 7631

Campingaz
Coleman UK Inc.,
Parish Wharf Estate,
Harbour Road,
Portishead,
Bristol BS20 9DA
Tel: 01275 845024
(Supplier of Campingaz butane and LPG appliances)

Camping International Superstore,
Clock Tower House,
Watling Street,
Gillingham,
Kent,
ME5 7HS
Tel: 01634 577326
(Display and sale of awnings)

Canvas Repair Centre,
121 Branston Road,
Burton-on-Trent,
Staffordshire,
DE14 3DD
Tel: 01283 541721
(Awning repairs and alterations)

Caralux Upholstery,
(The Company is no longer trading)

Carafax Ltd,
Rotterdam Road,
Sutton Fields Industrial Estate,
Hull,
HU7 0XD
Tel: 01482 825941
(Cartridge sealants)

Caralevel,
Springhill Farm,
Great Horwood Road,
Little Horwood,
Milton Keynes,
MK17 0NZ
Tel: 01296 713476
(Electrically operated automatic levelling system)

The Caravan Centre,
Steadmans Yard,
Tal y Wain,
Pontypool,
MP4 7RL
Tel: 01495 774999
(Specialist breakers supplying caravan products)

The Caravan Club
East Grinstead House,
East Grinstead,
West Sussex RH19 1UA
Tel: 01342 326944

Caravanparts.net,
Unit 5,
Grovehill Industrial Estate,
Beck View Road,
Beverley,
East Yorkshire HU17 0JW
Tel: 01482 874878
(Supplier of caravan parts and the Henry-GE water heater)

The Caravan Seat Cover Centre,
Kings Road,
Brislington,
Bristol BS4 3HH
Tel: 0117-9770797
(Re-upholsterer, loose covers, and foam supplier)

Carcoon Storage Systems Int. Ltd,
Orchard Mill,
2 Orchard Street,
Salford,
Manchester M6 6FL
Tel: 0161 737 9690
(Power & Charge System: Mail Order direct)

Carlight Caravans Ltd,
Church Lane,
Sleaford,
Lincolnshire NG34 7DE
Tel: 01529 302120
(The Company has ceased full scale production; repairs still undertaken)

Carver product spares – See Truma (UK) Ltd

CEC Plug-In-Systems,
Tower Street,
Hull,
HU9 1TU
Tel: 01482 659309
(Low voltage control components chargers and gauges)

Ceuta Healthcare Ltd,
41 Richmond Hill,
Bournemouth,
Dorset,
BH2 6H7
Tel: 0800 0975606
(Milton sterilising products and water treatment additives)

Coachman Caravan Co Ltd,
Amsterdam Road,
Sutton Field Industrial Estate,
Hull HU7 0XF
Tel: 01482 839737
(Manufacturers of Coachman caravans)

Compass Caravans Ltd – See The Explorer Group

Cosmic Car Accessories Ltd,
Sadler Road,
Brownhills,
Walsall,
West Midlands,
WS8 6NA
Tel: 01543 452626
(Accessory supplier including "Big Foot" corner steady base)

CRiS
Dolphin House,
New Street,
Salisbury,
Wiltshire
SP1 2PH
Tel: 01722 413434
(Caravan Registration & Identification Scheme)

Crossleys,
Unit 33A,
Comet Road,
Moss Side Industrial Estate,
Leyland,
Lancashire,
PR5 3QN
Tel: 01772 623423
(Major body repair and rebuilding work)

Crown Caravans - See The Explorer Group

B. Dixon-Bate Ltd,
Unit 45,
First Avenue,
Deeside Industrial Park,
Deeside,
Clwyd,
CH5 2LG
Tel: 01244 288925
(Towing accessories including cushioned towball units)

W. David & Sons Ltd,
Denington Industrial Estate,
Wellingborough,
Northamptonshire,
NN8 2QP
Tel: 01933 227186
(David's Isopon resin, filler paste and U-Pol branded versions)

D.J. Russell Sales – See Miriad Products Ltd

Dometic Ltd,
99 Oakley Road,
Luton,
Bedfordshire,
LU4 9GE
Tel: 01582 494111
(Air conditioners, refrigerators, Seitz windows – formerly Electrolux Leisure)

Driftgate 2000 Ltd,
Little End Road,
Eaton Socon,
Cambridgeshire,
PE19 3JH
Tel: 01480 470400
(Manufacturers of XCell Mains inverters)

Elecsol Europe Ltd,
47 First Avenue,
Deeside Industrial Park,
Deeside,
Flintshire,
CH5 2LG
Tel: 0800 163298
(Elecsol batteries)

Electrical Contractors Association (ECA),
3 Buenavista Gardens,
Glenholt,
Plymouth
Tel: 01752 700981
(Mains supply system checking)

Electrolux Leisure Appliances – See Dometic Ltd.

Elddis Caravans - See The Explorer Group

Elsan Ltd,
Elsan House,
Bellbrook Park,
Uckfield,
East Sussex,
TN22 1QF
Tel: 01825 748200
(Manufacturers of toilets and chemicals)

EMC, Ltd,
Lamb Inn Road,
Racca Green,
Knottingley,
West Yorkshire,
WF11 8AU
Tel: 01977 676028
(Suppliers of lightweight ply and components for caravan DIY re-builds)

Eriba Ltd,
The Priory,
A417 Faringdon Road,
Lechlade,
Gloucestershire,
GL7 3EY
Tel: 01367 253452
(Importers of Eriba caravans)

Europa Specialist Spares,
Fauld Industrial Park,
Tutbury,
Burton upon Trent,
Staffordshire,
DE13 9HR
Tel: 01283 815609
(Vehicle trims, light clusters, and specialist vehicle parts)

Evode Ltd.
Industrial Division,
Common Road,
Stafford,
ST16 3EH
Tel: 01785 257755
(Manufacturers of Evo-Stik Adhesives)

Exhaust Ejector Co Ltd,
Wade House Road,
Shelf,
Nr. Halifax,
West Yorkshire HX3 7PE
Tel: 01274 679524
(Replacement acrylic windows made to order)

Exide Leisure Batteries Ltd,
Gate No. 3,
Pontyfelin Industrial Estate,
New Road,
Pontypool,
NP4 5DG
Tel: 01495 750075
(Exide Leisure Batteries)

The Explorer Group,
Delves Lane,
Consett,
Co Durham,
DH8 7LG,
Tel: 01207 503477
(Caravan manufacturer of Buccaneer, Elddis, Compass, Crown and Herald models)

Farécla Products Ltd,
Broadmeads,
Ware,
Hertfordshire,
SG12 9HS
Tel: 01920 465041
(Caravan Pride acrylic window scratch remover and GRP surface renovator)

Fiamma water pumps and water tanks
Contact your caravan dealer for Fiamma products.

Flavel Leisure,
Clarence Street,
Leamington Spa,
Warwickshire CV31 2AD
Tel: 01926 427027
(Flavel cookers and hobs)

Fleetwood Caravans Ltd,
Hall Street,
Long Melford,
Sudbury,
Suffolk CO10 9JP
Tel: 01787 378705
(Manufacturers of Fleetwood caravans)

FFC (Foam for Comfort) Ltd,
Unit 2,
Wyther Lane Trading Estate,
Wyther Lane,
Kirkstall,
Leeds,
LS5 3BT
Tel: 0113 274 8100
(New foam supplier, composite bonded foam specialist)

Franks Caravan Spares,
16/27 Wigmore Street,
Stopsley,
Luton,
Bedfordshire,
LU2 8AA.
Tel: 01582 732168
(Caravan breakers and sales)

Freedom Caravans,
Lichfield Road,
Stafford,
ST17 4NY
Tel: 01785 222488
(Importers of Freedom caravans)

Gardner of Wakefield Ltd,
76 Wakefield Road,
Flushdyke,
Ossett,
West Yorkshire,
W5 9JX
Tel: 01924 265367
(Portable showers, protective covers for components)

Gaslow International,
The Manor House,
Normanton-on-Soar,
Leicestershire LE12 5HB
Tel: 0845 4000600
(Gas leak gauges, refillable cylinders, LPG components)

General Ecology Europe Ltd,
St. Andrews House,
26 Brighton Road,
Crawley,
RH10 6AA
Tel: 01293 400644
(Nature Pure Ultrafine water purifier)

Gobur Caravans Ltd,
Peacock Way,
Melton Constable,
Norfolk NR24 2BY
Tel: 01263 860031
(Manufacturers of Gobur folding caravans)

Grade UK Ltd,
3 Central Court,
Finch Close,
Lenton Lane Industrial Estate,
Nottingham NG7 2NN
Tel: 0115 986 7151
(Status TV aerials and accessories)

Gramos Repair Kits, Mail Order,
Kingdom Industrial Supplies Ltd,
6/10 Bancrofts Road,
Eastern Industrial Estate,
South Woodham Ferrers,
Essex CM3 5UQ
Tel: 01245 322177
(Kits for repairing ABS plastic)

Grangers International Ltd,
Grange Close,
Clover Nook Industrial Estate,
Alfreton,
Derbyshire,
DE55 4QT
Tel: 01773 521521
(Awning proofing and cleaning products)

Grayston Engineering Ltd,
115 Roebuck Road,
Chessington,
Surrey KT9 1JZ
Tel: 0181 9741122
(Tow car spring assister kits)

Häfele UK Ltd,
Swift Valley Industrial Estate,
Rugby,
Warwickshire,
CV21 1RD
Tel: 01788 542020
(Furniture components and hardware)

Hammerite Paints
Available from DIY stores and automotive specialists.

HBC Systems UK,
12 Stuart Road,
Halesowen,
B62 0ED
Tel: 0121 421 4373
(Professional system for repairing aluminium body panels)

Hella Ltd,
Wildmere Industrial Estate,
Banbury,
Oxfordshire,
OX16 7JU
Tel: 01295 272233
(Hella towing electrical equipment)

Herald Caravans - See The Explorer Group

F.L. Hitchman,
46, The Trading Estate,
Ditton Priors,
Near Bridgnorth,
Shropshire,
WV16 6SS
Tel: 01746 712242
(Aquaroll and Wastemaster carriers and cleaning chemicals)

Hodgson Sealants,
Belprin Road,
Beverley,
North Humberside HU17 0LN
Tel: 01482 701191
(Manufacturers of caravan sealants)

Isabella International Camping Ltd,
Isabella House,
Drakes Farm,
Drakes Drive,
Long Crendon,
Buckinghamshire HP18 9BA
Tel: 01844 202099
(Awning alteration, repair and reproofing)

Johnnie Longden Ltd,
Unit 24,
Dawkins Road,
Poole,
Dorset BH15 4JD
Tel: 01202 679121
(Caravan Accessories including components for older caravans)

Kenlowe Ltd,
Burchetts Green,
Maidenhead,
Berkshire SL6 6QU
Tel: 01628 823303
(Radiator cooling fans and automatic transmission oil coolers)

Knott (UK) Ltd – See Miriad Products Ltd

Labcraft Ltd,
22B King Street,
Saffron Walden,
Essex CB10 1ES
Tel: 01799 513434
(Lighting units)

Peter J Lea Company Ltd,
Peterlea Works,
Shaw Road South,
Shaw Heath,
Stockport SK3 8JG
Tel: 0161 480 2377
(Manufacturers of the Scott Stabiliser)

Leisure Accessories Ltd,
Britannia Works,
Hurricane Way,
Airport Industrial Estate,
Norwich,
NR6 6EY
Tel: 01603 414551
(POSIflow, FLOking water pumps)

Lunar Caravans Ltd,
Sherdley Road,
Lostock Hall,
Preston,
Lancashire,
PR5 5JF
Tel: 01772 337628
(Manufacturer of Lunar caravans)

MAD tow car spring assisters - See Ashley Banks Ltd.

Marlec Engineering Ltd,
Rutland House,
Trevithick Road,
Corby,
Northamptonshire,
NN17 5XY
Tel: 01536 201588
(Wind and solar systems)

Magnum Mobiles and Caravan Surplus,
Unit 9A,
Cosalt Industrial Estate,
Convamore Road,
Grimsby,
DN32 9JL
Tel: 01472 353520
(Caravan surplus stock)

Maxview,
Common Lane,
Setchey,
King's Lynn,
Norfolk,
PE33 0AT
Tel: 01553 810376
(Maxview TV aerials)

Merlin Equipment,
Unit 1,
Hithercroft Court,
Lupton Road,
Wallingford,
Oxfordshire,
OX10 9BT
Tel: 01491 824333
(PROwatt Inverters)

Mer Products Ltd,
Whitehead House,
120 Beddington Lane,
Croydon,
Surrey,
CRO 4TD
Tel: 0181 401 0002
(Distributor of Mer Car Care products)

Milton Sterilising Products – See Ceuta Healthcare

Miriad Products Ltd,
Europa House,
Wharf Road,
Burton-upon-Trent,
Staffordshire,
DE14 1PZ
Tel: 01283 531541
(UK distributor of Knott running gear, BPW chassis spares, Peitz Axle spares)

Monroe tow car spring assister systems - See Ashley Banks Ltd.

Morco Products Ltd,
Morco House,
59 Beverley Road,
Hull,
HU3 1XW
Tel: 01482 325456
(Instantaneous Water Heaters)

Munster Simms Engineering Ltd,
Old Belfast Road,
Bangor
BT19 1LT
Northern Ireland.
Tel: 01247 270531
(Whale semi-rigid pipework system & all plumbing accessories)

The National Caravan Council,
Catherine House,
Victoria Road,
Aldershot,
Hampshire,
GU11 1SS
Tel: 01252 318251

National Inspection Council for Electrical Installation Contracting, (NICEIC)
Vintage House,
36–37 Albert Embankment,
London,
SE1 7UJ
Tel: 020 7564 2323
(Certification to confirm a caravan is correctly wired for mains electricity)

The Natural Mat Company,
99 Talbot Road,
London,
W11 2AT
Tel: 0207 9850474
(Slatted sprung beech bed systems, anti-condensation underlay)

Navarac,
1 Montana Road,
Kesgrave,
Ipswich,
Suffolk,
IP5 1ER
No telephone contact
(Water Geezer)

Nikwax Ltd,
Unit F,
Durgate Industrial Estate,
Wadhurst,
East Sussex,
TN5 6DF
Tel: 01892 786400
(Awning proofing products)

O'Leary Spares and Accessories,
314 Plaxton Bridge Road,
Woodmansey,
Nr Beverley,
East Yorkshire,
HU17 ORS
Tel: 01482 868632
(Retailer of surplus stocks purchased from caravan manufacturers)

Peitz axle, chassis and over-run couplings - See Miriad Products

PGR Products Ltd,
16 Crofton Road,
Lincoln,
Lincolnshire,
LN3 4NL
Tel: 01522 534538
(Sectional TV mast, wheel clamps, winter wheels)

Phoenix Power & Equipment
(Generator Servicing – Company no longer trading)

Plug-in-Systems – See CEC

Protimeter plc,
Meter House,
Marlow,
Buckinghamshire,
SL7 1LX
Tel: 01628 472722
(Caravan moisture meters)

Pyramid Products Ltd,
Unit 1,
Victoria Street,
Mansfield,
Nottinghamshire,
NG18 5RR
Tel: 01623 421277
(Patriot wheel clamp and accessories)

Remis UK,
(Blinds for caravans – Order through dealer accessory shops)

RoadPro Ltd,
Stephenson Close,
Drayton Fields Industrial Estate,
Daventry,
Northamptonshire NN1 5RF
Tel: 01327 312233
(Suppliers of chargers, inverters, satellite TV systems, electrical accessories)

RT Marshall,
Woodside Industrial Estate,
Bayton,
Kidderminster,
Worcestershire DY14 9NE
Tel: 01299 832533
(Satellite TV systems)

Ryder Towing Equipment Ltd,
Mancunian Way,
Ardwick,
Manchester M12 6HW
Tel: 0161 2735619
(Electrical towing equipment & 'The Practical Guide to Towbar Electrics')

Safe and Secure Products Ltd,
Chestnut House,
Chesley Hill,
Wick,
Bristol BS30 5NE
Tel: 0117-937 4737
(SAS stabilisers, security devices, posts & Dart spare wheel carrier)

Sargent Electrical Services Ltd,
Unit 39,
Tokenspire Business Park,
Woodmansey,
Beverley,
Hull,
HU17 OTB
Tel: 01482 881655
(Electrical control systems and low voltage panels)

Scotch Gard Upholstery Products
Available from DIY Superstores e.g. B & Q

Selmar Guardian Chargers
Tadmod Ltd,
Galliford Road,
Malden,
Essex,
CM9 4XD
(Selmar stage chargers, sold Mail Order direct from M.A.C. Tel: 01621 859444)

Sew 'n' Sews,
42 Claudette Avenue,
Spalding,
Lincolnshire,
PE11 1HU
Tel: 01775 767 633
(Bespoke awnings, cover systems, bags and generator covers)

SF Detection Ltd,
Hatch Pond House,
4 Stinsford Road,
Nuffield Industrial Estate,
Poole,
Dorset,
BH17 ORZ
Tel: 01202 665330
(SF330 Carbon monoxide detector)

Shurflo Ltd,
Unit 5,
Sterling Park,
Gatwick Road,
Crawley,
West Sussex,
RH10 2QT
Tel: 01293 424000
(Shurflo diaphragm water pumps)

Sika Ltd,
Watchmead,
Welwyn Garden City,
Hertfordshire,
AL7 1BQ
Tel: 01707 394444
(Sikaflex Cartridge Sealants)

The Society of Motor Manufacturers and Traders,
Trade Sections Department,
Forbes House,
Halkin Street,
London,
SW1X 7DS
Tel: 020 7235 7000
(Publishers of SMMT booklet Towing and the Law)

Solar Solutions,
Unit 1,
565 Blandford Road,
Hamworthy,
Poole,
Dorset,
BH16 5BW
Tel: 01202 632488
(Suppliers of solar panels)

Sold Secure Trust,
5c Great Central Way,
Woodford Halse,
Daventry,
Northamptonshire,
NN11 3PZ
Tel: 01327 264687
(Test house conducting attack tests to verify the integrity of caravan security devices)

Spinflo domestic appliances – See Thetford

The Stabiliser Clinic,
Holme Grove,
Bypass Road,
Garstang,
Preston,
Lancashire,
PR3 1NA
Tel: 01995 603745
(Stabiliser test kits and complete overhaul service)

Stain Devils Information Service,
107-111 Fleet Street,
London,
EC4A 2AB
Tel: 020 7353 4499
(Guidance on stain removal)

Sterling Caravans - See The Swift Group

Stoves plc,
Stoney Lane,
Prescot,
Merseyside,
L35 2XW
Tel: 0151 426 6551
(Stoves, cookers and hobs)

Superpitch,
Conduit Road,
Conduit Industrial Estate,
Norton Canes,
Cannock,
Staffordshire,
WS11 3TJ
Tel: 01543 270987
(Superpitch motorcaravan conversion accessories)

Swift Group Ltd,
Dunswell Road,
Cottingham,
Hull,
HU16 4JX
Tel: 01482 847332
(Manufacturer of Abbey, Bessacarr, Sterling & Swift caravans)

Technicol Ltd,
The Studio,
112 Hardwick Lane,
Bury St Edmunds,
Suffolk,
IP33 2LE
(Ventair 15 mattress anti-condensation underlay)

Tetroson brake and clutch cleaner
Available from automotive factors.

Thetford Ltd,
Unit 19,
Oakham Drive,
Parkwood Industrial Estate,
Rutland Road,
Sheffield,
S3 9QX
Tel: 01142 738157
(Manufacturers of refrigerators, toilets and chemicals)

Thompson Plastics (Hull) Ltd,
Bridge Works,
Hessle,
East Yorkshire,
HU13 0TP
Tel: 01482 646464
(Manufacturer of acrylic-capped ABS caravan components)

Tockfield Ltd,
Pitt Lane,
Shirland,
Nr. Alfreton,
Derbyshire,
DE55 6AT
Tel: 01773 834968
(Re-upholsterer and foam supplier)

Tri-Flow Suppliers - See WYKO Industrial Services

Towsure Products Ltd,
151-183 Holme Lane,
Hillsborough,
Sheffield,
S6 4JR
Tel: 0870 60 900 70
(Accessory supplier and towbar manufacturer)

Truma UK,
Truma House,
Beeches Park,
Eastern Avenue,
Burton-upon-Trent,
Staffordshire,
DE13 0BB
Tel: 01283 511092
(Space and water heating system, gas cylinder changeovers)

Trylon Ltd,
Unit J,
Higham Business Park,
Bury Close,
Higham Ferrers,
Northamptonshire, NN10 8HQ
Tel: 01933 411724
(Resins, glass and guidance on glass reinforced plastics)

Tyron Safety Band (UK) Ltd,
Manor House Stables,
Normanton on Soar,
Leicestershire,
LE12 5HB
Tel: 0870 744 6911
(Distributor of Tyron Safety Band)

Vanmaster Caravans,
Unit 57C,
Bradley Hall,
Bradley Lane,
Standish,
Wigan,
WN6 0XQ
Tel: 01257 424999
(Manufacturer of Vanmaster caravans)

Vanroyce Caravans,
(No longer in manufacture; contact Auto-Trail V.R. Ltd Tel: 01472 571000)

Varta Automotive Batteries Ltd
Broadwater Park,
North Orbital Road,
Denham,
Uxbridge,
Middlesex UB9 5AG
Tel: 01895 838993
(Gel-type, non-spill leisure batteries)

Ventair mattress anti-condensation underlay – See Technicol

V & G Caravans,
107 Benwick Road,
Whittlesey,
Peterborough,
Cambridgeshire PE7 2HD
Tel: 01733 350580
(Replacement replica panels in GRP)

W4 Ltd,
Unit B,
Ford Lane Industrial Estate,
Arundel,
West Sussex BN18 0DF
Tel: 01243 553355
(Suppliers of 230V kits, double-pole switched sockets, socket testers, and ribbon sealants)

WAECO International,
Unit G1,
Roman Hill Business Park,
Broadmayne,
Dorset,
DT2 8LY
Tel: 01305 854000
(Battery chargers, inverters and electrical accessories)

Watling Engineers Ltd,
88 Park Street Village,
nr. St. Albans,
Hertfordshire,
AL2 2LR
Tel: 01727 873661
(Designer/manufacturer of towing brackets)

West Riding Leisure,
Unit 19,
Perseverance Mills,
Lockwood Scar,
Lockwood,
Huddersfield,
HD4 6BW
Tel: 01484 451760
(Specialists in repairing ABS panels and caravan repair work)

Whale Products - See Munster Simms Engineering Ltd,

Winterhoff coupling head stabilisers - See Miriad Products Ltd and BPW Ltd

Witter Towbars,
Drome Road,
Deeside Industrial Park,
Deeside,
CH5 2NY
Tel: 01244 284500
(Towbar systems and cycle carriers)

Woodfit Ltd,
Kem Mill,
Whittle-le-Woods,
Chorley,
Lancashire,
PR6 7EA
Tel: 01257 266421
(Hinges, fittings, hardware, wire storage baskets and catches)

WYKO Industrial Services,
Amber Way,
Halesowen,
West Midlands,
B62 8WG
Tel: 0121 5086000
(For address of nearest WYKO branch retailing Tri-Flow moisture inhibitor spray)

ZIG Electronics Ltd,
Saxon Business Park,
Hanbury Road,
Stoke Prior,
Bromsgrove,
Worcestershire,
B60 4AD
Tel: 01527 577800
(Low voltage control components, chargers, and gauges)

INDEX